THE ENCYCLOPEDIA OF
KNITTING
TECHNIQUES

THE ENCYCLOPEDIA OF
KNITTING
TECHNIQUES

Debby Robinson

Rodale Press, Emmaus, Pennsylvania

For Agnes Coe

Published in The United States of America by
Rodale Press, 33 East Minor Street, Emmaus, PA 18049.

Note: Throughout this book, American terms are given in parentheses
after their British equivalents on the first occasion they occur
in each entry. Where the title of an entry itself differs, the
American term is signalled by a solidus, eg **Stocking/Stockinette stitch.**

Printed in Italy

Conceived and produced by
Swallow Publishing Limited
Northdown House, Northdown Street,
London N1.

Editor: Anne Yelland
Art director: Elaine Partington
Designer: Patricia Walters
Assistant editors: Laura Buller, Geraldine Christy
Assistant designers: Su Martin, Kate Simunek
Illustrators: Eugene Fleury, John Hutchinson,
Kate Jaspers, Kevin Jones, Su Martin,
Coral Mula, Stan North, Kate Simunek
Photography: Tim Imrie
Picture research: Liz Eddison
Studio: Del & Co.

Library of Congress Cataloging-in-Publication Data
Robinson, Debby
    The encyclopedia of knitting techniques.
    1. Knitting. I. Title.
TT820.R73   1986   746.9′2   86–21972

ISBN 0-87857-661-4   (paperback)

2 4 6 8 10 9 7 5 3 1 paperback

CONTENTS

FOREWORD

The last few years have witnessed a renaissance in hand knitting. Hand knits have become high fashion in the 1980s, and because they are usually so expensive to buy in the shops more and more of the 12 million or so people who can knit are taking up their knitting pins again, often after an interval of many years, and producing their own. The sales of hand-knitting yarns to private knitters – excluding commercial hand knits – have been climbing steadily in Britain: in 1980 12.5 million kilos of hand-knitting yarn were sold, which works out at an average of 250 tonnes a *week*; in 1985 it was about 21 million kilos – or 420 tonnes a week.

Spinners and magazines compete to produce knitting patterns, which are today markedly more attractive than they were just a decade ago; more and more books of patterns come off the publishing presses. Meanwhile the new yarns take advantage of improvements in man-made fibres to give lightness to cotton and strength to delicate natural fibres like mohair and angora; even pure wool is now machine-washable – unthinkable in the not so distant past. The range of novelty yarns increases season by season. Together, patterns and yarns make it possible for us to knit comfortable, covetable clothes – hand knits we should be proud of.

Yet the garments which many of us produce just don't look as good as they do in the photographs. They look fatally home-made – rather than good enough to pay a lot of money for in a shop.

That, Debby Robinson believes, is because you need to be more than a good knitter to produce a first-class piece of work. You have to be able to finish a garment to a professional standard, and there are all kinds of tricks of the trade which even some of the best amateur knitters don't know, and which the knitting books, appealing as they do to the beginner, don't get round to mentioning.

Which is where *The Encyclopedia of Knitting Techniques* comes in. It will help the amateur knitter achieve a professional standard. It covers the basics, of course: casting on, casting off, increasing, decreasing (but remembers to tell you which type is best for which purpose). But it also covers the knotty question of how to dispose of ends properly; how to block garments; which seaming methods to use when making up; the proper way to alter garments or how to unravel; facings, fairisle, frills – indeed, anything and everything, not forgetting bead knitting and even shoulder pads (two particularly valuable entries).

I first met Debby Robinson when the *Sunday Times Magazine* was preparing its Born-Again Knitting series in 1984. She'd caused a stir at that year's International Fashion Show at London's Olympia with her extremely original coats and hoods in vertical bands of stocking stitch and reverse stocking stitch, and we jumped at the chance of commissioning a coat and jacket from her for a special kit offer in our series. The kits were truly simple to knit (even if they took a long time); but you had to get the tension right, you had to know the secret of keeping the sleeves the right length, you had to know how to look after the finished garment. Even for something so simple, method mattered.

Like most of us, Debby can't remember learning to knit, though it certainly went no further than garter stitch squares, but she is quite clear that she only learnt to knit properly when she was grown up. She went to Greece as a girl to teach English, and was 'bowled over by those lovely chunky Greek sweaters'.

She bought 'some knobbly handspun yarn on Mykonos and knitted my first proper garment'. Not only that, but being by nature an entrepreneur she began to import Greek hand knits to the U.K. (teaching English by this time forgotten) – then realized it would be simpler and cheaper to get the sweaters knitted up in Britain. Back home she recruited her own knitters – at one time she had 200 – and for ten years ran her own business; for five of those years she ran a shop. So there's not much she doesn't know about hand-knitting from the point of view of the designer, the retailer, the customer and the knitter.

She says her knitters all knew much more than she did: 'I learnt from them.' The results of that learning process, and the further skills she acquired during a long process of trial and error in order to achieve perfection, are in this invaluable book.

Susan Raven,
London 1986

INTRODUCTION

During the time that I have been employing knitters to produce my hand-knit designs and selling knitting kits to the public, it has become clear to me that there is a world of difference between having sufficient grasp of the basics to produce straightforward sweaters and perfecting the art of knitting so as to create a professional-looking finish. The high-quality merchandise which I was aiming to produce under the 'The Hand Knit Company' label necessitated the strictest standards of production control. Necessity being the mother of invention, I soon found the best techniques for dealing with a particular styling problem or new yarn, and if a method did not exist, I worked one out. This meant that each one of my knitters received detailed instructions, covering every aspect of making the garment, from basic stitch instructions to specific finishing methods, enabling them all to work to a uniformly high standard.

Unfortunately, most patterns available for the home knitter stop short of providing this kind of information, leaving the knitters to fend for themselves and interpret the instructions as best they can. Since very few knitters possess the gift of clairvoyance, I have written this book to provide all that extra information, and much more, so that the very best results may be obtained from today's patterns and yarns; it is particularly necessary as these are more diverse and stylish than ever before.

Before the pattern of family life had started to change as dramatically as it has done over the last decades, knitting knowledge was passed on directly from one generation to another. This meant that there was usually an auntie or a granny ready with assistance. During the renewed interest in knitting which has blossomed during the last few years, many younger knitters were attracted to the craft by the designer patterns and yarns which appeared for the first time. This new generation of fashion knitters are very often self-taught, however, and as such are on their own. No amount of practising blanket squares and teddy bear's scarves can equip a knitter for perfect buttonholes or invisible seams. Disheartened by the absence of detailed technique instructions and lacking the knowledge to 'have a go', many knitters abandon their work, unable to finish it.

Even experienced knitters can be stumped when they come across a technique with which they are not familiar, especially if they do not possess the confidence to experiment and trust in their own judgement. So, I hope that this book will help knitters at every level, from absolute beginners right through to true craftspeople wanting to polish up their skills. My main aim is to engender confidence so that knitters with any degree of experience can feel able to tackle any project, however complicated. Nobody is born with a genetic inability to cope with fairisle, for instance, although a lot of knitters would have you believe it. What they are born with is a fear of the unknown.

The entries are specifically designed with speed and simplicity of reference in mind, to provide a back-up at every stage with cross references wherever necessary. The tricks of the trade may be picked up with a few moments' careful reading with the help of step-by-step illustrations rather than years of painstaking trial and error. The book also provides help in dealing with the enormous variety of new yarn types and styling variations, since the mastery of plain double knitting wool will not stand you in good stead when handling the exotic yarns which the spinners are continually developing. Contrary to popular opinion, the producers of knitting patterns have not cornered the market in technical expertise and design ability – both are easily within any knitter's grasp.

Once the mystique of the knitting process has been cracked, confidence will develop naturally. As with any task, faith in your own ability is the most important factor in producing satisfactory results, though unfortunately this is exactly what the vast majority of knitters lack. Knitting is, after all, simply a series of loops, the structure, neatness and design of which are totally under the control of the knitter. It is the knitter who controls the needles and yarn, not the other way round. When the anxiety brought on by the fear of a bodged job has been dispelled, knitting can become one of the most enjoyable pastimes – which, as well as being useful and highly creative, has such an extraordinary therapeutic value that it can often become addictive.

A HISTORY OF KNITTING

J udging by the archaeological evidence to hand, the Middle East seems to have been the 'cradle' of knitting. The hypothesis is based largely on examples of sandal socks, dating from the 4th century, found preserved in Egyptian tombs. The fact that only these examples have been found does not necessarily mean that the craft of knitting was not being developed in other parts of the world at that time; it simply means that no other evidence has survived. There have been archaeological hints from other civilizations, however – the system of loops, built up using a single needle, found in Peru or the 'sprang' from Viking tombs which is a cross between weaving and knitting – but no true knitting needle. In fact, much of the early Arab knitting may have been produced on small frames, rather like the bobbins of today, but the structure of the fabric would have been the same as needle knitting.

It has been generally accepted that the craft of knitting spread from the Arab countries along the trade routes, through Spain and then the rest of Europe. By the Middle Ages, knitting had become firmly established on the continent of Europe; historical records show that the creative skills found among members of the French and Italian guilds were the most highly regarded.

By the time the continent of North America was being settled, most European countries had developed their own distinctive knitting traditions. These skills, which included the texture patterns of Dutch, and the colour work of the Scandinavians, travelled with the settlers, creating a broad base from which modern American knitting has developed.

Possibly the earliest representation of someone knitting is the altarpiece painting entitled 'The Visitation of the Angels to Maria', attributed to Meister Bertram von Minden and dating from about 1400 (now hanging in Hamburg). This shows the Virgin Mary knitting in the round using a set of double-pointed needles – this was, in fact, the only way that knitting was produced until the 19th century. Much traditional knitting, such as Fair Isle, is still produced using that method today: two-needle, 'flat' knitting is a relatively modern invention.

The original forte of knitting was in its ability to produce garments which needed a considerable degree of elasticity and shaping. Socks, stockings, gloves and hats were all far more practical and comfortable if knitted, rather than cut from woven cloth and seamed. During the Elizabethan era the knitting of stockings in both wool and silk became a thriving industry in England and continued to be a very lucrative occupation despite the invention of the stocking frame, the earliest knitting machine, in 1589. One would assume that such a mechanical breakthrough would have had a devastating effect on the knitting trade but it took a couple of centuries and the Industrial Revolution before the machine finally killed commercial hand knitting. The inventor, William Lee, appears to have died in poverty at a time when human labour was still far cheaper than any machine.

Over the next two hundred years, industrially produced hose (and eventually knitwear) gradually took over the knitting trade. Professional hand knitters survived only in rural areas which had a strong knitting tradition, such as the Yorkshire Dales, and by 1900 this was virtually non-existent.

During the 19th century, as the trade of hand knitting – which had been a business frequently carried out by entire families, including the male members and small children who would all have learned their patterns by heart – declined, the hobby of hand knitting emerged as a genteel pastime for ladies. To cater for this trend, the first knitting books appeared towards the middle of the 19th century and it was around this time that yarn spinners became aware of a specific hobby market.

In 1896 John Paton and Co. began to produce patterns specifically for their own yarns, the first spinners to do so. Since then, the yarn manufacturers have largely dominated the design and publication of printed knitting instructions. The 20th century has seen the proliferation of spinners specifically geared to the manufacture of yarns for amateur hand knitters. In order to compete in the market it has become essential for them all to produce their own knitting patterns to promote specific brands of yarn.

It was not until the First World War that styles of dress changed so dramatically and the sweater, as we know it, first took shape. With the formality of Victorian dressing left behind, the twenties, thirties

A *Pueblo Indian cotton shirt.*

and forties saw a burgeoning of knitwear design. For a time in the thirties there was even a revival in the trade of hand knitting and many Parisian designers, most notably Schiaparelli, employed immigrant workers to produce high-fashion knits.

The postwar 'brave new world' atmosphere which dominated the fifties saw hand knits banished to the realms of home-spun anachronism. It was so much more sophisticated to wear perfectly plain, uniform, machine-produced knitwear – attractive examples of fairisle only being seen in the potting shed. The hallmark of the country bumpkin was a home-made sweater worn under the jacket. The only exception was the 'sloppy joe' of the beatnik era which has become a modern classic.

The patterns of the sixties were also very dull. High fashion at the time was far more interested in PVC and perspex than wool or silk. Knitting was something grandmother did. Synthetic yarns burst on to the market as the new saviour and hand knitting has never produced so many cheap and nasty-looking garments.

The seventies brought with them a new awareness of the environment and a movement towards natural fibres and ethnic styling. Fairisle, guernsey, aran, and lace knitting were all resuscitated by the longing for nostalgia. Younger designers became aware of the immense design potential of hand knits. The combination of these two factors created a blossoming of hand-knit design which we are still enjoying today. Knitters were recruited and hand-knit production

companies sprang up all over the place. This new high-fashion approach to knitting has filtered down to the hobby knitters, attracting an entirely new set of people to the craft. The popularity of designer hand-knit garments, produced commercially, and stylish home knitting have developed hand in hand.

As leisure time expands and our society becomes more and more style orientated, the hobby of hand knitting may continue to grow, demanding ever more up-to-date yarns and patterns. It has taken British spinners ten years to wake up to the fashion market within hand knitting but they are finally getting somewhere near the standards of excellence in colour, style and technical development of spinners on the continent of Europe.

'Der Besuch der Engel bei Maria' – the first representation of someone knitting.

ABBREVIATIONS

Since all designers have their own variations, all spinners producing patterns have their own house styles, and trends vary over the years, this glossary is as comprehensive as possible. Before starting a pattern, however, always check the very beginning as it will normally explain all the abbreviations which have been used.

alt	alternate(ly)
b	bobble
beg	begin(ning)
blw	below
bo	bobble
C	cable
CB	cable back
CC	contrast colour
CF	cable front
cm	centimetre(s)
cont	continue/continuing
cr b (cross b)	cross back
cr f (cross f)	cross front
cross 2RK (RP)	cross 2sts to the right, knitting (or purling)
cross 2LK (LP)	cross 2sts to the left, knitting (or purling)
dec	decrease/decreasing
DK	double knitting (worsted)
dp	double-pointed
foll	following
g	gram(s)
gms	grams
gr	group
g st	garter stitch
in(s)	inch(es)
inc	increase/increasing
k	knit
kb	knit into back of stitch
kfb	knit into front and back of stitch
k1B (k1 blw)	knit into the stitch below the next stitch to be knitted
k wise	knitwise
LH	left hand
lp(s)	loop(s)
MB	make bobble
MC	main colour
mm	millimetre(s)
M1	make one
oz	ounce(s)
p	purl
pat(t)	pattern
pfb	purl into front and back of next stitch
pnso	pass next stitch over
psso	pass slipped stitch over
p wise	purlwise
rem	remain(ing)
rep	repeat
ret	return
rev st st	reverse stocking (stockinette) stitch
RH	right hand
rnd(s)	round(s)
RS	right side
skp	slip one, knit one, pass slipped stitch over
skpo	slip one, knit one, pass slipped stitch over
sl	slip
sl st	slip stitch
ssk	slip, slip, knit
st(s)	stitch(es)
st st	stocking stitch
tbl	through back of loop(s)
tog	together
tw	twist
wb	wool back
wf	wool front
won	wool over needle
wrn	wool round needle
WS	wrong side

wyib	with yarn in back of work
wyif	with yarn in front of work
ybk	yarn back
yfwd	yarn forward
yo	yarn over
yon	yarn over needle
yrn	yarn round needle

The following are crochet terms but since knitting patterns frequently call for some crochet at the finishing stage, here are the basics:

ch	chain
dc	double crochet
sc	single crochet
tr	treble (triple) crochet

ADJUSTING PATTERNS

The knitting patterns on the market today provide the knitter with the greatest variety of styles and sizes which has ever been available. Very few of us, however, are lucky enough to possess bodies which are totally in proportion and conform to standard size specifications, and so adjustments are often necessary. On basic designs, these present no problem. If, however, you are attempting to work on a more adventurous shape – say, a cardigan with asymmetric fastening – shapings can get extremely complicated and are best left alone. It is usually easier to draft a pattern from scratch than get involved in a complicated reworking (see *Designing*).

Adjusting plain designs
On a one-colour garment worked in a simple stitch, accurate adjustments can be achieved by using the most basic of aids – a pad of graph paper and a sharp pencil. If the piece of work you wish to adjust has no shapings, even these are not necessary.

Non-shaped work To adjust the length of a piece without shaping, if the instructions quote measurements, simply add or subtract the required number of centimetres or inches. If the length is calculated by the number of rows, use the row tension (gauge) to work out the adjustment. If, for example, you wish to lengthen by 5cm (2in.) and you are working to a tension of 24 rows to 10cm (4in.), then add 12 rows.

Note: When adjusting body length on a garment which later becomes shaped, such as at armholes, neck or shoulders, always work the alteration *before* the start of any shaping.

To adjust width, once you have decided how much you need to add or subtract, refer to the tension to work out how many stitches this will involve. If, for example, you wish to remove 2.5cm (1in.) from the width of the work and you are working to a tension of 28sts to 10cm (4in.), then subtract 7sts.

Note: After adding or subtracting stitches on a garment which later becomes shaped, remember to allow for the addition or subtraction of these stitches when following subsequent instructions.

Shaped work Whether you wish to adjust the length or width of a shaped piece of work, it will probably involve respacing any increasings or decreasings. This is where graph paper comes into its own, making what can be fairly tricky mathematical calculations simply a matter of redrawing.

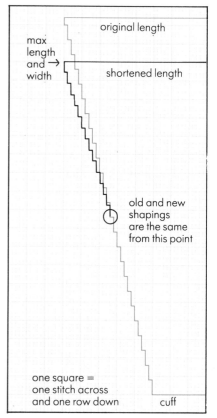

A shortened sleeve showing the before and after increase sequence.

Take one square to equal one stitch across and one row down, and draw the original shape of the piece to be altered, in ink. Here a sleeve with a straight top has been used to illustrate the method (for sleeve details, see *Sleeves*). To save time and space, put an imaginary fold line down the centre of the piece so that you need only draw half of it (remembering to double all your stitch numbers).

With a pencil (not another pen since a certain amount of trial and error may be necessary), mark the extreme points of the alteration, that is, the maximum length and width. Now, working back from this point, respace the shapings, spreading them out or condensing them, as required. Always try to distribute any shapings as evenly as possible since this will make them far easier to remember once you have started the knitting, and will make the work itself as neat as possible. If at first you don't succeed, just erase it and try again. It may seem like a terribly random procedure but it is, in fact, far easier than attempting to work it out arithmetically. Once you have the shape on paper, file it for future reference in case further adjustments are necessary.

Although a very simple use of this method is shown, naturally it can be applied to any part of a garment, a sleeve head (cap) for instance. This, however, involves simultaneous depth and width considerations and would be best tackled after consulting some of the basic tailoring rules outlined in *Designing*.

Adjusting fancy patterns and coloured designs

Here it is not always possible to make the precise adjustment required since the stitch and/or colour pattern repeats must be taken into account. If these cannot be broken up easily, your adjustment will have to be made to the nearest whole repeat.

There are obvious examples where repeats cannot be tampered with, such as lace patterns, cables and colour motifs, but when in doubt, work your tension sample large enough to contain a whole repeat. Using graph paper again, you can then work out how many repeats there are on the entire piece and where neck shapings, armholes, pockets, and so on will come in relation to them.

The alpaca, a relative of the llama and vicuna, prized for its soft coat.

On some patterns, it will be acceptable to have a small plain border of added stitches at either side of the work. Wherever possible, however, keep all new stitches in pattern as you go.

ALPACA

Alpaca yarn does actually come from an animal called the alpaca, a grazing animal of the camel family, which is herded in Peru and Bolivia and closely related to the llama and vicuña. It thrives at extreme altitudes and has consequently developed an extremely long, straight and soft coat, which provides a fine fibre of a very high quality which is spun for use in weaving and knitting.

Although not as expensive as cashmere, alpaca is a luxury yarn and is very rarely spun into weights heavier than double knitting (worsted). When knitted, it has a very soft handle (feel)

but also a slight hairiness which, although nowhere near as extreme as a fibre like mohair, can irritate some sensitive skins.

ALTERATIONS TO FINISHED GARMENTS

Knitting is a fabric, just like any other, and once the structure of the stitch being used has been recognized and understood, alterations become a far less daunting prospect. Naturally, there are limitations, as with any fabric, and before starting an alteration it is advisable to ask yourself if the time and effort required might not be better spent in reknitting the garment from scratch. With a very complicated stitch or colour pattern, this is usually the case. The more simple knitted fabrics, however, can often be altered fairly easily.

> **HINT**
>
> *If you anticipate that an alteration may be likely in the future – children's garments are an obvious example – and the pattern which you are using lends itself to such a trick, it can be very useful to work a garment upside-down so that the stitches can be easily picked up from the bottom when alteration is necessary.*

Altering widthways/widthwise

The possibilities here are rather limited since stitches cannot just be picked up, as they can for shortening and lengthening. It is not totally impossible to take a pair of shears to a large sweater and remove the unwanted centimetres, but as it involves cutting across the rows and producing numerous unfastened ends, there are hazards. The alternatives are to bind the raw edges produced or to run several rows of machine stitching along them – neither of which produces an acceptable finish on the average sweater seam.

A trick which can sometimes work wonders, especially on woollen garments, is to unpick all the seams of the knitting and reblock the pieces to the desired measurements (see *Blocking*).

If you are trying to make the pieces wider, however, excessive widthways stretching may 'take up' too much of the length and mean you have to lengthen the garment as well. And if you are trying to make them narrower by stretching lengthways, shortening the garment may be necessary. If a considerable size alteration is required, take these factors into account before you become involved in a 'push me, pull you' struggle.

Altering lengthways/lengthwise

Shortening If the knitted front and back have been worked in the usual manner, that is, from the bottom to the top, and without armhole shaping, the cast (bound) off shoulder edge may be unpicked and the garment unravelled back to the required length. On a non-shaped garment this method is ideal. It is not acceptable, however, where shapings have been worked. On a standard crew-neck sweater with set-in sleeves, for example, shortening from the top would destroy the shape of the neck opening and reduce the depth of the armholes (unless you unravel to below the armholes). In such cases, the shortening should be tackled from the bottom:

1. Measure the length which you wish to remove, and mark this row. On a garment with a welt (finishing border) or hem this should be measured from the last row of welt/hem upwards.
2. Divide the work along the marked row by either:
a. pulling a thread out with a tapestry needle, snipping it and then carefully picking it out, leaving two rows of loops. This method is not recommended with a slippery yarn such as polyester, or a heavily textured

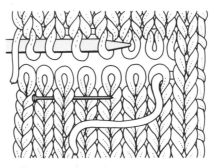

Pulling out a thread to open rows.

one such as a bouclé, as you will end up by unevenly unravelling far more rows than required, and it will prove virtually impossible to pick up the loops. Or:
b. picking up the loops along the marked row with a smaller needle than the one used for the original work and then cutting across, two rows below. The little ends can then be picked off, leaving a row of loops already neatly on the needle, without any dropped stitches. This method is essential if

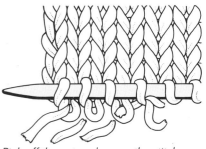

Pick off the cut ends once the stitches are on a needle.

you are being adventurous and tackling a pattern which involves more than simple knit and purl stitches as you will get in a mess when you try to pick up unheld loops.
3. If you wish to reknit the welt/hem/edging, work it downwards. This method is advisable if the original pattern had shapings immediately after the welt as they can then be worked in reverse.
4. If you prefer to graft the old welt back on, divide the work again one or two rows above the welt, and pick up the stitches on the row immediately above the welt. Then, take back the one or two rows which were allowed as a safeguard only. If both pieces have exactly the same number of stitches, they can then be grafted together

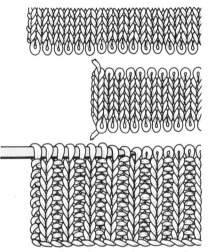

A section of stocking stitch removed, with the rib and remainder of the garment ready for grafting.

using a tapestry needle (see *Grafting*). If the number of stitches differ, such as on a shaped sleeve where increases usually start straight after the welt, then knitting together enables you to decrease the correct number of stitches as you work along the row (see *Seams*). Even using larger needles this will definitely form a ridge, which can be a drawback if the welt or cuff is already a close fit.

Lengthening As long as you have the correct yarn, or one which will form an acceptable contrast band, non-shaped garments can be extended at will. Shaped garments must be tackled from the bottom, as with shortening.
1. Open up a row of loops, as for shortening but immediately above the welt/hem/edging.
2. Double check that none of your stitches have dropped and that they are all on the needle the correct way round (twisted stitches will show up later).

3. If you are working with stocking (stockinette) stitch or garter stitch, provided that the garment is not too well worn and faded compared with the new yarn being used, you can start knitting in the opposite direction without the work looking any different from that knitted in the first place. Take great care to match the original tension (gauge).
4. If you are working a more complicated stitch or your yarn is not a good match, the best way to lengthen is to start at the same point but work a new welt/hem/edging, and extend it to the length you want. Although this limits the degree to which you can lengthen (very few sweaters can take a 15cm/6in. welt, for example), it does give by far the most professional finish.

ANGORA

Angora yarn comes from the angora rabbit, not the angora goat which only produces mohair. These two, quite different, animals simply share the name which is derived from the Angora (Ankara) region in Turkey. Today China is the world's major producer of angora.

Angora rabbits are albino, so produce only white hair, which is thick and silky. This is gathered, by either combing or shearing, every three or four months. Since the underhairs are very short and naturally slippery, angora is very difficult to spin without the addition of other fibres such as wool and nylon. This problem with spinning, and the fact that the animals are so small, make pure angora one of the most expensive yarns on the market; it is usually used either in

Angora comes from the angora rabbit.

conjunction with other yarns or as a trimming, rather than for an entire garment.

Mixing it with other fibres reduces the degree of fluffiness, so when you are buying an angora yarn, decide just how fluffy a garment you wish to produce. Delicate texture stitches will be lost in the fluffy finish and heavily textured stitches will take up extra yarn, making the garment even more expensive. Colour patterns can be effective, provided that very sharp lines are not required since any design will become fuzzily blurred. Angora should never be pressed.

Although angora garments are extremely luxurious, the short hairs are very prone to shedding which can induce allergic reactions in anyone who is susceptible. It is claimed that refrigeration will cut down on the degree of shedding but there is no conclusive proof, and who really wants to put on a chilled sweater?

ARAN KNITTING

Aran knitting is instantly recognizable by its unique use of cables, in all their variations and forms. On true arans, these are worked in panels, often with the addition of bobbles and moss (seed) stitch 'fill in' areas, so that the entire garment is covered in texture.

The popularity of 'folk' crafts since the age of technology created a market for nostalgia has increased the romanticism that surrounds 'traditional' skills. Knitting is no exception. Although aran is probably the most popular form of classic knitting that we now have, the assumption that the tradition goes back into the mists of time appears to be erroneous.

Situated off the west coast of Ireland, the Isles of Aran, unprotected from the blasts of the Atlantic, have always been harsh and inhospitable. For the isolated communities living there, life was a continual struggle for survival with, presumably, little time for arts and crafts. In contrast to many of the fishing communities around the British Isles, the Aran islands have no early photographic records of the local people in their work clothes. Furthermore, none of the people taking part in Robert Flaherty's 1934 documentary film *Man of Aran* wears a 'traditional' aran. The first documented example dates from 1936 when Heinz Kiewe (best known as the author of *The Sacred History of Knitting*) gave a garment to Mary Thomas, who then featured it in her knitting book.

Nearly all the native inhabitants of Aran have now migrated to areas which provide a less spartan existence and, since virtually no knitting is now done on the islands, the researcher comes up against a brick wall. The sweaters which are available locally for the tourist trade are made on the mainland and no historical examples are known. Naturally, this does not prove categorically that the aran does not have the pedigree claimed for it. The traditions of aran knitting would

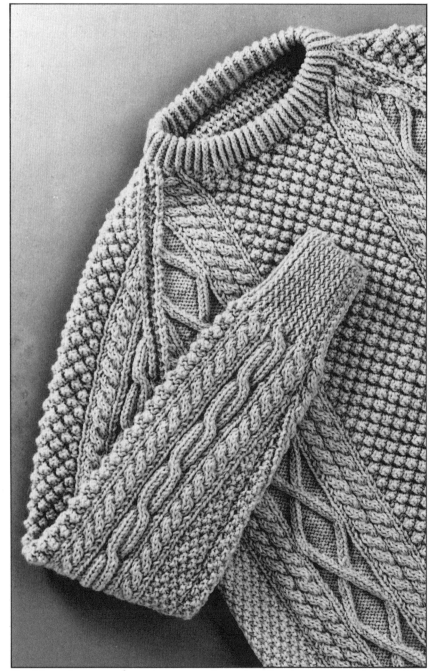

The 'classic' aran sweater, showing traditional stitches (such as trinity) and cables.

have been passed on verbally from generation to generation and since a work garment has even less chance of survival than a painting or a piece of furniture, the mystery is wide open.

Theories regarding the cultural origins of aran knitting must remain just that – theories – and, as such, a matter of personal interpretation, although the visual debt to ancient Celtic art is undeniable. The interlocking, serpentine designs found in historical sources such as *The Book of Kells* are definitely echoed in the criss-crossings of cable designs but any concrete link, going back over a thousand years, is supposition – as is the religious significance attributed to stitches such as 'trinity stitch' and 'the tree of life'.

As a style of knitting, rather than a tradition, however, aran has been worked and reworked as it has drifted in and out of fashion over the last fifty years. Although garments were originally worked only in the natural off-white colour or 'bainin' yarn, a vast selection of dyed wools and even tweed effects are now being marketed as 'aran' yarns. Aran-type patterns can also be worked in virtually any other type of yarn, as long as tension (gauge) adjustments have been made. The same stitch configurations can be used for garments as diverse as a masculine sports sweater and a delicate evening top. Modern interpretations have included calf-length chenille dresses and even lurex versions – a far cry from fishermen's work garments.

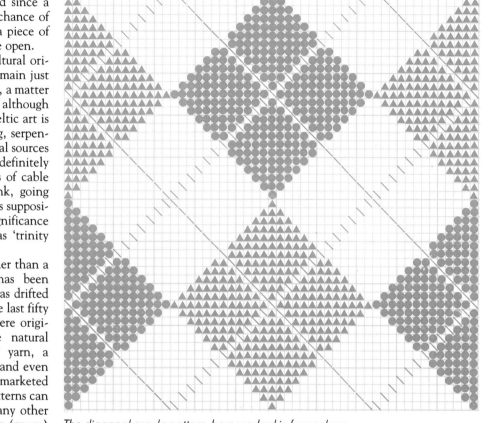

The diagonal argyle pattern, here worked in four colours.

ARGYLE

Argyle patterns originally took their name from the socks which were knitted as part of the traditional highland dress of Scotsmen, but the basic design is now used on almost any type of knitwear. The pattern consists of large, diamond-shaped areas in two or three colours, transversed by diagonal lines of another contrast colour. Argyle patterns are worked in stocking (stockinette) stitch and always involve more than two colours in any row. A combination of colour knitting techniques must, therefore, be used – fairisle for the diamonds, and intarsia for the diagonal lines. (See *Fairisle* and *Intarsia* for a discussion of these techniques.)

Such patterns are really not for beginners unless they possess a talent for colour knitting.

ARMBANDS

Any sleeveless garment, unless knitted in a neat-edged, non-curling stitch, will require bands to finish the armholes. These can be knitted up or worked separately; follow the general advice detailed in *Bands or Borders*.

When knitting (picking) up stitches

around a shaped armhole, extra care should be taken in distributing the stitches around the curve – always allow more stitches here than on the straight. This prevents the armhole from pulling uncomfortably when the garment is worn. The armband should be worked after the shoulder seam has been completed. The band seam should be a continuation of the side seam, unless the band is worked in the round when no seam is necessary.

ARMHOLES

As with any other part of a garment, armhole and sleeve shaping change with variations in fashion, and as designers become more individual, the number of permutations becomes endless. For obvious reasons, these descriptions are limited to the more classic shapes.

Drop shoulder

No armhole shaping is required for a drop shoulder style with a straight sleeve top but it is very important to work the seams in a particular order (see *Drop Shoulders*).

Raglan

The classic raglan shaping is a straight diagonal produced by a uniform decrease sequence to form a non-variable angle. Because the shoulder is formed by the top of the sleeve, the raglan cannot be called an armhole in the true sense of the word (see *Raglans*).

Saddle/Saddle yoke

The armhole required for a saddle shoulder is as for a set (set-in) sleeve but not so deep to make allowance for the shoulder yoke, which is worked as

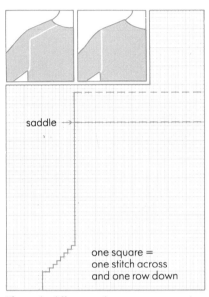

saddle →

one square =
one stitch across
and one row down

The only difference between set and saddle armhole shaping is the depth.

part of the sleeve. It produces a flat square-finished shoulder shape and is traditionally used more for menswear than womenswear.

Set/Set-in sleeve

This is the most commonly used shaping and can be worked with a shaped or straight shoulder, adjusting the armhole depth accordingly. The sleeve is set in *after* the side and sleeve seams have been worked, and any fullness in the sleeves eased to the top of the shoulder.

If you are working a set sleeve style, always double check that it is exactly the correct size. The fit is far more precise than with any other shape. If you prefer baggy styling, then look for an alternative armhole.

Sleeveless

Unless a cap-sleeved appearance is required on the finished article,

sleeveless garments require the same armhole shaping as a set sleeve, except that the armhole needs to be deeper than on a sleeved garment if bands are to be added. The shaping may also have to be slightly deeper in the front than in the back so that the armhole will sit properly when you are moving your arm.

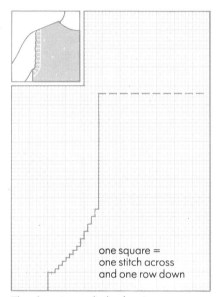

one square =
one stitch across
and one row down

The deeper armhole shaping on a sleeveless garment allows for borders.

Square (semi-set)

This armhole is shaped with a few cast (bound) off stitches on just one row, and takes a straight-topped sleeve. It is suitable for heavyweight yarns since it creates less fabric under the arm than a drop shoulder style, and is best made up using a flat seam (see *Seams*).

The changing shapes of knitwear design through the decades from the shapeless belle of the 1900s, to a Patricia Roberts' modern classic.

1900's

1920's

1930's

1940's

1960's

1950's

1970's

BACKSTITCH

See *Seams*.

BALL BANDS/ LABELS

The term ball band refers to the label which is wrapped around a standard-shaped ball of yarn or the tag which is attached to skeins and flat balls. It contains a great deal of very useful information and should not be discarded. On standard balls, ball bands can also help to keep the ball of yarn tidy while you are working; start with an end carefully teased out from the centre of the ball rather than the outside. This stops the ball jumping around as it unravels.

Although the information contained on a ball band will vary from manufacturer to manufacturer, most

Four sweaters, including a 'bainin' classic aran, worked in both wool and cotton, illustrating numerous different cables used with other fancy stitches.

are becoming standardized on an international basis. The most important information is the individual dye lot number (see *Dye Lots*), the washcare instructions (see *Washcare*), the fibre content and the suggested tension (gauge) details. In addition, it may have the metreage, that is, the length of yarn you can expect from a particular weight. This can be useful for comparison of quantities required when substituting one yarn for another.

The recommended needle sizes are very good as a guideline but should not be treated as hard and fast rules since everyone's tension varies, especially on the fancy textured yarns where there can be enormous variation. The tension you can expect will usually be indicated on a small grid which represents an area 10cm by 10cm (2½in. × 2½in.). The figure across will represent the number of stitches and the figure down the number of rows you can expect from this sized sample (see *Tension/Gauge*).

Take particular note of the fibre content if you find some fabrics, angora for example, irritate your, or the potential wearer's, skin.

BANDS OR BORDERS

The main drawback with most knitted fabrics is their tendency to curl; this makes bands or borders almost essential in the finishing of such garments. Bands or borders are either worked separately, or knitted (picked) up at the final stage, since smaller needles are used than for the main work for extra neatness and firmness. The main non-curling band and border stitches are ribs, moss (seed) stitch and garter stitch. Since garter is the loosest of these stitches, only use it if you are a very even knitter. If you are following an old pattern which uses garter stitch edging worked as part of the garment (very popular in the thirties), try – it isn't easy – to adjust your tension (gauge) as you go for maximum neatness.

When working bands or borders at right angles to the main fabric, it is essential to get the number of stitches or the measurement absolutely accurate. Bands which are too full will give a 'frilly' appearance and cause the garment edge to stretch; those which are too tight will pull necks, or armholes, out of shape and perhaps pucker the garment. A band which is the wrong size can completely ruin an otherwise beautifully knitted garment.

Knitted/Picked up bands

Worked after picking up stitches (see *Knitting/Picking Up Stitches*), knitting up a band is the normal method for finishing necks and armholes. A rib stitch gives the most flexibility around curves – moss and garter stitch have to be shaped at these points if the band is more than a few rows deep (see *Corners* and *Curves*).

When you are measuring the depth of a vertically ribbed band, always allow for the fact that it will stretch widthways (widthwise) after casting (binding) off (see *Casting/Binding Off* for appropriate methods). If it looks the correct depth while it is still on the needle, add a couple of rows to compensate for this.

If you are working horizontally ribbed cardigan bands, remember that they will have far more elasticity than vertically ribbed ones. This is one instance where the bands should look too short to begin with to allow for inevitable stretching.

Double bands

These can be used where a stocking (stockinette) stitch border is specifically required as they are worked from picked up stitches and then doubled over, as with a hem (see *Hems*).

If a double band is to be worked around a curve, then decreasings should be worked across the top layer, followed by increasings on the part which is to be folded over so that it may be stitched back around the original line of the curve. Alternatively a band may be worked diagonally, that is on the bias.

Bias bands

Worked in stocking stitch, these may be knitted separately or as part of the garment since it is not essential to use a smaller needle. The bias twist is formed by increasing one stitch at one edge and decreasing one stitch at the other. This can be done on alternate rows or on every row if an extreme angle is required. Since the cast on and cast off edges will also be angled, unless they are to be joined as for an armband, they must also be shaped. This is done by casting on and off the required number of band stitches in small sets rather than all in one go. Bias bands may then be attached in the same way as bias binding is used in dressmaking although flat, rather than backstitched, seams should be used.

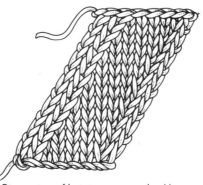

Bias strips of knitting are worked by combinations of increases and decreases on each side.

Bands worked and attached simultaneously

When worked vertically, bands can be knitted and joined to the main garment at the same time. If working in stocking stitch, work a simple slipped stitch (single chain edge) selvedge to create a chain edge to work into (see *Selvedges*). On a right side row, work across the band stitches, except one.

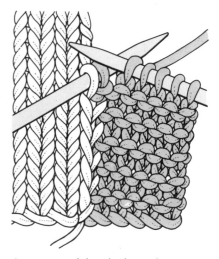

A garter stitch border knitted on to a stocking stitch selvedge.

Slip this on to the right-hand needle, pick up the main work edge stitch with the left-hand needle, return band stitch to the left-hand needle and work these two together. Turn the work and work band stitches to end. There will be more rows on the band (since it is on smaller needles) than on the main work, so this method cannot be worked row for row. An average ratio is two band rows to one main work row, that is, you should work a

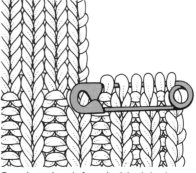

Band stitches left on hold while the stocking stitch is completed.

selvedge stitch every alternate band row. As this ratio will vary according to the tension produced by the yarn and needles which you are using, do a short test run first to see if this technique is suitable.

Cardigan/coat bands

Technically, these can be knitted up horizontally but as so many stitches are involved they are far easier to handle if they are knitted separately and stitched on.

If the welts (finishing borders) and bands are in the same stitch, and worked in the same direction as the garment, all the stitches can be cast on together. Once the welt has been worked, put the band stitches on to a safety pin or stitch holder while the rest of the front is completed. These stitches can then be picked up and the band knitted up from them.

If knitted completely separately, vertical bands can be knitted in one continuous length from one front hem to the other. Knitting them in two pieces, which will be joined at the centre back neck, however, makes any alterations easier to make without having to undo the entire band.

Do not take on trust the length the pattern says the bands should be. Pin them to the fronts as you go, making sure they are neither too stretched, nor too loose. The finished bands will then be exactly the correct length. As with any knitting, keep checking your work and use your own judgement for perfect results.

Take the greatest possible care when stitching the bands to the garment. *The front edges are the focal point of any cardigan or coat.* The seam used here should always be a flat one and all ends must be invisibly secured (see *Seams*).

BEAD KNITTING

There are two main categories of bead knitting: the incredibly intricate, all-over beading of the 18th and 19th centuries which you see in Victorian bead purses; and the more modern use of beads, spaced out over the knitted fabric in random or geometric designs.

The former method used tiny glass or ceramic beads which were knitted into every single stitch, with the knit stitches twisted to keep them in place. Tiny metal wires rather than knitting needles were used and the beading was so dense that the fabric itself was not visible. The delicacy of the designs and the number of different colours used must have meant that the threading of the beads was a Herculean task.

There are many different methods of bead knitting, the variations depending on the stitch you are using and whether you wish to have the bead placed horizontally or vertically on the finished fabric. Traditionally, they have all necessitated threading the beads on to the yarn before starting work, either by threading a whole ball at a time, or continually breaking the yarn into manageable lengths. If more than one colour bead is to be used this is very tedious, since each bead has to be threaded in the correct order, according to the design. Included below, however, is a method which does away with the chore of threading and which, I think, is my own invention, although with knitting methods one can never be sure who thought of something first.

When choosing beads for bead knitting, choose ones of a suitable weight for the fabric you will be working and, more important, which have a hole large enough to pass the yarn through (with the non-threaded method this must be large enough to take two thicknesses of yarn). The rounded wooden type is perfect. If beads with small holes must be used with thicker yarn, it is sometimes possible to work with two ends of yarn – one very fine. Thread the beads on the finer yarn, then knit this together with the heavier one.

Avoid working to a loose tension (gauge) as the beads may slip through to the wrong side of the work. A firm fabric will keep them in place.

Threaded methods

Garter stitch When you come to the bead position, on a wrong side row, push the bead up the yarn, as close to the work as you can get it and knit the next stitch as normal. The bead sits in between the stitches, horizontally.

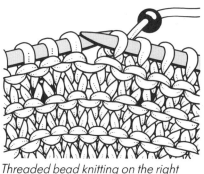

Threaded bead knitting on the right side of garter stitch.

Reverse stocking (stockinette) stitch When you want the bead to sit on the purl side of stocking stitch, the method is as above but the yarn should be at the front of the work.

Stocking stitch There are two ways to place a bead horizontally in stocking stitch.

1. On a purl row, knit the stitch before the bead position, place the bead as for the garter stitch method, knit the next stitch, purl to the end of the row and continue in stocking stitch.

2. This can be worked on a purl or knit row. Work to the bead position, put the yarn to right side of work, bring the bead up and slip the next stitch. Continue in stocking stitch. The strand at the front of the slipped stitch holds the bead.

Threaded beads: (above) flanked by knit stitches, (below) held on a strand in front of a slipped stitch.

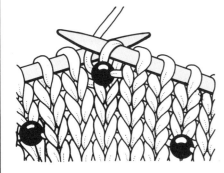

It is also possible to place a bead vertically in stocking stitch, although with the threaded method, the bead is never truly vertical in position. Since it has to be worked on part of the actual stitch, the bead will always have a slight angle to it.

To place the bead, on a knit row, work to the bead position. Put the point of the right-hand needle into

the back of the next stitch and make the loop large enough for you to bring the bead up and push it through the loop as the stitch is knitted.

This twisted knit stitch method was the one used by the Victorian bead knitters who placed a bead on every stitch, pushing the beads through to the right side on the purl rows.

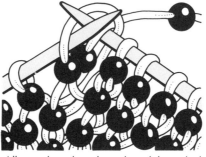

All-over bead work – a bead threaded on to every single stitch.

Non-threaded bead knitting

This method can be used on knit or purl stitches equally effectively, and results in a vertically placed bead.

Work to the stitch immediately below the bead position. Work it, winding the yarn twice around the needle. On the next row, when you come to this enlarged stitch, slip it off the needle and, using your thumb and forefinger, pass the entire loop

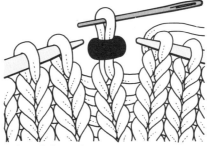

A bead slipped over a stitch, not threaded on to the yarn.

The stitch holding the bead is then knitted as normal.

through the bead (a tapestry needle can be of help in pulling the loop through). Now, place the loop back on to the left-hand needle and work it as normal. The bead will sit perfectly straight with the entire stitch running through it.

Naturally, this technique is not suitable for beads which have small holes. It does, however, allow you to alter the design or simply make it up as you go along since the order in which you work your beads is not predetermined by the order in which they have been threaded.

■ BINDING OFF

See *Casting/Binding Off.*

■ BLOCKING

This is the term used for the technique – involving steam, pressing, damping down, or any combination of these three – whereby each individual piece of knitting is set to a specific size and shape, or pattern 'block'. It is usually carried out after the knitting is complete but before the making up (assembling).

During periods when styling has demanded a perfectly tailored fit from all knitwear, and before the advent of so many synthetic yarns, blocking was *de rigueur*. Today, however, with so many textured stitches, baggy shapes and speciality yarns, it has become almost forgotten and is often regarded with suspicion.

There are two major uses for blocking: flattening fairisle or colour motif work which can look uneven, despite careful knitting; and adjusting the size or shape of a garment without reknitting. It is amazing how far a knitted garment can be stretched or reduced without harming the fabric in the slightest, as long as blocking is carried out properly, with due care and attention to the type of yarn used.

Method

Blocking should be carried out on a soft surface. If you cannot use an ironing board which has a padded top, put a thick blanket under the work, then pin it out to the desired measurements. Stretch it to make it larger, ease it to make it smaller. Use long pins with coloured tops – they are easier to handle – and use plenty of them, spaced evenly, or the pins themselves will pull the work out of shape. Do not block ribbing as this should already have sufficient elasticity. Always block on the wrong side of the work.

Different yarns respond to blocking with varying degrees of efficacy; always consult the instructions on the ball bands (labels) before you decide whether to dampen alone (using a fine plant spray/mister), press or steam. Very few natural fibres do not respond to blocking but wool is by far the best performer, allowing one to dampen, steam and even press – make sure that

Careful pinning out is essential to successful blocking.

the iron is at the correct heat setting.

With fluffy yarns such as angora or mohair or if the knitting is a heavily textured stitch, never let the iron come into contact with the fabric or you will squash the life out of it. If you have a steam iron, hold it a few centimetres above the work and allow the steam to enter the fabric from a distance. Alternatively use a kettle or iron a damp cloth over the fabric.

Always allow the blocked work to dry completely before moving it.

■ BOBBIN/SPOOL KNITTING

Bobbin or 'french' knitting is the technique of producing a knitted tube or cord, using a small frame which is sometimes called a 'knitting Nancy'. In the days of wooden cotton reels (thread spools), this was popular with schoolchildren, since the only equipment needed was an empty cotton reel and four nails. Now, bobbins of varying designs can be bought in craft shops.

Starting with a loop over each nail, the yarn is wound right around the outside of the nails. The loops are then hooked over the nails and the strand of yarn, with the aid of something like a tapestry needle, thus forming stitches as in normal knitting. The cord is then pulled down through the hole in the bobbin and the yarn wound round the nails again to form another row of stitches.

The size of the cord can be varied according to what weight of yarn you use, the frame you have and how many nails or pegs it will accommodate. Cord knitted in this fashion can be used for piping, belts, tie fastenings and for threading through eyelets (rounds). If you want an extra chunky knit, it can even be used as yarn, worked on very large needles.

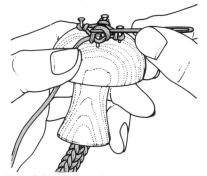

French knitting worked clockwise on a mushroom-shaped bobbin.

■ BOBBINS

Colour knitting which uses more than two colours per row presents the knitter with the problem of how to prevent the yarns becoming one large tangle. Each colour can be kept in a box, jam jar, or anything else that will keep it away from its fellows, but this necessitates careful turning at the end of every row, or spasmodic untwisting if you are working in the round.

Using bobbins, however, means that the yarn will just hang at the back of the work, ready for the next row. These can be bought ready-made in most good knitting shops. Alternatively, you can make your own out of stiff card (cardboard), making sure that the slit at the top will hold your yarn end securely and allow you to unwind a controlled amount at a time. Use a separate bobbin for each colour and, where possible, wind on sufficient yarn to complete the entire colour area. Do not overdo it since heavy bobbins will pull stitches out of shape.

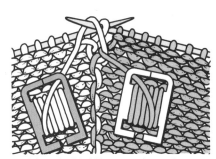

Bobbins hold different coloured yarns to prevent tangles.

BOBBLE STITCHES

Stitches which produce a raised bobble on a flat fabric vary from a simple knot – made by working twice into a stitch and then lifting the first stitch over – to large detached clusters which are worked over several rows. The basic principle is always the same, however: working more than once

The most basic bobble stitch – trinity or blackberry stitch.

into a single stitch and then decreasing those extra stitches which have been made to form a bump. Any one of these methods may be abbreviated to 'MB' although most patterns will specify which method is required at the beginning of the instructions.

The list of names, as with most fancy stitches, is endless – currant, gooseberry, pine burr, popcorn, berry-in-a-box are just a few of the variations. One of the most straightforward and commonly used varieties is blackberry or trinity stitch, so called because it works 'three into one and one into three', although some purists claim that they are two separate stitches, with a very slight variation between them.

MAKING A FIVE STITCH BOBBLE

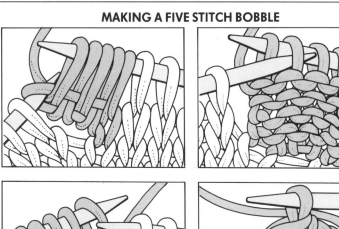

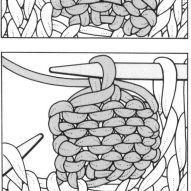

Make five stitches from one (top left), turn (above), and work four rows of stocking stitch over the bobble stitches only. Lift the stitches in order over the first (top right), until one remains (above).

This type of stitch is used as an all-over texture since the bobbles produced do not have great individual definition. If you want a more definite and dramatic bobble, to be scattered or used in clusters on a flat fabric, often in a contrast colour for even greater effect, the bobble must be scaled up in size.

Larger bobbles are formed by making more stitches out of the original one, then turning and working additional rows over the bobble stitches only. Any variations depend on the number of stitches and rows worked and on which stitch is used. A basic five stitch bobble in reverse stocking (stockinette) stitch is worked as follows:

1. (RS row) Work to the st where the bobble is to be made. Knit into its front, then its back, then front again and so on until 5sts have been made on the RH needle. Then, slip the original st off the LH needle.

2. Turn the work, k5.

3. Turn the work, p5.
Repeat steps 2 and 3.

4. Lift the bobble sts, in order, over the one nearest the point on the RH needle, starting with the nearest but one and working away from the needle point until only 1st remains on the needle. Work the rest of the row as normal. In this way, the bobble is worked separately from the main fabric, and there will be a small gap between the two, but this is hidden by the bobble itself.

If you are experimenting with bobble stitches using a pattern which was written for a plain stitch, there are two important things to remember. Firstly, allow enough yarn – bobbles take far more than a non-textured stitch. Secondly, take time and thought when it comes to any shaping. Re-

> *HINT*
> *Although the styling of the garment and the type of yarn you are using will dictate the approximate size of your buttonholes, always buy the buttons first – finding the correct colour and type can be one of the most difficult parts of the project. The buttonhole size can then be adjusted to suit the buttons, rather than the other way round.*

member that you have made more than one stitch out of the original stitch so that although you may have three stitches on the needle, as in trinity stitch, they are, in fact just one stitch and must be cast (bound) off, decreased, increased and so on as such. A short cut around this problem, provided it will not look too out of place, is to leave a border of plain stitches at either side of your work to accommodate all the shapings.

Although there are numerous variations to the bobble method, if you understand the basic principles and bear them in mind, even the most complicated 'MB' instructions become far less daunting.

BUTTONHOLES

Buttonhole making is yet another example of a finishing detail which is as important as the knitting itself. A beautifully knitted garment can be ruined by sloppy, untidy buttonholes which may pull cardigan fronts quite out of shape, besides losing any button-holding function they should have possessed.

There are numerous buttonhole methods but those described will produce a perfectly neat finish by knitting alone, without recourse to additional stitching or binding.

Vertical

A simple vertical slit can be produced by working to the required position and then joining in another ball of yarn so that you knit the work in two separate parts for a number of rows, according to how deep the buttonhole is to be. On the next row, work straight across all stitches with one ball of yarn and continue as normal. Use the two ends left at the top and bottom of the buttonhole to put a strengthening stitch at both points.

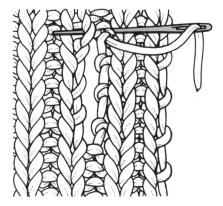

Use the ends left top and bottom to secure a vertical buttonhole.

If it is to be a deep buttonhole, worked in stocking (stockinette) stitch, work a small border of garter or moss (seed) stitch to prevent the edges from rolling (see *Selvedges*).

Eyelet/Round

At the buttonhole position, place the yarn over the needle, and then work the next two stitches together. Work the next row normally. This method produces a very small hole without any reinforcement, and is only suitable for small buttons and on garments which will receive minimal wear and tear.

Basic horizontal

This is the most commonly used method and is worked over two rows. On the first, the required number of stitches are cast off, and on the next row the same number of stitches are cast on, immediately above those which were cast (bound) off on the previous row. If the thumb (one needle) method of casting on is used, make sure that the first stitch is formed very tightly to avoid a loop at one side of the finished buttonhole. To allow the use of a two-needle method of casting on, the work must be turned.

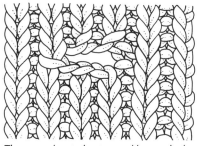

The most basic horizontal buttonhole, here worked in k1 p1 rib.

This method can look rather untidy at either end, especially when worked on k1 p1 rib. To neaten it, cast off one less stitch than is required, then slip the last loop from the right-hand needle back on to the left-hand needle and work it together with the next stitch, keeping in rib. When casting on, create one more stitch than is required and work this together with the next stitch to be worked after the

buttonhole, keeping in rib, as before.

Since buttonholes made using this method tend to stretch, it is best used when only a few stitches are to be cast off. Always work them as tightly as possible to compensate.

Self-reinforcing

This is worked over one row and is far firmer and neater than the basic

horizontal method. It can be worked on either side of the work.

Note: Put the yarn forward or back wherever necessary to keep the stitch in pattern.

1. Work to the start of the buttonhole. Put the yarn to the other side of the work from where it is required, eg on a RS row in st st the yarn should be brought forward.

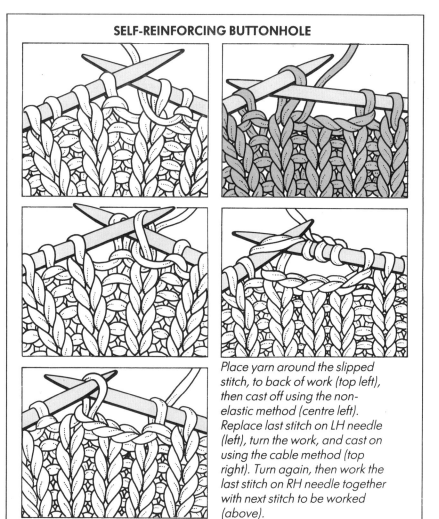

SELF-REINFORCING BUTTONHOLE

Place yarn around the slipped stitch, to back of work (top left), then cast off using the non-elastic method (centre left). Replace last stitch on LH needle (left), turn the work, and cast on using the cable method (top right). Turn again, then work the last stitch on RH needle together with next stitch to be worked (above).

2. Slip the next st and then put the yarn back into its correct working position. Leave it there.

3. Slip the next st from the LH needle to the RH needle and pass the first st over it, thus casting it off without working it. Rep this step until the required number of sts has been cast off.

4. Slip the last st back from the RH needle to the LH needle and turn the work.

5. Insert the RH needle between the last 2sts on the LH needle and cast on the same number of sts that were cast off, plus one, by the 'cable' method (see *Casting On*). Turn the work.

6. Slip the last st on the RH needle on to the LH needle and work it tog with the next st to be worked.

When the buttonhole is complete, work to the end of the row and continue as normal.

Open edge buttonholes

These lie flat and are ideal for buttonholes which are to be made on two thicknesses of fabric, such as when a knitted facing is being worked or when a doubled collar needs buttoning.

1. Work to the buttonhole position but make no opening, just work the required number of stitches in a contrast yarn. Join in another end of the working yarn and then continue as normal. Echo this on the facing, underside of collar or whatever you are working.

2. When the work is complete, double it over and pin it in position so that one buttonhole is lying directly above the other. Gently pick out the contrast yarn, leaving two rows of open loops on the top and bottom layer of work.

3. Using the yarn ends which were left at either side of the opening, graft the upper row on the top layer to the upper row on the bottom layer and the lower row on the top layer to the lower row on the bottom layer (see *Grafting*).

Contrast yarn is picked out to leave two rows of loops on both layers of fabric (above). These are then grafted together.

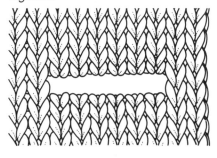

This method is also the one to use on garments which are to have fabric facings added, where the knitting is to be stitched to the backing.

Buttonhole stitch

If buttonhole stitching is used to cover up a really badly done buttonhole, it will always give itself away by looking bulky and untidy. *Always* try to get it right at the knitting stage.

On buttonholes which are going to take a great deal of hard wear or are already showing signs of strain, however, it can provide useful reinforcement.

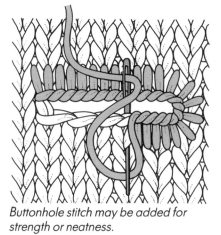

Buttonhole stitch may be added for strength or neatness.

■ BUTTONS

If you cannot find buttons which will match a knitted garment or if you prefer the softer appearance of buttons made from self (matching) yarn there are three ways of making them.

Covered buttons

These can be made in the same way as with any fabric. The metal bases which can be bought in haberdashery (sewing notions) shops are by far the easiest to use as the top, once covered, just clips on to the bottom. There is a limitation as to how much fabric the small teeth within the button can hold, however, which means that thick yarns cannot be used (double knitting/worsted is the heaviest weight that this type of base will hold). It also makes it important that the covering is a very snug fit so that there is not a lot of excess fabric which will prevent the back from clipping to the front.

If these ready-made bases are not available or are unsuitable, old buttons can be used as moulds but the piece of knitting used as a covering then has to be drawn up at the back to form a shank.

It is important to work button coverings in a solid stitch and at a firm tension to avoid the base showing through when the covering is pulled taut over it. Use any stitch you feel is appropriate but remember that only a small area of it will be visible so that a large pattern will be lost.

For circular buttons, work an octagonal covering of a suitable size, depending on your tension (gauge). For example, cast on 4sts, inc 1st each end of every row until it is the required width (remember that although no excess fabric is required, you must leave enough to turn under a clip-on base or form a shank under an old button), work a few rows straight and then dec 1st each end of every row until you are back to the original number of sts. Cast (bind) off.

Other shapes are not recommended since they will involve a lot of fabric having to be bunched at the back of the button, unless you are prepared to go in for some really fiddly shaping.

Button frames

Good craft and yarn shops now sell plastic button 'frames' of varying sizes which have their own shank. Yarn can

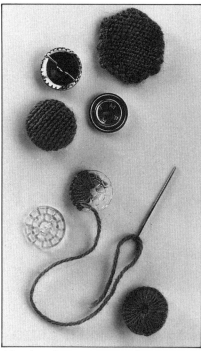

Matching buttons are made using bases which clip together, or by winding yarn round button frames.

be wound around these in a number of ways – using buttonhole stitch (see *Buttonholes*) – to produce self-coloured 'covered' buttons without having to knit a covering. As with covered

buttons, the thickness of the yarn is a limiting factor, since the yarn must be pulled through the holes of the frame over and over again, filling them as it is worked.

Crochet buttons

Using a crochet hook it is possible to make large bobbles without any mould by repeatedly working into the same stitch. There is a limit to how large these can be worked and, without a solid base, they are best used for decoration rather than on a garment which will receive heavy wear.

Sewing buttons

When attaching any type of button to knitted fabric, it is advisable to place a very small, lightweight button or a piece of fabric on the inside of the garment to take the strain off the stitches themselves. Use self yarn wherever possible but if this is too thick or textured, use a single ply or a matching button thread.

If you are buying buttons individually, always buy one or two more than you need to safeguard against loss or breakages. If you don't keep a button box, the spare can be stitched on to the inside of a seam for safekeeping.

CABLES

Cables are the embossed 'plaits' (braids) which are the unmistakable signature of aran knitting but which have a multitude of design uses, including anything from men's sport sweaters to delicate evening tops.

Cables are formed by setting aside a certain number of stitches on a spare needle, working a few more stitches from the main work and then working the stitches which have been held. The held stitches have been moved from their original position to the left or right of it, according to whether they were held at the back or front of the work. Every cable, however intricate it may look, comprises combinations of these front and back stitch swaps, worked over varying numbers of sets of stitches and row repeats.

Cables are most commonly and traditionally worked in stocking (stockinette) stitch with a reverse stocking stitch background. If the ground is worked in stocking stitch, a few stitches in reverse stocking stitch are usually worked on either side of the cable to give it greater definition.

Stitches which are being cabled can be held on a spare double-pointed needle or even a crochet hook of a suitable size. The weight of these, however, can pull the stitches out of shape and make handling unnecessarily difficult, so it is preferable to use the short, very lightweight needles made specifically for this task. Try to buy the ones which have a slight kink (wave) in the middle as this is a great help in keeping the stitches on the needle. Use the same size cable needle as you are using for the main work (a smaller one will not hold the stitches and a larger one will enlarge them) and move the held stitches with care to avoid twisting or stretching them.

Front cross cable (to the left)

This is the most basic cable, here worked over 6sts.

1. (RS) Work to the 6sts which are to be cabled. Place next 3sts from the LH needle on to the cable needle. Let this lie at the front of the work.

2. Knit the next 3sts on the LH needle, as normal.

3. Take up the cable needle and knit the 3 held sts from it, taking care not to twist them.

4. Work to the end of the row and then work 7 more rows in st st. Repeat the cross on the 8th row.

Back cross cable (to the right)

This is worked in exactly the same way as the front cross, but the cable needle is held at the back, rather than the front, of the work.

Mock cables

Twisted (crossed) stitches Very small mock cables can be worked over two

A mock cable worked as a separate strip of garter stitch.

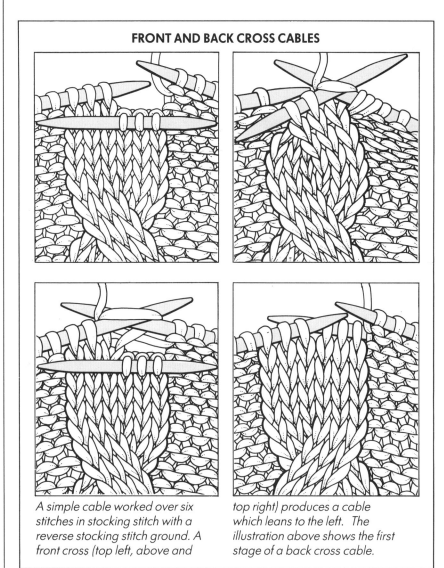

FRONT AND BACK CROSS CABLES

A simple cable worked over six stitches in stocking stitch with a reverse stocking stitch ground. A front cross (top left, above and

top right) produces a cable which leans to the left. The illustration above shows the first stage of a back cross cable.

main work to the desired length, allowing extra rows for twisting. Once twisted, the strip can be attached by knitting it together with the main working stitches — either directly above, or at a diagonal slant. If a long strip has been worked, it can be stitched down where necessary to keep it attached to the main work.

Cables can be used as a decorative panel, by themselves or in conjunction with other stitches, or to form an all-over fabric, but their effect on the overall tension (gauge) and shape of the garment must always be taken into consideration. The tension of a cabled fabric will always be far tighter than a flat one. Heavily cabled bodies can shrink to a fraction of their intended size, giving welts (finishing borders) a frilled appearance unless allowance has been made by casting on fewer stitches for the welt, and then working a series of increases across the row before starting to work the cable pattern (see *Increasing*).

Since the crossover method of cabling involves virtually doubling the fabric every so often, cabled sweaters are never lightweight. Bear this in mind when choosing your yarn, and steer clear of the 'heavies' such as thick cottons, silks and polyester ribbons.

stitches without using a cable needle. The twist effect is produced by working the second stitch on the left-hand needle and then, without slipping it off, working the first. Both are then dropped off the left-hand needle (see *Twisted/Crossed Stitches*). This 'tw 2' (cross 2RK) can be used on right side

rows of k2 p2 rib to form a very attractive fancy ribbing.

Jumbo 'cables' Dramatic, giant 'cables' can be produced using a separate strip of knitting in a non-curling stitch – garter stitch is ideal. The strip stitches may be knitted up from the

CASHMERE

Synonymous with luxury, cashmere is surely the most gorgeous yarn available for knitting, since it is ultra soft yet has none of the hairiness of such yarns as mohair, alpaca and angora.

Cashmere is produced from the hair, and the even finer underhair, of

Cashmere goats – their coats provide the most luxurious knitting fibre.

a breed of goat found in central Asia. This coat gives the animal resistance to extremely low temperatures, allowing it to survive in the most inhospitable terrain such as the Himalayas and the Gobi desert. Once a year, the underhair is removed by combing and the remaining coat is shorn.

Although the word 'cashmere' comes from Kashmir in northern India, it is likely that the connection was with the precious cashmere shawls produced there, rather than that Kashmir was the goat's original home. Today, China dominates the world market in cashmere and demand always exceeds supply, keeping the price at a constantly high level. The yarn is so rare that spinners who decide to introduce a cashmere yarn must book the raw material some years in advance. As the price of pure cashmere is almost prohibitive, most cashmere yarns have a high percentage of wool added. Besides bringing the price down to earth, this also adds strength since cashmere is not as strong as wool.

If you are lucky enough to find a cashmere yarn, choose your pattern carefully and treasure your finished garment. Once you have worn cashmere there is no looking back – you will be spoiled for life.

◼ CASTING/ BINDING OFF

Never let the euphoria which can be overwhelming when you finish a piece of work blind you to the fact that casting off must be tackled just as carefully as any other part of the knitting. It is so tempting to race along that final stretch, but take time to consider: What part of the finished garment are you dealing with? Will it be hidden in a seam or on full show, say on the edges of a collar? Does it need to be loose for ease of wear or firm to provide a base for knitting (picking) up stitches? Does the yarn or stitch method affect the degree of elasticity available?

As with so many knitting techniques, tension (gauge) is the most important factor. The most common fault is an over-tight cast off edge puckering the work and ruining the garment. In all but very few cases, the tension of the cast off edge should have the same 'give' as the knitted fabric itself and so it is essential to cast off in the same stitch as you were working: ribs must always be cast off in rib to allow elasticity, and even lace stitches should be kept in pattern, slipping, decreasing or making stitches wherever necessary to keep the cast off row in tension and to avoid puckering or frilling.

The basic method
The tension of this method is rather difficult to adjust without making the stitches uneven, especially if you are using a yarn with very little elasticity, such as cotton. It usually ends up too tight. To adjust this evenly, cast off with a larger needle than the ones you were working with. How much larger

depends on your own tension – experiment if you are not sure.

These instructions are for the knit side of st st.

1. Knit first 2sts. With the point of LH needle, lift first st over second.

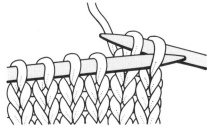

Lift first worked stitch over second.

2. Drop the first st between the points of the two needles. Knit next st from LH needle and repeat this lifting over. Continue along the row until you are left with 1st. Cut your yarn (leaving ample for seaming where needed), and pull through the st, fastening it off.

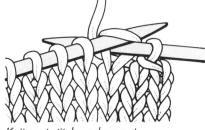

Knit next stitch and repeat.

The 'elastic'/suspended method

This is another way to regulate the size of your cast off stitch and a handy method if you have no access to a choice of large needles.

1. Knit the first 2sts. With point of LH needle, lift first st over second, but do not slip it off the LH needle.

2. Knit the next st, then slip the lifted st off. In this way, you enlarge

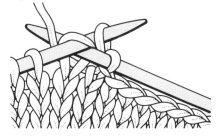

The elastic or suspended method regulates its own tension.

the cast off st by hanging on to it, rather than by using a larger needle.

Always use either the basic or the elastic method where a cast off edge

has to match the cast on one, as, for example, when you are working a garment sideways – starting with one cuff and finishing with another.

The English method

1. * Knit first 2sts tog.

2. Put this st just made back on to LH needle. Repeat from *.

This method produces an edge very similar to the basic method, but the way that it's worked makes it slightly more open.

Non-elastic

The movements involved in this method are very similar to those in the basic method, but instead of working the stitches and then slipping them one over another, the stitches are not worked at all.

1. Slip 1st k wise from LH to RH needle, slip another in the same way.

2. Lift the first slipped st over the second, leaving 1st on the RH needle.

THE ENGLISH METHOD

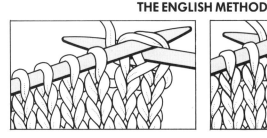

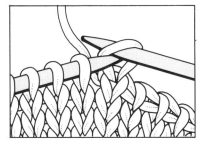

Knit the first two stitches together (left above), and replace the stitch made on to the right-hand needle (left). Repeat this movement (above). This produces a more open edge than the basic method.

Slip another st from the LH to the RH needle and repeat. Keep repeating until all sts are cast off. Since the yarn end is left at the beginning of the row, the last st to be cast off must be fastened with another end of yarn.

Although this is the fastest method possible, it allows no elasticity whatsoever since one stitch is simply being pulled over the next. It has its uses, however, when a very firm edge is required, say on the shoulder seams of a coat which will have to take a lot of weight. It is also useful when an 'anchoring edge' is needed on a garment which has been worked in a very loose or open stitch.

Elastic method for single rib/ Invisible bind off

Holding the sts on the LH needle, cut the yarn end so that it's four or five times the length of the row to be cast off. Thread up a blunt tapestry needle – avoid a pointed one, it will split stitches – with this end and use it to work the casting off.

1. * Put tapestry needle through the first st k wise and slip it off LH needle.
2. Ignoring the next purl st, put the needle through the next knit st, p wise. Return to the ignored purl st and put needle into it p wise, draw the yarn through and slip it off the needle.
3. Take the yarn behind the st still on the needle and bring it through to the front of the work. Put needle into next purl st, k wise. Pull yarn through, not too tightly. Rep from *.

This method is not half as fiddly as it sounds and produces a very neat, very elastic edge, once you get into the swing of it. It can be used wherever a really stretchy edge is required – on close-fitting necks, for example, especially polos.

Casting off on shoulders

The instructions given are for a shoulder with three steps, 8 cast off sts each.
Row 1: Cast off 8sts, work to end.
Row 2: Work 15sts, don't work last st, but turn work.
Row 3: Slip first st off LH needle on to RH needle and lift unworked st over it. Cont casting off normally until you get to the next 'step' then repeat the procedure.

This method produces a gradual slope, rather than an obvious 'staircase' and is the best to use where the shoulder seam is to be backstitched because the shoulder line will be kept smooth and not appear bulky when it is completed. If, however, the shoulder seam is to be a flat seam, take care with the slipped stitches as these become enlarged. (See *Turning* for the best method of ensuring a smooth shoulder slope.)

Casting off two pieces together

This method can only be used when the two pieces to be joined together have the same number of stitches, and forms a knitted seam (see *Seams*).

CASTING ON

Casting on appears to be the knitting technique with the most variations. Close analysis, however, reveals that

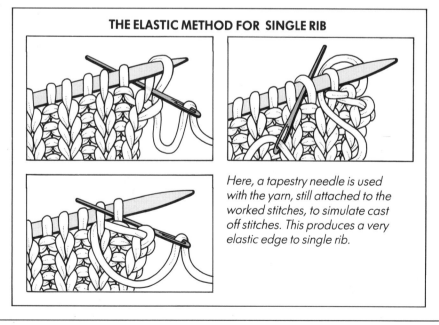

THE ELASTIC METHOD FOR SINGLE RIB

Here, a tapestry needle is used with the yarn, still attached to the worked stitches, to simulate cast off stitches. This produces a very elastic edge to single rib.

SIMPLE THUMB

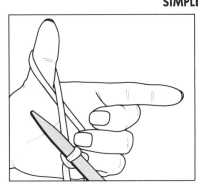

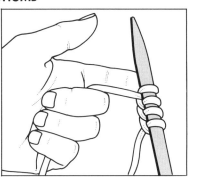

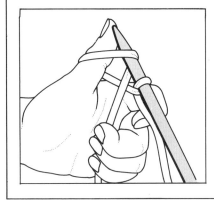

In this cast on method a loop is formed using the thumb only (left above), and the loop slipped on to the needle (left). This action is repeated until there are as many stitches as required on the needle (above). The edge produced is rather loose and loopy.

several methods are in fact the same, and the confusion arises from arbitrary naming.

All the major methods are covered here, although some are of academic interest only since few people need to use more than three or four of them in an entire knitting career. Try them all out, by all means, so that you can select the methods you feel most comfortable with and which suit the types of knitting and yarns that you work most often.

Simple thumb/One needle

This method uses only one needle, held in the right hand; the yarn is held in the palm of the left hand.

1. * Place the thumb of the left hand over the yarn and then back up under it to form a loop.
2. Put the needle into this loop from the bottom of the thumb, up.
3. Slip the loop on to the needle and pull it tight to form a stitch. Repeat from * .

This produces a rather loose, loopy edge which is not suitable as a finished edge. It is useful, however, if you need a row of loops to pick up later, as, for example, when forming a hem at the beginning of a piece of work.

Twisted thumb/Single cast on

The edge produced by this method is acceptable as a finished edge and it is particularly useful when working non-elastic yarns such as cotton.

1. Hold both needle and yarn as for simple thumb method, but place the left index finger down into the loop on the thumb.
2. Slip the loop on to the index finger.
3. Return the loop to the thumb; this twists the loop.
4. Lift the loop off the thumb, as for the simple thumb method. When it is slipped on to the needle it can be pulled up more firmly than in the simple method, and the twist keeps it in place on the needle.

Since the original loops are firm, it is easier to form a more regular stitch on the first row, creating a neater edge. As it produces a small knot effect, if you are working in stocking (stockinette) stitch, purl the first row. It is a little difficult to get the needle through the cast on stitches but it is worth doing for the extra neatness. Rib can be worked straight away.

Double cast on

This method is so called because it uses two ends of yarn to form each stitch.

1. Hold the yarn and needle exactly as for the simple thumb method, but make the first loop over the thumb some distance from the end of the yarn: the end left has to be long enough to complete the cast on row of sts.
2. The thumb is used just as a needle in the left hand would be. * Put the RH needle into the loop and knit a st using the main end of yarn.

Beading using purl beads, threaded on to the yarn before knitting, to create bands and highlight a fan of rib.

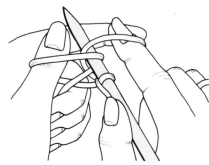

Knit the loop on the thumb.

3. Use the shorter end of yarn to form another loop over the thumb. Repeat from ***** .

If you are working in stocking stitch and purl the first row, this method produces an extremely unobtrusive edge, firm enough to be left as a finished edge. On rib, the effect is more irregular but still acceptable.

Continental method

In effect, this involves exactly the same yarn configuration as the double cast on above, but they are often dealt

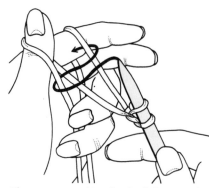

The continental method – following the arrows produces an edge similar to the double method.

Bobbles worked in angora, cotton, and a fancy spun cotton and acrylic.

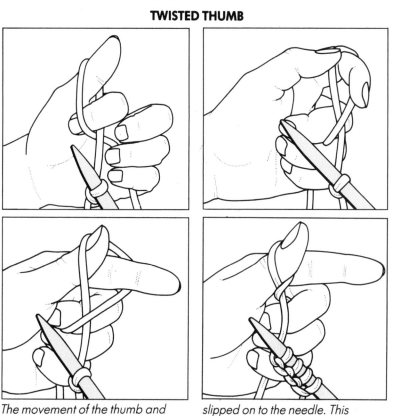

TWISTED THUMB

The movement of the thumb and index finger produces a twisted loop (top right), which is then

slipped on to the needle. This produces an edge with a 'knotted' appearance (above).

with as if they were two totally different methods.

As with all continental knitting, the working yarn is held in the left hand. This means that the short end forms a loop around the thumb and the working end forms a loop around the index finger. The RH needle is then passed in and around the loops to form a st, identical to that formed by double casting on. The difference is that the needle has been moved to form the stitch, rather than the working yarn, held in the right hand.

Two needle/Knitting on – simple

1. Make a slip loop (knot) and place it on LH needle. *****Hold both needles as for normal knitting and put the RH one into the loop and pull the working yarn through, as in a normal st.
2. Put this loop back on to the LH needle, forming a st. Repeat from ***** .

Although this is one of the most common methods used by British knitters (the one many are taught as children), it produces the most irregular and untidy edge. The knitter has

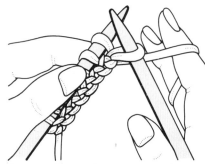

Two-needle simple casting on – basic and untidy.

virtually no control over the tension on the first row worked, which can result in a ghastly mess. The usual advice is to knit into the backs of the stitches on the first row but this produces an unnecessarily deep selvedge and is no help at all if the first row is to be ribbed. A method to avoid.

Two needle/Knitting on – cable

1. Form a loop and work the first st as for the simple two needle method.
* Then, instead of putting the RH needle point into the last st, put it in between the slip loop and the last st.
2. Pull the yarn through to form a

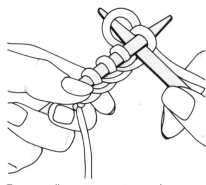

Two-needle casting on to produce a neat and even 'cabled' edge.

new st and place this on to the LH needle. Repeat from * .

This method produces by far the most even edge, sometimes described as 'corded'. It forms regular, firm stitches which require no special working on the first row. Since the whole stitch is used to form the next stitch, the very edge is doubled yarn which gives it extra strength and makes it suitable for garments which will receive hard wear. This double edge can sometimes be a problem – on very heavyweight yarns, for instance, it may be too chunky. It tends to give slightly too much fullness with some yarns and is unsuitable for yarns without any elasticity, for example cotton.

Open/Looped cast on

Work with one needle in the right hand, a length of contrast yarn and the main yarn.

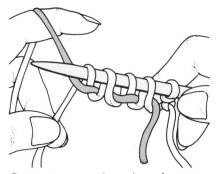

Contrast yarn used as a base for cast on loops.

1. Make a slip loop on a needle two sizes larger than those required for the main work.
2. * Loop the main yarn under the contrast yarn, over the needle from front to back, then under the contrast yarn. Repeat from * until sufficient sts have been formed. The work can then be continued. When the contrast

yarn is removed, a perfect set of loops is opened up.

Although getting the loops and contrast yarn in exactly the right positions, without them slipping around the needle, is rather tricky at first, this is the perfect technique for creating an open edge where an obvious cast on line is not desirable, such as with fine lace knitting, where the borders are knitted up from the open edge. If stocking stitch is worked, the row of loops can be picked up and knitted in the opposite direction without leaving a visible line.

Invisible casting on

There are three methods of casting on invisibly when working k1 p1 rib; they are listed in order of preference.

Double invisible This uses a single needle, two sizes smaller than those to be used for the ribbing, held in the right hand, and two ends of yarn.
1. Hold both yarn ends in the left hand and slip the yarn around the needle. Follow the arrows on the diagrams. Take the needle behind the

DOUBLE INVISIBLE

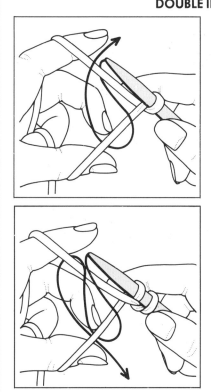

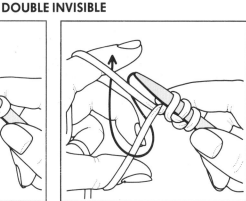

Although this method looks confusing, by following carefully the path of the arrow an extremely elastic and undetectable cast on edge is produced on k1 p1 rib. Use the right hand to steady the stitches being formed so that they do not swivel around the needle.

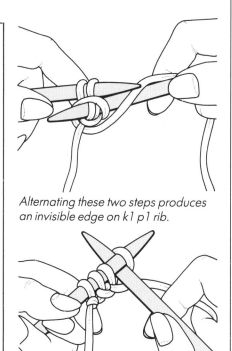

Alternating these two steps produces an invisible edge on k1 p1 rib.

upper yarn, then in front of and underneath the lower end of yarn.

2. * Take the needle in front of both ends of yarn, then under the lower end, and over and behind both ends.

3. Take the needle behind both ends of yarn, over the lower end, and behind and over the upper end. Repeat from * . Work the first row on the smaller needle and then change to the size required for the rest of the welt (finishing border).

This forms an edge which looks exactly like a machine knitted cast on and gives the welt the maximum amount of elasticity. It is not suitable for non-elastic yarns.

Two needle
1. Form a slip loop and place it on the LH needle. Cast on another st (using the simple two needle method).

2. * Place the RH needle between the 2sts from back to front. Place the yarn around it, as to purl it, and then draw a loop through. Slip this loop back on to the LH needle.

3. Cast on next st as for cable method. Repeat from * until you have the required number of sts. Start the next row with a purled st if the number is odd, a knitted st if it is even. With this method, you should also work into the backs of the knit sts on the first row only.

This is as neat as the double invisible method, but it produces a much firmer edge and is suitable for non-elastic yarns and delicate ones which need a little extra strength.

Tubular Although this method produces a neat finished edge, it works a double fabric for five rows and therefore tends to stick out. Using smaller needles for these rows can help but it is still not advisable for bulky yarns. (See *Double Fabric* for a description of the technique; here it is produced in k1 p1 rib.)

With two needles and a length of contrast yarn, cast on half the number of sts required, plus one, using the simple thumb method. Change to main colour.

Tubular cast on edge.

Row 1: * K1, yfwd, rep from * to last st, k1.

Row 2: * K1, yfwd, sl 1 p wise, ybk, rep from * to last st, k1.

Row 3: Yfwd, * sl 1, ybk, k1, yfwd, rep from * to last st, sl 1.

Row 4: As row 2.

Row 5: As row 3.

Row 6: * K1, p1, rep from * to last st, k1.

Row 7: * P1, k1, rep from * to last st, p1. Remove the contrast yarn and continue in single rib, as set.

Note: On the first row of this method, bringing the yarn forward and then knitting a stitch makes a stitch.

Before starting any work, take into consideration all the factors which are likely to affect the cast on edge. The type of yarn to be used, the behaviour of the stitch, and the degree of wear that the edge will receive will all make a difference to the method you choose, but it must be a method which you can handle with dexterity and which will produce a pleasing appearance on the finished garment.

CHARTS

Charts are most commonly used in conjunction with a pattern which will give you all the stitch numbers and

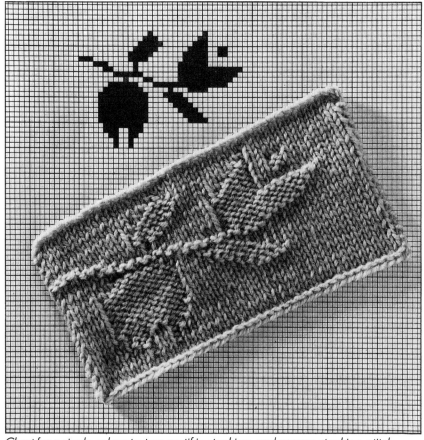

Chart for a single colour texture motif in stocking, and reverse stocking, stitch.

shaping details but will refer you to the chart or charts when it comes to a specific design on a part of the garment. If this is a self-coloured (one yarn) textured design, the chart will be straightforward to follow, using only one symbol or colour to denote the pattern.

Multicolour work which is charted gets more difficult. If you are lucky enough to be following a pattern which reproduces the chart in colour, you are halfway there. Charts reproduced in black and white, however, use symbols to represent each indi-

vidual colour (see page 49). This is where eye strain begins. It is no wonder the traditional Fair Isle knitters learned their patterns off by heart – such intricate charts, worked by candlelight, must surely have ensured premature blindness.

Before you knit a stitch, do yourself a favour and colour in your chart. Don't worry if you have not got the correct coloured pens or pencils – this is a guide only and can be reused with whatever colourway (colour scheme) you choose. If it still looks like a nightmare, you can copy it out on to larger squared paper, but that is a time-consuming process.

Assuming that you now have a legible chart, do not let it get the better of you. Remember that when you look at this flat piece of paper you are simply looking at a representation of the front of your piece of work. Read right side rows from the right to the left and wrong side rows from left to right. Each square across is a stitch, each square down a row. Bear this ratio in mind when the pattern begins to emerge on your work. If the design does not look in proportion, don't panic. Although the graph paper is squared, your tension (gauge) will hardly ever be. A standard 4-ply tension, for instance, is 14sts and 20 rows to 5cm (2in.). If it were like the graph paper, it would be 14sts and 14 rows to 5cm (2in.). Allow for this slight distortion when you compare your work to the chart.

Remember, too, that a chart for a design which is to be repeated will only show one repeat, and this may not look complete, depending on what point in the design you are to start working; for instance, a diamond in the design may have been cut in half in order to form a whole when it is repeated. The written pattern will always give you guidance as to the number of repeats which you must work, both horizontally and vertically.

At the end of the day, human beings fall into two categories – those who can relate to visual, graphic images and those who cannot. If you really cannot cope with a chart, then get someone to write it out for you:
Row 1: black 1, white 4, red 2, white 4, and so on.
Even better, if the kind soul in question is at a loose end, ask them to call the pattern out to you, as above.

For details on the actual knitting methods used, see *Colour Knitting*.

CHEVRONS

A chevron effect can be created using a variety of stitch and colour combinations, but there is only one way of creating a chevron by actually shaping the work so that the stitches lie in a zigzag pattern and the edge of the work is a distinct wavy line. This is achieved by working double decreases, spaced across the row, balanced out with single increases on either side to keep the number of stitches constant (see *Colour Knitting*). Worked in stocking (stockinette) stitch, this produces a subtle texture effect which may be highlighted with bands of texture stitches or lace effects.

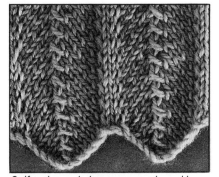

Self-coloured chevrons produced by working increases and decreases.

CHUNKY/BULKY WEIGHT YARN

Once yarns become thicker than double knitting (worsted), the naming of them becomes fairly arbitrary. Most spinners have their own ideas of terminology: double double, triple knit, quick knit and a vast array of fancy yarns may all be termed 'chunky'. This means that yarns with stitch tensions (gauges) of anything between 20 and 12sts to 10cm (4in.) can all be found in this category.

Many spinners make yarn identification even more difficult with the brand names which are used for each new yarn they produce. If you have chosen a pattern without seeing the recommended yarn, refer to the tension given on the ball band or label. Along with the needle size, this will give you a very good idea of just how chunky the yarn should be.

Every time you use a new yarn, try to memorize the tension so that, in time, yarn identification and substitution will become virtually automatic.

CIRCULAR KNITTING

Until the end of the 19th century, circular knitting – knitting worked in the round – was virtually the only method of knitting known. For a whole garment to be knitted using only two needles, turning back and forth, is still considered rather strange by the professional knitters of the Shetland Isles, who would rather cut openings in their work than knit with two needles.

It is probable that flat knitting increased in popularity as knitting became more of a leisure activity for amateurs, rather than an industry, and styling moved away from the traditional, and required more shaping and more detail. Since the great majority of knitters find sewing up (assembling) the least enjoyable task, it is strange that modern circular knitting is largely limited to socks, gloves, and the working of neck and arm bands.

Whether you use one circular needle or a set of needles, pointed at both ends, it is very important to use the correct length of needle for the number of stitches which you wish to work. Too many stitches will fall off double-pointed needles and crowd on a circular one, too few will not reach around the circumference of the circular needle or set of needles. This makes working the stitches very difficult, since the work is pulling away from the needle points, and results in odd tension (gauge) as the stitches are continually stretched. Double check

The completed cast on row on a circular needle.

the number of stitches which you will start *and finish* with before choosing the needle length. If the variation is very great, then flat knitting will be a more suitable work method. Alternatively, be prepared to buy more than one length of circular needle and change when necessary.

Cast on in whatever manner you would normally use, taking care not to twist the work as you do so – something very easily done. On sets of needles, divide the number of stitches by the number of needles minus one, and cast on that many across each needle being used. Since the usual number of needles is four, three for holding stitches and one for working, these will form a triangle. The first stitch of the first round is the first stitch which was cast on. To avoid twisting, you could cast on using two normal needles, work one row, and then transfer the stitches to the double-pointed needles.

Although double-pointed needles are usually only sold in sets of four, it is possible to use whatever number you, and your stitches, are comfortable with. Traditional rural knitters are said to have used up to ten, those in the Shetlands use only three. Whatever number you choose, take care when moving from one needle on to the next, as a stretched stitch will form a visible line right up the work. A good safeguard is regularly to move this changeover point by a couple of stitches or so. Move it in the same direction and by the same number of stitches each time or your work will become unequally divided between the needles, and remember to take increased and decreased stitches into account.

Circular knitting has many advantages, most notably speed, especially

Circular knitting on double-pointed needles.

when you are working stocking (stockinette) stitch. Since the work is never turned, every row is a knit row. For knitters who tend to work their purl rows more tightly than their knit rows, this also evens out the tension. When working a texture or colour design, it is also far easier to keep track since you are always looking at the right side of the work. In fairisle work this can be extremely helpful. It also means that the colour not in use is always at the back of the work, and that both colours are brought around to the starting point again so that they are always in the correct position when next needed, rather than having to be broken off at one side of the work and brought round to the other, as in flat knitting.

Another valuable use for circular knitting is if you are ad-libbing a pattern, working in different bands of stitches and/or colours (a good way of using up scraps of different types of yarn). By working the body in the round you avoid the time-consuming task of noting down what you are doing or having to use guesswork when it comes to duplicating the same effect on front and back. To make sure the sleeves match each other, work them simultaneously, on the same needle, on the flat.

When working a garment in the round, there are obvious points where the work must be divided and worked flat, for instance at armholes. It is still possible to produce a garment with no sewn seams, however (see *Guernseys* and *Cutting*).

To adapt a 'flat' sweater pattern to be worked in the round, add the front and back stitches together to calculate the number which you need to cast on. Most garments have stitches added as seam allowances, so these must be subtracted. Extra edge stitches may also have been added if a full repeat of the pattern being used would not fit in the row. Work out the number of stitches in a repeat as it may be possible to work another full repeat if the front and back provide enough spare stitches. This avoids having a plain band up either side of the garment.

Very few stitches do not lend themselves to circular knitting and the only method which actually becomes far more problematic is intarsia colour knitting since the number of separate balls of yarn in use is doubled when you work the front and the back of the garment simultaneously.

If you find seams difficult, or would simply like to speed up your knitting, do try this technique. Start off with a plain stocking stitch pattern written specifically for circular knitting, and then as you become familiar with thinking 'in the round', experiment with suitable 'flat' patterns which will lend themselves to adaptation.

COLLARS

This section is limited to a consideration of the most basic collar shapes in order to illustrate the techniques involved in their production. For reasons of space, a list of the range of design possibilities has been avoided.

Collars are normally worked in non-curling stitches, since the addition of borders can often prove too fiddly. If they are to be attached to a close-fitting neckline, they must be worked in two pieces to allow for either a front or back opening so that the garment will fit over the wearer's head.

Straight collars

These are used in conjunction with rounded necklines, which have been shaped as for crew necks (see *Crew Necks*). If the collar is small – up to a maximum depth of approximately 7.5cm (3in.) – it can be worked as a totally straight strip. If it is to be any deeper than this, it is advisable to add a slight degree of shaping by changing the size of the needles which you are using. Take the cast on edge as the outer edge, and change to needles one or two sizes smaller, halfway through the collar so that the cast (bound) off edge (which will be attached to the neckline) is slightly narrower, because it has been worked at a tighter tension (gauge). If you are knitting up the collar from the neck stitches, reverse the procedure. This allows the collar to sit on the shoulders without pulling out of shape.

Stitching the edges of the collar together for a few centimetres or inches at the front opening will make it stand up to a certain degree so that its points will aim downwards rather than to the sides.

Split roll collar

Usually quite deep, this type of collar can be worked in exactly the same way as a straight collar. The difference is that it is attached asymmetrically, with the opening to one side rather than centred at the front.

Eton-type collar

This is worked as for a straight collar, but the rather more exaggerated points are shaped by decreasing along the collar edges rather than changing needle size. The greater the number of decreases worked, the more extreme the collar points will appear.

Peter Pan collar

Since this is a very small, rounded collar, it is always put on to a close-fitting neckline which will require an opening at the front or back. If the opening is at the back, then the collar is worked in two identical pieces. The shapings which produce the curve should be very carefully worked, to keep the continuity of the stitch which you are using.

Basic shawl sweater collar

There is an endless variety of shawl shape collar variations, some of which involve complicated shapings. The one illustrated, however, consists of a wide, straight band which must be knitted separately. The trick is to attach it to the square neckline with the end of row edges sewn down to the horizontal front edge, one on top of the other. In this way, they overlap,

COLLARS

basic shawl collar for a sweater

cowl

polo

split collar

side split

Peter Pan collar

front split with small seam

eton-type shaped collar

basic shawl collar for a cardigan

causing the rest of the collar to fold back over itself.

Cardigan shawl collar

This shape may be achieved in a number of different ways, by working vertically or horizontally to form an elliptical shape. It is then attached to a 'V'-shaped neckline and turned back on itself. The deeper the collar, the greater the degree of shaping required to allow the turn back (lapels) to sit on the shoulders.

When attaching a collar like this which is shaped along one edge but straight along the other, always sew the shaped edge to the neckline edge, and leave the neater, straight edge as the outer one.

Classic roll/Turtleneck

This is used with the standard shallow crew-neckline shape and consists of a straight tube which can be knitted in the round or on two needles and seamed on completion. Since the roll must double back on itself, its height must be determined by taking the length of the wearer's neck into consideration. Also, consider the suitability of the yarn being used and any possible irritation which may be caused by the friction of the roll against the skin of the neck.

Cowls

These are tube shaped, as for roll necks, but are wider and considerably longer, and the extra fabric is folded back over itself more than once. This

Charts. A fairisle design which has been expressed in chart form using black and white symbols in one version and full colour in another. Both reproduce exactly the same pattern.

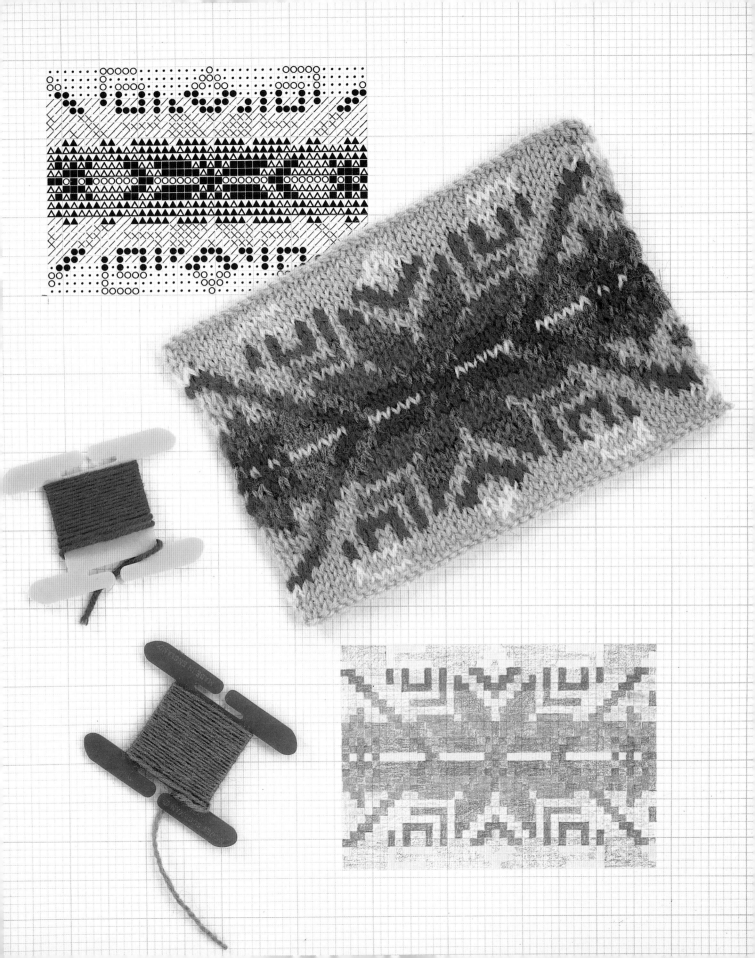

loose fall is also encouraged by a wider, more scooped, neckline than for a roll collar.

Even with these few basic shapings, endless permutations can be produced simply by altering the shape of the neckline to which the collar is to be attached, and varying the depth of the collar – they will often sit in a totally different way when the size is altered. Because they are small and quick to knit, collars provide a perfect area for experimentation and change since a sweater can be given a total revamp by removing the old collar and attaching a new variation.

COLOUR KNITTING

This term covers an enormous diversity of design but it can be loosely divided in two: vertical colour change, that is stripe effects which use only one colour in any row, and horizontal colour change, where more than one colour is used across a row.

There are two main methods of working horizontal colour knitting. Fairisle involves using two colours in a row, with the one not in use being carried at the back of the work. Intarsia allows for a number of colours to be used per row, with separate balls of yarn used for each area of colour.

The blue sweater here shows a four-colour design, which has been applied using Swiss darning, after the knitting is completed. The butter-coloured one shows embroidered smocking which has been applied all over the body on to a k2 p6 rib.

Some designs which use more than two colours in a row but have small areas of each colour, such as argyle patterns, incorporate both methods. For detailed explanations of the two techniques, see *Fairisle* and *Intarsia*.

Slipped stitches

These can be used in a variety of ways to create a two-colour effect across a

This slipped stitch pattern uses only one colour per row to produce a two-colour effect.

row, although only one colour is being worked at any one time. A basic method for achieving this is:

Cast on a multiple of 4sts plus 3.
Row 1: (WS) Using colour A, purl.
Row 2: Using colour B, * k3, sl 1 k wise, rep from * to last 3sts, k3.
Row 3: * P3, sl 1 p wise, rep from * to last 3sts, p3.
Row 4: As row 2.
Row 5: Purl.
Rows 6, 7, 8: Using A, rep rows 2, 3, and 4.
These 8 rows form the pattern.

In this pattern, the slipped stitches carry one colour up into a stripe of the contrast colour. By varying the colours used, number of rows worked and knit/purl stitches, quite intricate-looking colour patterns can be produced using this very simple technique.

Horizontal stripes

These speak for themselves, although there are a few tips worth noting. If a colour stripe is to be repeated at intervals throughout the work, make sure that you have an even number of rows in between so that the yarn will be at the correct side of the work when you next need it. If there is some distance between each stripe, the colour can be carried up the side of the work, weaving it in every few rows. **Note:** Only do this on garments which are to have backstitch seams to hide any untidiness (see the section on weaving in *Fairisle*).

When changing colour on the right side of the work, a knit row will produce a clean line and a purl row will produce a broken line. This should be taken into account if you

Horizontal stripes: change colour on knit rows for a 'clean' line, purl rows for a 'dotted' line. Moss stitch produces a 'broken' effect.

HINT
Always bear in mind when using several colours that every time you break off your yarn it will produce yet another end to secure at the end of your work. Preplan the colourway (colour scheme) as far as possible to avoid making unnecessary work for yourself.

are working stripes in ribbing. To produce a clean line, change colour on a right side row, knitting rather than ribbing it. If you specifically want broken-edged stripes, then use reverse stocking (stockinette) stitch, garter stitch or, even more subtly, moss (seed) stitch.

Chevrons

This 'wave' effect is created by working double decreasings (dipping

In a two-colour chevron, the shapings produce a wavy line.

points), and increasings (rising points), along every alternate row (see *Chevrons*) while working different coloured stripes.

Cast on a multiple of 13sts plus 2.

Row 1: (RS) * K2, inc 1 by picking up the loop between the needles, putting it on the LH needle and knitting into the back of it, k4, sl 1, k2 tog, psso, k4, inc 1, rep from * to last 2sts, k2.

Row 2: Purl.

These 2 rows form the pattern. Change colour every so many rows, as required.

Entrelacs

Although this creates a patchwork colour effect, an entrelac is worked in one piece. For details of the method, see *Entrelacs*.

CONTINENTAL KNITTING

In regular knitting the yarn is held in the right hand and wrapped around the needle to form the stitch. The continental method differs in that the yarn is held in the left hand and the needle moved around the yarn to form the stitch.

Individuals have their favourite ways of holding the yarn, but for continental knitting it helps to wind the yarn around the index finger at least once. On the knit stitch, the right-hand needle is placed through

CONTINENTAL KNITTING

In the knit stitch, the needle is placed around the yarn (top left) and the loop pulled through to form a stitch (above).

The action is similar in the purl stitch (top right and above) but the yarn is held more to the front of the work than in the knit stitch.

the stitch to be worked from front to back. It pulls the yarn, held behind, back through the stitch to form the new loop, and the old loop is slipped off the left-hand needle in the usual way. On the purl stitch, the needle goes through the stitch from back to front to catch the yarn, which is still held by the left index finger but more to the front of the work.

Since the yarn is held very close to the working stitches, movement is minimal. This means that, once the method has been mastered, phenomenal speed can be built up. The technique is common on the Greek islands, where the skill of the ladies in black is such that their hands become a blur before the eyes. Besides speed, its other main advantage is in two-colour fairisle knitting. If the continental and regular methods are combined, it means that one colour can be held in the right hand and the other, quite separately, in the left. Thus, neither yarn has to be dropped when you are not using it, making the knitting twice as fast and avoiding twisted and tangled yarns.

If you have always knitted in the normal way, attempting to change to the continental method takes a lot of perseverance. Don't practise on anything that matters since, at first, your stitches will be incredibly loose and uneven. If speed is important to you or, indeed, if you are taking up knitting for the first time, keep at it — it is well worth the effort.

CORNERS

When borders and the main work are knitted in one piece, corners present no special problems. The only point to

note is that the depth of the rows worked as the top or bottom border should correspond to the width of the stitches worked as the side border. This is easily calculated by comparing the row and stitch tensions (gauges) so that the borders match.

If the borders are to be knitted up at a later stage, or worked separately, or if hems which will meet at a corner are to be worked, then different techniques are required.

Knitted mitres

These are used when the horizontal and vertical borders are worked simultaneously; the stitches lie at right angles to one another. Depending on how long the borders are and whether or not more than one mitre is to be worked, it is usually advisable to use sets of double-pointed needles.

Inner corners On a square neckline, for example, knit (pick) up both your horizontal and vertical border stitches; one stitch right in the corner will act as the central 'axis' st.

Work to 2sts before the axis st, work 2 tog, work axis st, work 2 tog, work to end. Work next row without any decreasings. Repeat decrease row on next and every alternate row until

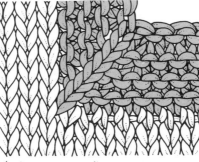

An inner corner mitre on a square garter stitch neckband.

the border is the required depth. Cast off.

Outer corners On jacket edges, for example, knit up both border stitches, as for inner corners.

Work to st before axis st, inc 1, work axis st, inc 1, work to end. Work next row without any increasings.

An outer corner mitre worked on a hemmed stocking stitch border.

Repeat increase row on next and every alternate row until the border is the required depth. Cast off. Take care to cast off loosely around the point of the corner, so as not to make it rounded; alternatively, turn a hem and reverse the shaping, decreasing one stitch on each side of the axial stitch.

Both types of mitre can be worked on separately knitted borders which are to be stitched to the main work. The stitch which you are using and the type of decreasings or increasings which are worked will give the mitres a variety of appearances, including some quite ornamental ones (see *Decreasing* and *Increasing*).

Cast/Bound off mitres

If both edges are to be turned under, as on a jacket with a hem and front edge facing, a mitre can be formed by decreasing or increasing one stitch at the end of every row. When they are turned under, join the mitre with a slip-stitch seam (see *Seams*).

Held mitres

This is used when the first border is knitted as part of the main work and the second is knitted up, at right angles to the first, after the main work has been completed.

If working the horizontal border first, cast on the number of stitches for the main work plus a number which corresponds to the width of the vertical border. Work in whatever stitch is to be used, placing one stitch at the corner edge on to a holder on every alternate row. When the border is the required depth, continue with the main work, as normal.

After completion, knit up the stitches along the vertical edge. Transfer the held stitches to a thread. Work the vertical border incorporating one held stitch on every alternate row until all the held stitches have been taken up. Cast off.

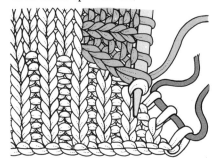

Mitre worked across vertical rib incorporating held stitches from the horizontal border.

Turned mitres

This technique is used when the horizontal and vertical border stitches are to be worked in the same direc-tion, rather than at right angles to each other. Work the horizontal border to the corner point, finishing a row at the outside edge.

Next row: Work to last st and turn without working it.

Row 2: Work normally.

Row 3: Work to last 2sts and turn without working them.

Continue as set, leaving an extra unworked st on every alternate row until only one st is left to be worked.

Next row: Work 2sts, turn.

Row 2: Work normally.

Row 3: Work 3sts, turn.

Continue as set, adding an extra held st to the working sts on every alternate row until you are working across all the held stitches. Now continue to work straight to produce the vertical border (see *Turning*).

■ COTTON

Since it is a natural plant fibre, after processing cotton is virtually 100 per cent cellulose. Grown in suitable climates throughout the world (USSR, USA, China and India are the major producers), it represents two-thirds of the total world consumption of all textile fibres. It is, therefore, rather surprising that cotton hand-knitting yarns are a relatively recent innovation.

The cotton plant (*Gossypium*) is ready to harvest when the 'bolls', or seed pods, split open to reveal the characteristic fluffy white wadding which surrounds the seed. Once the cotton has been separated from any impurities, the spinning process is much the same as for any other fibre although cotton's exceptional strength means that various chemical finishes can be used to lend it additional properties. With yarns for knitting, the most common process is mercerization. This involves immersion in a concentrated solution of caustic soda followed by restretching and the removal of the alkali. This gives the cotton a smooth lustre, prevents further shrinkage and increases its affinity for dyes.

As cotton is non-allergic, incredibly absorbent and desorbent (it will absorb an average of 40 per cent of its own weight in moisture, keeping the wearer cool and dry) and has excellent laundering qualities, it is a mystery why, for so many years, the only cotton yarns available were the very fine ones traditionally used for fancy lace crochet. Following its enormous growth in popularity in recent years, however, cotton yarns are now available in many weights and textures. A wide variety of other fibres are also mixed with it for reasons of greater economy, elasticity, or warmth. These mixes are some of the most interesting yarns to appear on the market for some years. If you've never knitted in cotton before, overcome any fears you might have since the yarns now being produced for hand knitting are gorgeous, and can be used for virtually any garment you would consider working in wool.

When knitting with cotton, it is important to remember that it does not have the elasticity of wool. This means that you must take greater care to work an even stitch at a constant tension (gauge) since any irregularities will not even themselves out as they do in wool. This is particularly applicable when working intarsia or fairisle as gaps can easily appear when you change colour.

Cotton welts (finishing borders)

The fluffy wide wadding of newly picked cotton, here in Peru.

picked up when the neckband is being worked. Each side of the neck is then worked separately; the total number of decreased stitches must equal the required number for the width of the neck (when calculating how large the neck opening should be, always remember to make enough allowance for the depth of the finishing border or band you intend to work).

Although there are no hard and fast rules as to the decrease sequence, the best curve is produced by dividing the depth of the neck roughly into three. Over the first third, decrease one stitch at the neck edge on every row. Over the second third, decrease one stitch at the neck edge on every alternate row and work the remaining third straight.

When working a raglan-sleeved garment or one with a saddle shoulder, this final portion, worked straight, is either shortened or omitted altogether since the sleeve top provides the side neck depth. When calculating the overall depth of the neck on such garments, this should always be taken into account.

The back neck can be worked straight – after any shoulder shaping, simply cast off all remaining stitches. More correctly, it should be given a very slight curve to echo that on the

can also become very baggy unless knitted at an extremely tight tension. It is usually preferable to use shirring elastic (elastic thread) to control the amount of elasticity that you require (see *Elastic*).

 COWL NECKS

See *Collars*.

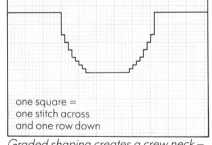 CREW NECKS

Viewed from the front, a crew neck – the classic round neck shape – should make a half circle. The exact shaping sequence depends on the number of rows between the start and finish of the neck, that is, its depth.

To start with, the centre front neck stitches are either cast (bound) off or placed on a holder so that they can be

one square =
one stitch across
and one row down

Graded shaping creates a crew neck – the classic round neckline.

front of the garment. This can be achieved by casting off the centre back neck stitches, minus a few stitches, a few rows short of the complete length. Decrease the few stitches which are necessary to complete the full width of the back neck over these last rows. **Note:** Be careful not to cast off the full number of stitches for the back neck otherwise the decreasings will make the neck too wide.

To finish neck, see *Neckbands*.

CURVES

When shaping a curve on a main piece of work, try to achieve as smooth a line as possible, by carefully graduating the decreasings or increasings to avoid sharp angles. Also, keep the edge itself neatly rounded by working the shapings a few stitches in from the edge, rather than on the actual edge stitch.

If a straight border is to be attached to a curved edge, such as at the bottom edges of a curve-fronted jacket or the beginning of the neck shaping on a cardigan with a deep 'V' neck, allow ample fullness at these points so that the border can be eased around. If the garment is to have deep borders, shaping will be necessary at these points so that the border has enough 'give' on the outer edge, when it is stretched around the curves. If this is not done, the border will tend to curl under on itself.

On a border worked vertically, extra fullness can be given to the outer edge by leaving a varying number of

inner stitches on hold while extra rows are worked over the outer stitches (see *Turning*).

If the border is being worked sideways, the shaping needed depends on the stitch used. A k1 p1 rib will usually have enough natural elasticity to fan out on convex curves and contract on concave ones. Garter or moss (seed) stitch, however, will require a few invisible increasings or decreasings at various points on the curve – how many depends on the degree of the curve to which the border will be attached.

If you are working the border from knitted (picked) up stitches, make the cast (bound) off outer edge as loose as possible around the curves. If working a border separately, always attach it to the main work by the cast off edge as the cast on edge will provide more elasticity for the outer edge.

CUTTING

Cutting along a row of knitting is fairly easy (see *Alterations to Finished Garments*), but cutting across rows is another matter since it leaves a raw edge with numerous ends. In certain places, this can be bound with fabric or even machined over to prevent the ends from unravelling, but the end result is very rarely acceptable, being too bulky, too untidy, or both. They are methods to be used in emergencies only.

There are, however, two ways of preparing the work for later cutting, at the knitting stage.

A steek

This is a plain band of several extra stitches, used by traditional fairisle knitters who work everything in the round, cutting afterwards where openings are required. When the garment is completed, the steek is then cut up the centre. If this is used on a cardigan, for example, the front bands are then knitted (picked) up from where the steek meets the pattern. The ends are then secured.

Loops

A gap in the pattern is produced in the same position as with a steek, but rather than working extra stitches, the yarn is wound around the needle several times before the next round is started. On the next row this loop is slipped off the needle and another loop is formed for that row. After completion, the loops can then be cut and the ends secured.

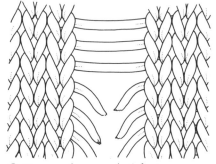

Cutting produces ends to fasten.

If you are knitting a garment in the round and then cutting, bear in mind that the benefits of seamless knitting have to be weighed against sewing in all these loose ends.

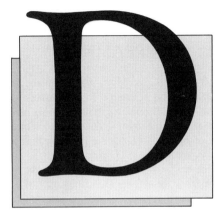

DARTS

Knitted darts provide one of the best illustrations of just how much more flexible knitted fabric, compared to tailored woven fabric, can be. Rather than removing a wedge of fabric, as you would with tailored darts, knitted darts are simply worked by turning rows or using increases and decreases. When calculating the size and positioning of a dart, however, it is useful to see an imaginary wedge in your mind's eye, since any shaping will, in effect, be disposing of rows or stitches in just such a triangular configuration.

Such shapings within the work are only suited to single colour stocking (stockinette) stitch. They will throw out any stitch or colour pattern unless allowance has been made for this.

Horizontal darts

These are suitable, for example, for side bust darts, and are worked by turning, within rows, to leave sets of stitches unworked (see *Turning*). When you have decided the exact position of the dart at the seam edge, work out how deep it needs to be and convert this into the number of rows, according to your row tension (gauge). Halve this number since you can only turn on every alternate row. Now calculate how many stitches long the dart is to be and divide these stitches by the number of turning rows to be worked. Don't worry if the number of stitches doesn't divide equally – the sets can vary by a stitch.

By leaving sets of stitches unworked at the seam edge, the wedge shaping is formed over the rows being worked for the dart. When completed, all stitches are worked across and the work is continued as normal.

When measuring work which has horizontal darts, do so on the side seam to get an accurate result.

Vertical darts

These are used, for example, at the waistline, and are worked by decreasing or increasing stitches at different ratios. Once again, bear in mind the wedge shape when you plan the dart as the increases/decreases must echo this shape. The widest part of the wedge corresponds to the maximum number of stitches increased or decreased. On a garment where the fabric has to be reduced, working from the bottom up, the dart starts at the pointed end of the 'wedge' and then widens out.

Decide where the dart should be positioned and mark the central stitch with a marker loop. Start shaping with very sparse decreasings (for example, work a decrease before and after the centre stitch on every sixth row), and, gradually, over the following rows, work these more regularly so that the dart finishes with a decreasing on every alternate row (see *Decreasing*).

If you are shaping a fitted waist and want the work to expand again after the waistline, work another dart above the first by working increasings at the same position in relation to the centre stitch and at the same ratio as the previous decreasings, but start with frequent increasings and finish with sparse increasings. In this way, two wedge shapes should be produced one on top of the other.

Use these two types of dart according to whether the fabric needs to be reduced or widened but always remember that the dart must be tapered to avoid the work becoming puckered.

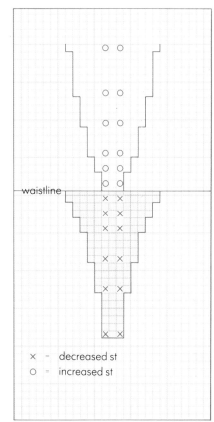

× = decreased st
○ = increased st

A double dart shaped in to the waistline and then out again above it, using a sequence of decreases and increases within the work. The shaded areas represent the imaginary wedges produced by the shaping.

Darts can be used at any point on a garment where shaping is required to form a curved fabric, the degree of that curve being controlled by the length and depth of the dart. This type of shaping within the work is totally different from the flat shaping achieved by simply increasing or decreasing at the edges of the work. In effect, it allows the work to become three-dimensional, and opens up numerous design possibilities.

■ DECREASING

A decrease is when the number of stitches on your needle is reduced by working stitches together to form one out of two (a single decrease), or one out of three (a double decrease). If a larger number of stitches is to be reduced, it is advisable to use a method of casting (binding) off rather than to repeat decreases, one after another, and produce an untidy fabric.

There are numerous methods of decreasing: which you choose depends on how obvious you wish the decreases to appear; where they are required – at an edge or within a piece of work; and if you wish them to have a specific 'tilt'. All finished decreases (with the one exception of 'raised vertical', see below) lean to the left or right.

The normal rule is that if the shape of the fabric slopes to the left then so should the decrease, and if it slopes to the right then the decrease should too. When you are shaping the back of a raglan sweater on right side rows only, for example, you would work a left-sloping decrease at the beginning of the row and a right-sloping decrease at the end of the row. In other words, certain methods provide pairs – one sloping one way, one the other, with the same finished appearance. Decreases which go against the slope of the work can be chosen to give a 'fully fashioned' appearance, and left and right slope methods can also be alternated to provide a decorative zigzag decrease line.

Try to avoid working decreases right on the edge stitches of a piece of work, unless there is no alternative – if, for instance, you are working over very few stitches or the stitch being used dictates edge shapings. Decreases also tighten the work and may create an edge with virtually no elasticity unless great care is taken to work them loosely. On edges, avoid methods which involve twisting stitches since these produce the tightest decreasings.

Wherever possible, work decreases at least one or two stitches in from the edge as this creates a far neater appearance, whatever method is used. This is essential if the garment is to be made up with flat seams, as edge decreases produce stitches which are far too loopy to form the basis of an acceptable seam. Decreases worked three or four stitches in will create a good border, perfect when working raglan shapings.

Note: For all methods involving slipped stitches, assume that all knit stitches are slipped knitwise and all purl stitches slipped purlwise, unless otherwise stated. This is important to remember to avoid unnecessarily twisted stitches. (See *Slipped Stitches.*)

Single decreases

Knit or RS rows For a right slope, K2 tog.

This is the most obvious and straightforward method, the two stitches are knitted together, exactly as if they were one.

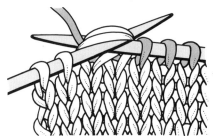

Knitting two stitches together is the most basic decrease but not always desirable since it always slopes to the right.

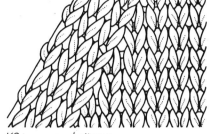

K2 tog every knit row.

There are three ways to produce a left slope in knit (right side) rows:
1. Sl 1, k1, psso.

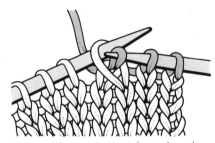

Slip one, knit one, pass slipped stitch over.

When you get to the stitch which is to be decreased, slip it from LH needle to RH needle, without working it. Knit the next stitch from LH to RH needle and then lift the slipped stitch over the one just worked. This method is best 'paired' with a K2 tog to produce a right slope, since they have the same appearance.

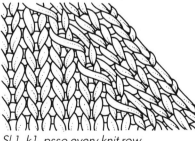

Sl 1, k1, psso every knit row.

2. K2 tog tbl.

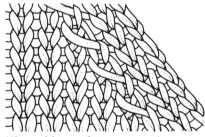

Knitting two stitches together tbl.

When you get to the stitch which is to be decreased, knit it and the next stitch on the LH needle together but instead of putting the right needle point into the fronts of the stitches to do so, put it through the backs of the stitches. Working into the back of a stitch is known as 'through the backs of loops' or tbl. This has the effect of twisting both stitches and is, therefore, a tight method, only suitable for knit stitches. It also produces a pronounced sloping strand, unlike method 1.

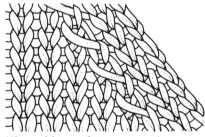

K2 tog tbl every knit row.

3. Mixed stitch.
When you get to the decrease position, insert the RH needle point purlwise into the first stitch on the LH needle and then knitwise into the next stitch. Work both stitches knitwise, pulling the new loop through both of them before slipping them off the LH needle.

This method produces exactly the same appearance as method 2 but only twists one of the stitches. This makes it marginally looser and considerably

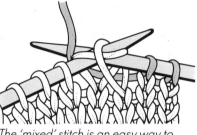

The 'mixed' stitch is an easy way to produce a left slope.

easier to work on stitches other than knit stitches, since it avoids the difficulty of getting the needle points into the backs of the stitches.

Purl or WS rows For a right slope (as it appears on the right side of the work), P2 tog.
Purl two stitches together as if they were one. This has the same finished appearance as K2 tog (above).

Purling two stitches together.

For a left slope (as it appears on the right side of the work), work to decrease position. Slip last worked stitch from RH needle back to LH needle. Lift the second stitch on LH needle over it. Put this stitch back on to RH needle.
This has the same finished appearance as K2 tog tbl (above).

59

Single decreases can be worked on both right and wrong side rows to form a continuous line on the right side of the work but if decreases are preferable on right side rows only, double decreases can be worked to reduce the same number of stitches.

Double decreases

Knit or RS rows There are two ways to produce both right and left slopes. For a right slope:

1. K3 tog.

Knit three stitches together in exactly the same way as if you were knitting one or two. This has the same finished appearance as K2 tog (above).

2. Sl 1, k1, psso, ret LH needle, pnso.

Work to the three stitches to be used for decrease. Slip next stitch, knit the following stitch and pass the

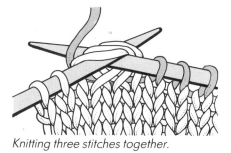

Knitting three stitches together.

slipped stitch over. Return knitted stitch to LH needle and pass next stitch on LH needle over it. Replace stitch on to RH needle.

SINGLE DECREASE

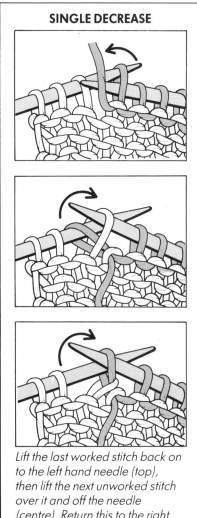

Lift the last worked stitch back on to the left hand needle (top), then lift the next unworked stitch over it and off the needle (centre). Return this to the right hand needle (above).

SL 1, K1, PSSO, RET LH NEEDLE, PNSO

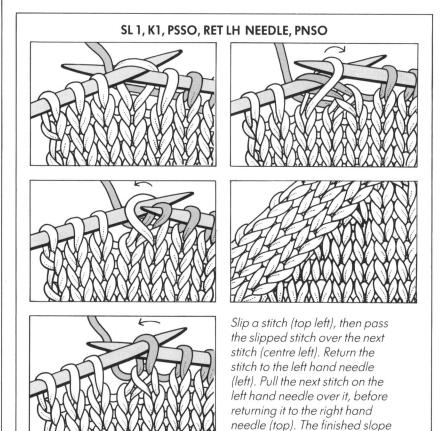

Slip a stitch (top left), then pass the slipped stitch over the next stitch (centre left). Return the stitch to the left hand needle (left). Pull the next stitch on the left hand needle over it, before returning it to the right hand needle (top). The finished slope is illustrated above.

For a left slope:
1. K3 tog tbl.

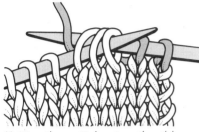

Knitting three stitches together tbl.

Knit three stitches together through the backs of the loops. This can be rather cumbersome, especially if you are working a stitch with a tight tension (gauge) or stitches other than stocking (stockinette) stitch.

This has the same finished appearance as K2 tog tbl (above).
2. Sl 1, k2 tog, psso.

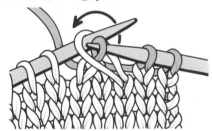

The slipped stitch is pulled over the two stitches which have been knitted together.

Work to the three stitches to be used for the decrease. Slip one, knit the next two stitches together to make one. Pass the slipped stitch over this one. This is much easier to work than method 1 and has the same finished appearance as Sl 1, k1, psso, ret LH needle, pnso (above).

Purl or WS rows Here, there are two ways to produce a right slope (as it appears on the right side of the work):
1. P3 tog.

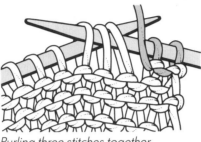

Purling three stitches together.

Purl three stitches together, in exactly the same way as if you were working one or two. This is difficult on tightly worked stitches, and the finish feels rather lumpy, although the appearance is acceptable.

This has the same finished appearance as K2 tog (above).
2. Sl 1, p1, sl 1, psso twice.

Work to the three stitches to be used for the decrease. Slip one, purl one and then slip the next stitch knitwise and immediately replace it on the LH needle, twisting it as you do so. Slip purled stitch back from RH needle to LH needle. Slip the twisted stitch over it. Return it to the RH needle and slip the original slipped stitch over it. This produces a flatter finish but has to be worked with the points of the needles only to avoid stretching the stitches.

This has the same finished appearance as Sl 1, k1, psso, ret LH needle, pnso (above).

> ### HINT
> *For chevron knitting, the raised vertical method of decreasing provides by far the best finish. It is also perfect for any fabric which requires central, ornamental shaping, such as some lace patterns.*

SL 1, P1, SL 1, PSSO TWICE

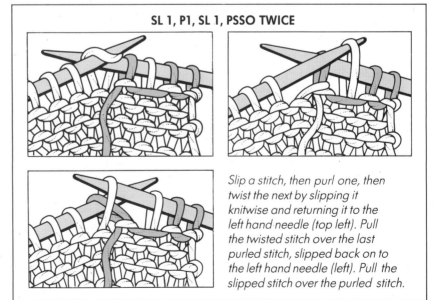

Slip a stitch, then purl one, then twist the next by slipping it knitwise and returning it to the left hand needle (top left). Pull the twisted stitch over the last purled stitch, slipped back on to the left hand needle (left). Pull the slipped stitch over the purled stitch.

For a left slope (as it appears on the right side of the work), P2 tog, sl 1, psso.

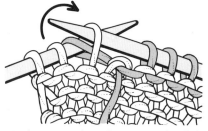

Purl two together, slip one, and pull the next stitch over.

Work to the three stitches to be used for the decrease. Purl two together and replace the stitch made back on to LH needle. Slip the second stitch on the LH needle over the one you've just replaced. Return this stitch to RH needle.

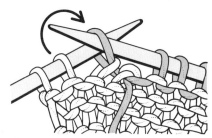

Return the stitch to the right hand needle.

This has the same finished appearance as K2 tog tbl (above).

Raised vertical This differs from all previous methods in that it is a double decrease which produces a neat line of vertical stitches which progresses up the work with the fabric on either side sloping in towards it.

On a RS row, work to the three stitches to be used for the decrease. Slip the next two stitches knitwise,

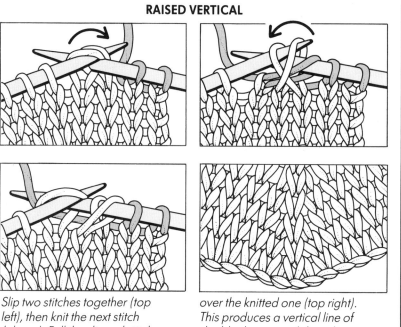

RAISED VERTICAL

Slip two stitches together (top left), then knit the next stitch (above). Pull the slipped stitches

over the knitted one (top right). This produces a vertical line of double decreases (above).

both together rather than singly. Knit the next stitch and then pass both the slipped stitches over it. If the line of stitches produced by this method is not vertical, check that you are slipping them knitwise and both at the same time. Twisted or individually slipped stitches will not create a straight line. Also make sure that you are working the decrease at exactly the same point on each row so that they line up one on top of the other.

DESIGNING

Designing knitwear deserves an entire book dedicated to the subject. If it could be dealt with adequately in a short section of an encyclopedia of

knitting techniques then the fashion students at art colleges and the design teams employed by the major spinners would be wasting their time. Unfortunately, the ability to draw a satisfactory representation of a sweater and the skill required to create a written set of instructions from which that sweater can then be reproduced are often taken to be one and the same thing. To compare the two is rather like mastering 'chopsticks' on the piano and calling yourself a composer. This is not to say that creating original patterns to suit your own size and taste is beyond the average knitter, but it does involve more than simple drawing. In this section, when discussing 'designing' we will, in fact, be considering something far less glamorous-sounding – pattern drafting.

Taking measurements

A. The bust/chest, measured over fullest part.

B. The waist, measured over narrowest part.

C. The hips, measured around fullest part.

D. The shoulder width, measured to the imaginary line **E**, that is, where a seam would come on a set sleeve style – not to the full width which would include the top of the arm.

E. Armhole depth, measured in a straight line from the level of the armpit to the highest point of the shoulder.

F. Length, measured from the highest point of the shoulder to the required lower edge.

G. Neck width, measured at the back of the neck, not the front.

H. Neck drop, measured from the imaginary line **G** to the front of the collar bone.

I. Sleeve seam, measured from armpit to cuff edge.

J. Upper arm, measured around the fullest part.

K. Wrist, measured around the point at the required sleeve length.

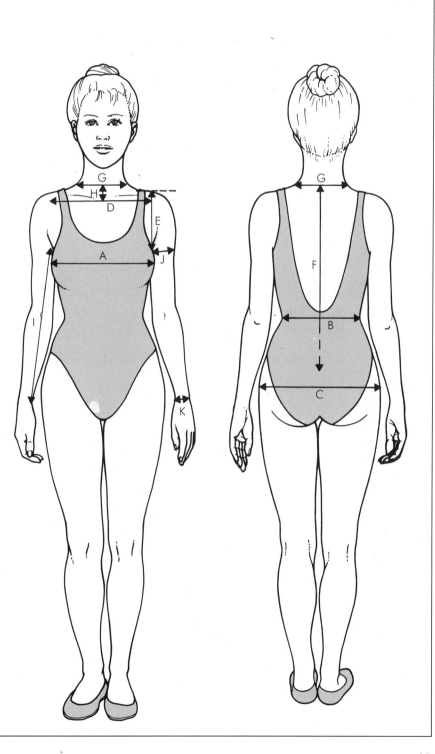

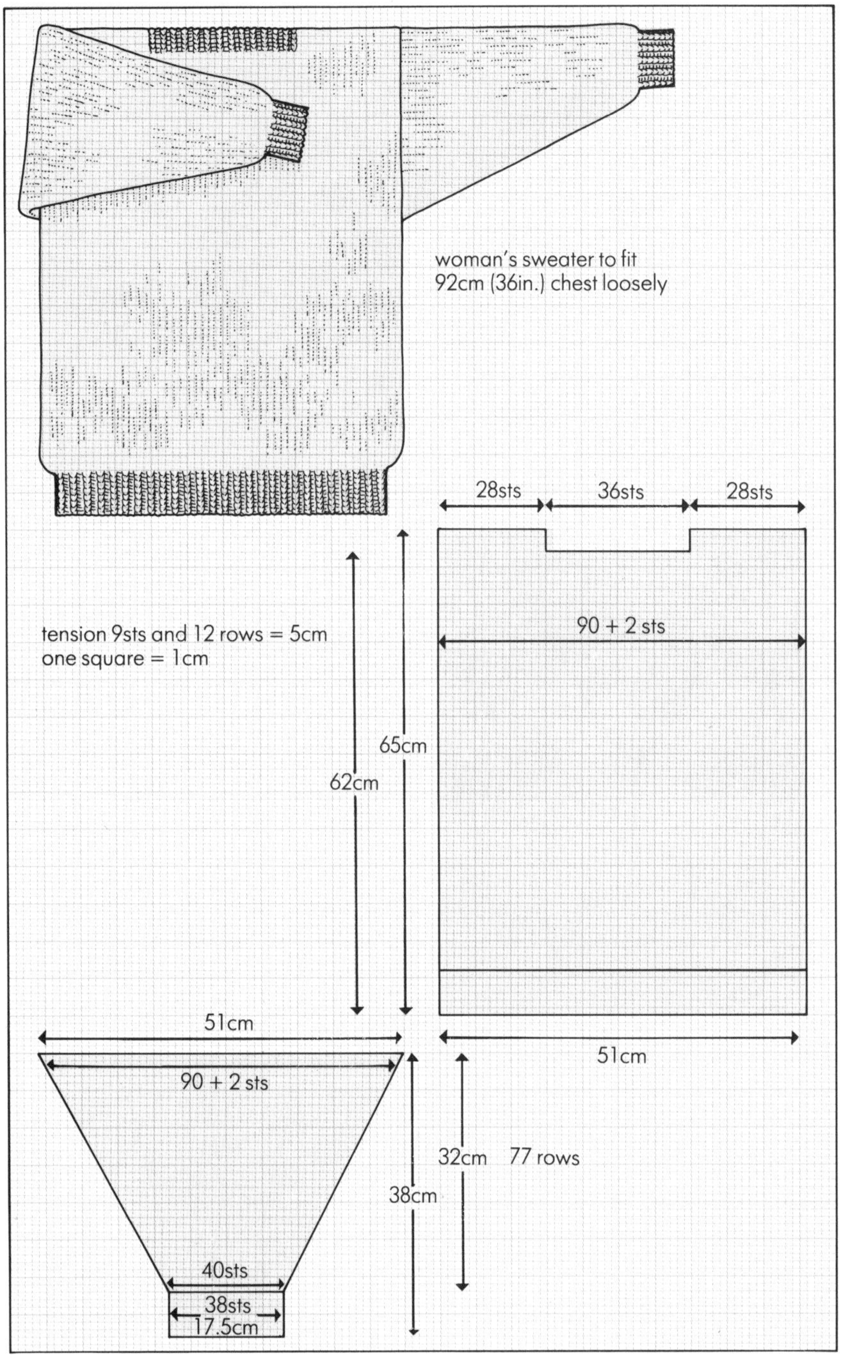

woman's sweater to fit
92cm (36in.) chest loosely

tension 9sts and 12 rows = 5cm
one square = 1cm

28sts   36sts   28sts

90 + 2 sts

65cm

62cm

51cm

90 + 2 sts

51cm

32cm   77 rows

38cm

40sts

38sts
17.5cm

The extraordinary number of permutations of stitch, yarn, needle size, and styling mean that the basic techniques guides which are to be found in this book are merely starting points. It takes years of experience (in other words, trial and error) to produce a truly competent designer with the ability to draft patterns and, even then, mistakes are all too common – we are only human, after all.

It would be impossible to start on a list of all the knitwear styling variations available – there wouldn't be a book large enough and since any such list would be partially, if not wholly, out of date by the time that the book appeared on the shelves, the task would be pointless. For that reason, here the most basic sweater shape – not much more than four rectangles – will be used to illustrate the basic mechanics of pattern drafting: the creative processes of true designing must be left for another book.

Even when creating the most simple garment, fit is vitally important. You may, for instance, want something loose and easy to wear, but there is baggy and *baggy* and although it may be acceptable to have an over-sized body, nobody really wants floor-length sleeves. Although the standard sizing tables are an invaluable guide when it comes to quick reference – such as the average width of a back neck opening, for example, or usual waist to hip differences – they cannot help with the allowances to be made for fit, since fashion and personal preference make hard and fast rules impossible. Although you may want a garment for a 92cm (36in.) chest, the extra width to be added so that the garment does

Basic measurements translated into stitch numbers, according to tension.

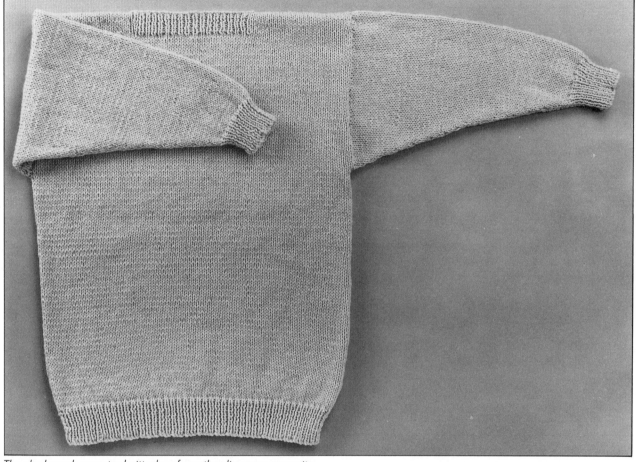

The slash neck sweater knitted up from the diagram opposite.

not actually fit like a second skin could be anything from 6 to 60cm (2½–25in.).

When calculating fit, the best method by far is to take the overall measurements from a garment which you, or the potential wearer, already possesses. It doesn't even have to be a sweater, if the fit and styling are similar there's no reason why measurements shouldn't be taken from a shirt, coat, or even a nightdress. If you have nothing which is near the correct fit,

then just go into a shop armed with a tape measure, try something on and measure it up.

Measurements

Once you have a list of the basic measurements required for the finished garment, draw each piece of the garment in plan with the working measurements – a 102cm (40in.) bust, for example, will be 51cm (20in.) across the front, plus any seam allowances. In a fairly heavyweight yarn,

the seams will be flat rather than backstitched and so no seam allowance is necessary although one or two extra stitches should always be added since the edge stitches do not count as full stitches when you are measuring tension (gauge).

Tension/Gauge

Ascertain the stitch and row tension suitable for the yarn which you are using. On most branded yarns the stocking (stockinette) stitch tension will be quoted on the ball band (label). Use this as a guide when checking your own tension. *This is the most important part of the pattern.* All the subsequent calculations which you will make will be based on these measurements (see *Tension/Gauge*).

This sweater will be worked at a tension of 9sts and 12 rows to 5cm (2in.) over stocking stitch on 5mm (size 8) needles. By dividing the width of the work by the tension measurement (51cm ÷ 5 = 10), and then multiplying this by the number of stitches to this tension (10 × 9 = 90), the number of stitches required to work the front can be calculated. Adding two stitches to compensate for the edge stitches gives a total of 92 stitches. Since there is no shaping on the body, this is the number of stitches which should be on the needles from the end of the welt (finishing border) right up to the shoulder point.

Welts/Finishing borders

K1 p1 (or single) rib is the most common border stitch. If the sweater is to be quite a long one, sitting on the hips, a tight welt is not required: 4.5mm (size 7) needles, just one size smaller than those required for the main work, can be used. For a welt which pulled in, smaller needles could be used and a smaller number of stitches than those needed for the overall width of the garment cast on; the extra stitches would be increased on the first row after the completion of the rib. For this sweater 92 stitches will be cast on and this number will be kept constant throughout the length of the work as no side shaping is to be worked.

When working in single rib it is important to have an even number of stitches so that the seams appear neat.

The last stitch on the first row of the front will be purl and the first stitch on the first row of the back will be knit, thus keeping in pattern right around the garment. If an odd number has been calculated then either add or subtract one stitch to make the number even. If you add a stitch, it can be decreased after finishing the rib if it is not needed on the rest of the body. An average single rib welt depth is 6–7cm (2½in.). A narrower welt will not give quite so much control and may cause the bottom edge to become baggy on a long-line sweater where the welt will take more strain than if it was situated at waist level. A deeper rib will give a more figure-hugging effect around the hips. After completing a sufficient number of rows in rib, change the needle size to that needed for the main work. It is at this point that stitches would be increased, evenly across the row, if the full number had not been cast on in the first place.

Front and back

On a drop shoulder sweater with no armhole or shoulder shaping and a straight, slashed neck, the back and front can be worked identically until the point where the neck edging is worked. This should be about 3cm (1¼in.) short of the full length. Mark both measurements on the plan.

Since there is no armhole shaping on a drop shoulder style, the sleeves will be shorter than those required where armhole shaping has been worked. This is because the shoulders are wider than on a set in sleeved garment – approximately 10cm (4in.) on a medium woman's size. This extra width is, in effect, extra sleeve length, and adds about 5cm (2in.) to the finished length. The wider the fit of

the body, the more allowance you must make when calculating the required length of the sleeves. This is why, in plan, the sleeves of this type of garment look rather stubby.

Neck border

A slash neck does not require semi-circular shaping, as a scoop or crew neck does. Since no allowance is made for the shape of the head, however, the neck opening itself must be wide enough to allow the garment to be pulled over the head. At the same time it should not be too wide or the neck will tend to slip off the shoulders. On an average woman's garment approximately 20cm (8in.) is about right. At a tension of 9sts to 5cm (2in.) this means that the neck will be 36 stitches wide.

On a garment worked in stocking stitch, a neck edge cast off and left unfinished would curl back on itself. The simplest way of finishing a slash neck is to work an inset border so that the finished line of shoulder and neck is still straight across. The alternative is to work the full length of the garment, and then work extra rows which can be turned in and stitched down as a facing. Here an inset border will be worked. Any non-curling stitch can be used (see *Bands or Borders*), but when deciding which stitch to use, the stitches used on

Contemporary fairisle method designs. The multicolour one uses several colours of alpaca, but never more than two on any given row. The black and white and grey sweater is knitted in mohair and uses a slight texture stitch in addition to working two colours per row. The techniques are identical to those used for traditional Fair Isles.

other parts of the garment should be taken into consideration. Naturally, there are no strict rules governing the choice of stitch, but since single rib is already being used for the welts and cuffs, it is far more appropriate to use it at the neck than moss (seed) stitch, for instance, unless another moss stitch feature, say pocket flaps, had been incorporated.

As border stitches should always be worked on a smaller needle, wherever possible, it will be necessary to put the 36 neck stitches on a holder when the work reaches the border point (62cm/ 25in.). Both sides of the neck will be continued, straight, until the full length (65cm/26¼in.) is reached. The held stitches are then slipped on to a 4.5mm needle, as for the welts, and 3cm (1¼in.) of single rib worked before casting (binding) off to form the actual neck edge. At the making up (assembling) stage, each end of the border will be stitched to the main work, using a flat seam. A few over-sewn stitches can also be placed at each side of the neck opening to give it a little extra strength.

Shoulders

The width of the neck and the number of stitches for each shoulder should be calculated at the same time, so that you know how many stitches to work before slipping the neck border stitch-es on to a holder. Subtract the neck stitches from the total (92–36), and

---

Classic Fair Isle designs, the cardigan colours reproducing chemically one of the original, hand-dyed colourways. The cuff of the snowflake sweater shows the use of colour pattern across welts, the 'V'- neck slipover illustrates a random use of colours.

then divide the remainder by two – that gives 28 stitches for each shoulder.

When the required length has been reached, the shoulder stitches can be individually cast off or, since they are straight and both fronts and backs have the same number of stitches, they can be cast off together to form the shoulder seams (see *Seams*).

Cuffs

These should be worked in single rib for 6–7cm (2½in.) to match the welts. The cuffs on a normal sweater have to fit fairly closely so the wrist measurement should not have any extra allowance added. On this swea-ter, 36 stitches are cast on to fit a 17.5cm (7in.) wrist. Stitches can be increased after the ribbing to widen the sleeve.

Sleeves

On a normal sweater sleeve, the cuff measurement is always smaller than that at the top of the arm. This means that, working from the cuff up, shap-ing is necessary to increase the number of stitches on the needle.

On your plan, mark the width of the sleeve at the cuff point and at its widest point – the very top. Also mark the full length of the sleeve, and its length minus the depth of the cuff. Convert the width measurements into stitch numbers and take one from the other to calculate how many stitches have to be increased. On this sleeve, the top of the sleeve is quite wide at 51cm (20in.), to echo the looseness of the body shape. This means that 56 stitches must be increased. The choice is whether to increase these stitches across the first row of the sleeve after the cuff or to spread the increasings up the length of the sleeve.

Working increasings across the first row and then working the rest of the sleeve straight creates a puff effect above the cuff and produces a very full sleeve right from the start. Increasings which are spread over the length of the sleeve, worked at the ends of the rows, create a shape which gradually widens out. Both types of shaping can also be combined, according to the shape of sleeve and how many stitches have to be increased over the number of rows available.

Calculate the number of rows with-in the main sleeve (always remember to subtract the depth of the cuff since the shapings will not be worked over these rows) by dividing the length by the row tension measurement (32cm ÷ 5cm = 6.4), and then multiplying that by the actual tension (6.4 × 12 = 76.8, rounded up to 77 rows). From this, we know that the 56 increased stitches must be achieved over 77 rows or thereabouts. Since shapings are nearly always worked at either end of a row, to assist in calculation and in keeping track of the working, we are, in fact, talking about 28 pairs of increasings. Therefore, 77 should be divided by 28 to find out on which rows the increasings should be work-ed. The answer is 2.75, which must be rounded up or down to provide a workable solution. Working pairs of increasings on alternate rows creates a very steep angle which will produce a dolman sleeve shape – it is more appropriate to round the figure up so that increasings are worked on every third row.

This is where we must start to work backwards in order to neaten things up. Multiplying the ideal increase sequence – every third row – by the number of increase pairs – 28 – gives 84 rows. This gives us the choice of lengthening the sleeve by seven rows so that we have enough rows to complete all the shapings, or increasing the necessary stitches across the row after the welt.

Lengthening the sleeve is not desirable, so the extra stitches to be increased are calculated by dividing the number of rows by the increase sequence (77 ÷ 3 = 25.6). Rounded up to 26, this is the new number of increase pairs required. This leaves us with four stitches to be increased, evenly (one every nine stitches), across the first row of the stocking stitch. By increasing one stitch at each end of the next and every following third row and by adding just one more row, making 78 in all, 92 stitches will have been reached by the time that the sleeve is 38cm (16in.) long, and may be cast off.

Unfortunately, much of the juggling about, rounding up, rounding down, adding odd stitches and rows here and there can make the whole process appear incomprehensible. It isn't. Pattern drafting is simply the marriage of logical, arithmetical calculations with the skill and experience to interpret those figures in a flexible way.

◻ DOUBLE FABRIC

One colour

This is a method of tubular knitting without using circular or double-pointed needles. By slipping alternate stitches along each row, two stocking (stockinette) stitch fabrics can be knitted simultaneously. These are joined at the sides, and at the cast on and cast (bound) off edges.

Note: For all methods involving slipped stitches, assume that all knit stitches are slipped knitwise, and all purl stitches are slipped purlwise, unless otherwise stated.

Row 1: * K1, yfwd, sl 1 p wise, yb, rep from * .

Row 2: K all the sts which were slipped on row 1 and slip those which were knitted. If you cast off straight along the row this will join the work at this edge.

This method is useful where a tubular piece of work is required but circular or double-pointed needles are not available. It can be used where plain stocking stitch is to be worked without any borders. Because it is double, the fabric will not curl.

Contrast lining

If you are working each fabric in a different colour, to form a contrast lining, double-pointed or circular needles must be used. To keep the colours separate, two rows are worked in each:

Cast on an even number of sts.

Row 1: Colour A * k1, yfwd, sl 1, ybk, rep from * to end. Don't turn, start at beginning again.

Row 2: Colour B * ybk, sl 1, yfwd, p1, rep from * to end. Turn work as in normal two-needle knitting.

Row 3: Still using B, rep row 1. Don't turn.

Row 4: Colour A, rep row 2. Turn. These 4 rows form the pattern.

Take care to twist the yarns around one another at the ends of the rows when you turn the work, otherwise the sides will not be joined. Cast off as for the single-colour method.

Although the work produced by both these methods is knitted as two fabrics and joined on all four sides, it cannot really be called double-sided or

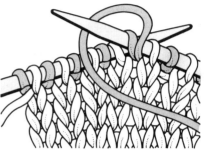

Working a purl stitch from the back layer of fabric.

reversible since the front and the back remain quite separate and can be pulled apart from one another.

Reversible fabric

By working a colour pattern which involves the same two colours on both sides of the work, the two halves become one fabric which cannot be separated, since the same yarn is used on both front and back fabrics. The pattern on one side will appear as its own negative on the other side of the fabric. Circular or double-pointed needles are required for this method. A simple chequers (checkerboard) pattern can be worked as follows:

Cast on a multiple of 16sts plus 8.

Row 1: Colour A * (ybk, k1, yfwd, sl 1) 4 times, (ybk, sl 1, yfwd, pl) 4 times, rep from * to end. Don't turn work, return to beginning of the row.

Row 2: Colour B * (ybk, sl 1, yfwd, pl) 4 times, (ybk, k1, yfwd, sl 1) 4 times, rep from * to end. Turn work, as normal.

Row 3: Still using B, rep row 1. Don't turn.

Rows 4 & 5: Using A, rep rows 2 and 1.

Rows 6 & 7: Using B, rep rows 2 and 1.

Row 8: A, rep row 2.

Row 9: B, rep row 1.

Row 10: A, rep row 1 but turn work.
Row 11: A, rep row 1. Don't turn.
Rows 12 & 13: Using B, rep rows 2 and 1.
Rows 14 & 15: Using A, rep rows 2 and 1.
Row 16: B, rep row 2.
These 16 rows form the pattern.
Note: Pay great attention to which rows are turned and which are not.

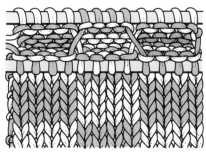

Reversible fabric opened to show the exchange of yarns.

Cast off straight across all the stitches using whichever colour you prefer. Fasten the other colour off.

Patterns such as these, because they are truly reversible, can be used to great effect as linings. On collars, cuffs and even whole garments the positive/ negative sides of the fabric can be used to the full advantage.

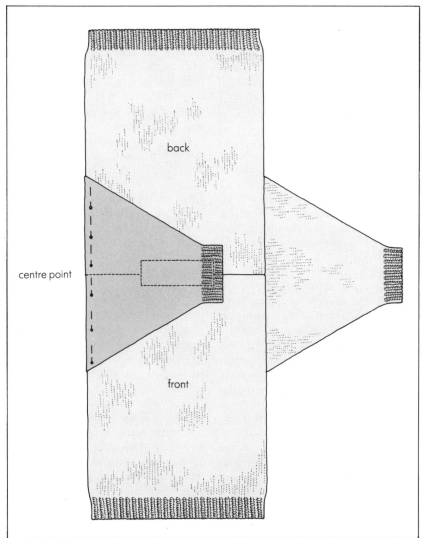

The correct way to attach sleeves in a drop shoulder sweater.

 **DOUBLE KNITTING/ WORSTED YARN**

This is a very versatile medium-weight yarn – heavier than a 4-ply and lighter than an aran weight – which can be used for anything from a baby's romper (play) suit to a man's outdoor sports cardigan. The term can be used for yarn of any fibre and is usually abbreviated to DK. In the UK it is the most commonly used yarn: about 40 per cent of all hand knitting yarn produced is double knitting.

The usual tension (gauge) achieved in DK is approximately 24sts and 32 rows to 10cm (4in.), measured over stocking (stockinette) stitch on 3.75mm (size 5) needles.

DROP SHOULDERS

A drop shoulder style is one which has no armhole shaping and a sleeve with little or no shaping at its top. The seam which joins the sleeve to the body therefore falls much lower than the same seam on a set sleeved gar-

HINT

Producing double fabric to line a large garment is a lengthy process, since it involves moving the yarn back and forth on every row. It is far quicker to knit a separate lining and stitch it to the original.

ment. Since it depends on the width of the garment, the seam can sit anywhere from the shoulder line to the elbow, depending on the fit of the body. The shoulders themselves can be shaped or non-shaped. The style is best used on loose-fitting, non-tailored garments.

Although a drop shoulder shape requires no armhole shaping, extra care must be taken at the making up (assembly) stage to ensure that the sleeve is correctly set. The garment must be sewn up in a specific order. Do not make an armhole and then set the sleeve in. First complete the shoulder seams and open the work out flat. With the sleeve seam still unsewn, mark the centre point of the sleeve top and place this down on the shoulder seam line. With the sleeve *fully* extended, either side of the shoulder line, carefully pin and stitch the two pieces, avoiding any puckering or stretching. The sleeve and side seams can then be completed.

DROPPED STITCHES

Accidental

Accidentally dropped stitches are one of knitting's major nightmares and the main reason for continually checking back on your work, every row or two, to spot anything untoward before it's too late. Keeping a regular eye on your work takes a fraction of a second each time but can save you hours of unnecessary work if a dropped stitch sneaks through without being noticed within a few rows.

If it is caught soon enough, a dropped stitch in stocking (stockinette) stitch can easily be remedied by using a crochet hook. Pick up the stitch on the hook and work it up the ladder which has been left, then place it back on to the needle at the correct place on the working row. The formation of each new stitch on the ladder will pull in the yarn from the stitches on either side of it. Because of this, the dropped stitch gets tighter on each progressive row and so there are limitations as to how far down this method can be used. If the knitting is to a loose tension (gauge), a stitch can be worked up several rows in this manner, since the surrounding stitches will 'give' yarn to the new stitch without pulling it too tight. After a few more rows, a tug around the picked up stitch will make the stitches in this area settle down so that no difference in tension should be noticeable.

If you are working to a firm tension, however, it is only advisable to go one or two rows down when picking up a dropped stitch. Any further and the surrounding stitches will not provide sufficient 'give' to work the new stitch without pulling it in far too tightly. This will result in a visible area of over-tight, even puckered, stitches. In such cases there is no alternative but to take the work right back to the dropped stitch and rework it.

Dropped stitches can also be saved

HINT

If you want to work a plaid or tartan type pattern, try using the dropped stitch technique. By adding the vertical stripes after the work has been completed, the knitting itself can be worked simply in horizontal stripes, without necessitating the use of fairisle or intarsia colour knitting techniques.

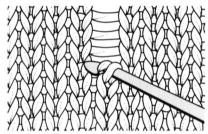

A dropped stitch reworked with the aid of a crochet hook on knit (above), and purl (below) fabric.

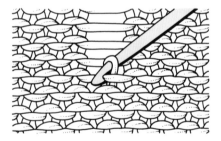

on patterns which involve combinations of knit and purl stitches, by using the appropriate knit or purl hooking action for each new stitch.

More complicated stitches usually require unravelling, but if the repeat sequence has been thrown out by the loss of a stitch, this should become apparent fairly early on so that only a few rows need to be taken back to rescue the dropped stitch (see *Un-ravelling*). When your pattern does become mysteriously out of 'sync', a dropped stitch is the first thing to look for.

Naturally, if the dropped stitch was one which should have been involved in any increasings or decreasings, once again, the work will have to be taken back so that these can be worked correctly.

Intentional

Stitches are sometimes dropped intentionally in order to provide a ladder up which a stitch of another colour can be worked, using the crochet hook method. If a stitch is to run right down a garment from the shoulder seam to the top of the welt (finishing border) it is simply slipped off the needle when the other shoulder stitches are being cast off. Wiggling the fabric will make it run down to the required position, where it can be stopped by putting a safety pin through it. A contrast colour can then be joined in, making a stitch through the one which has been held using a crochet hook, as for picking up an accidentally dropped stitch, and then continuing up the ladder to form a vertical stripe.

The same method can be used to create a simple, openwork pattern by leaving the ladders as they are. Since no other yarn is joined in to hold the dropped stitch, a break must be made to prevent it running further than is required. This is done at the knitting stage by working an increase (see working the strand method in *Increasing*) at the exact point where the run is to stop. The increased stitch is then dropped to where it originated.

Such an open ladder can also be used for threading different yarns, ribbons, and so on. This should only

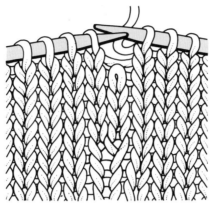

An intentionally dropped stitch working down to an increase break.

be used for decoration, however, and not to gather up the garment since the single strands of the ladder will not be strong enough to take any strain.

DRY CLEANING

There is an artsy-craftsy prejudice against dry cleaning for hand knits. Unless the ball band or label on a yarn specifically states that it is not dry cleanable or bears the ⊠ symbol (which means the same thing), there is no reason why any knitwear has to be hand washed.

In a comparison of the effects of dry cleaning and washing on virtually every natural fibre which can be used for knitting, dry cleaning wins every time. Dry-cleaned garments maintain their shape, colour, body and texture to a far greater degree than those which have been washed. In addition, the element of risk is removed (see *Washcare*).

There are three minor drawbacks to dry cleaning. Firstly, it can be expensive, although this has to be compared

to the cost in time wasted by hand washing. Hoarding your cleaning, taking 5 kg (10lb) loads (five to ten sweaters) to a launderette with a do-it-yourself dry-cleaning machine will cut your cleaning bills in half. Secondly, there is the question of freshness – sometimes dry-cleaned garments have a lingering smell of solvent. This is usually only a problem if the chemicals used are dirty; by picking a reputable cleaners where the solvent is changed regularly you should be able to avoid this. Thirdly, dry-cleaned items may be pressed. Consult the fibre care instructions before allowing any pressing to be carried out, and give specific instructions for it to be omitted if the garment is heavily textured – commercial presses can completely flatten a fabric (another reason to go for do-it-yourself cleaning machines where pressing is not included).

DYE LOTS

All yarn, even colours described as 'natural', have to go through chemical scouring and dyeing processes. The deeper the colour, the longer the dyeing process. The differences in the chemical dyestuffs used and the length of dyeing time required, make for considerable variations in bulk, even when exactly the same raw yarn has been used. This variation can often be sufficient to create a difference in tension (gauge) between one colour and another when knitted, especially on fine yarns where a great many stitches might be in use. Even if you have checked your tension for a specific yarn, if you are about to work another piece or another garment in a very different colour in the same yarn, it is well worth taking the time to work another tension sample.

When buying branded yarns, you will find the colour name (or code number) and number which refers to the dye lot on the ball band or label. Most reputable spinners go to great lengths to ensure colour consistency over every batch of dyeing which they carry out but a slight variation is inevitable. Always make sure that you have sufficient yarn of the same dye lot to complete the entire garment to avoid the risk of noticeable dye variation. If you are using guesswork to estimate how much yarn you will need for a garment, buy too much rather than too little. Even if the yarn is all labelled with the same number, accidents do happen at the winding stage and different dye lots do sometimes become mixed up. This is yet another

good reason for keeping a close eye on your work every few rows.

If you find that you are short of yarn for a specific project and are unable to match the dye lot number at any stockist, you will have to use another dye lot. Whatever you do, don't change lots within a piece of work. Use the different dye lot for a separate piece of the garment, and try to choose an inconspicuous part (the back of the cardigan, for example, rather than one of the fronts). Ideally, the odd lot should be used on differently patterned parts of a garment, such as ribbed welts (finishing borders) and cuffs or a fancy stitched inset, since the different texture will disguise the difference in colour. On a garment with a colour pattern, divide the different dye lots with another colour so that the variation will not be detectable.

Fancy dyeing

Intentional variegated colour effects are produced by random dyeing and yarn printing. In random dyeing hanks of yarn are only partly immersed in a series of dyes so that the colour varies throughout the hank. When knitted up, the colour is dispersed at regular intervals throughout the work. Yarn which is print dyed has the colour applied to it, much the same as in any other printing process. The areas of colour tend to be less gradually dispersed than with random dyeing.

Such multicolour yarns can be very useful in producing simplified fairisle designs. By using a plain colour for the base and a variegated yarn for the pattern, apparently multicoloured work can be produced using only two yarns. This saves all the extra time involved in joining colours and securing ends at the finishing stage.

EDGES

See *Selvedges*.

EDGINGS

Straightforward bands and borders are covered in the section so named. Detailed below, however, are some different edgings which you may like to use to add variety to your work.

Picot edging

Since this is worked in stocking (stockinette) stitch and then doubled over as for a hem, the needles used should be one or two sizes smaller than those used for the main body of the work. When knitting (picking) up the stitches from the main work, even greater care than usual should be taken over the even distribution of the stitches, especially around curves. Uneven spacing will look far more obvious on a picot edge than on rib, moss (seed) or garter stitch, as it will tend to twist the picot points in different directions. The same applies to the number of stitches – too many

will cause the edging to stick out, too few will stretch it out of shape.

After knitting up an odd number of stitches, work in stocking stitch until the edging is the required depth, finishing on a purl row. Now work the eyelet (round) hole row:

   * K1, yfwd, k2 tog, rep from * to end.

Continue in stocking stitch working one row short of the original number of rows.

For straight edges, such as cardigan fronts, the edging can be cast off loosely but on curves where elasticity is required, as around necks without openings, slip-stitch down without casting (binding) off (see *Neckbands*).

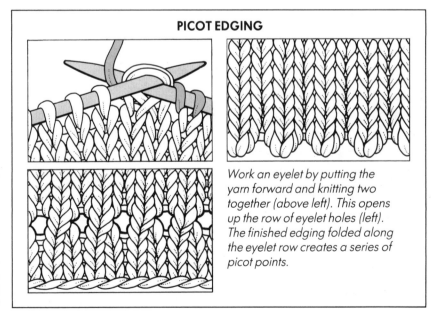

PICOT EDGING

Work an eyelet by putting the yarn forward and knitting two together (above left). This opens up the row of eyelet holes (left). The finished edging folded along the eyelet row creates a series of picot points.

If you do cast off, take great care when you turn in the edging to stitch it down, since any twisting at this stage will pull out of shape the little points which have been formed between the eyelets.

If all the instructions have been followed so that the picot edging does lie flat, it gives a pretty finish suitable for delicate styles and babywear.

Mock crochet

As so many knitting patterns which require a narrow, plain border give instructions for working one or two rows of double crochet, it is well worth mastering the basics of the craft. If you cannot – and there are many skilled knitters to whom crochet remains a closed book – the very simple knitted edging below can take the place of a row of double crochet.

First work out the number of stitches which are to be knitted up (see *Knitting/Picking Up Stitches*). Knit these up so that your first working row will be a right side row. Instead of knitting the next row, take a size larger needle and cast off, using the basic method.

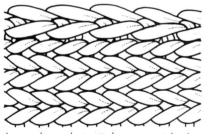

In mock crochet, stitches are picked up then cast off to simulate crochet edging.

Rouleaux

This type of edging takes advantage of the natural tendency of stocking stitch to curl upon itself. Edges knitted horizontally will appear in reverse stocking stitch on the right side of the garment, because the fabric will roll back on itself. On those knitted vertically, the stocking stitch edges will roll under, leaving the knitted side exposed.

Knitted up To create a small reverse stocking stitch rouleau, at a round neck for instance, knit up enough stitches to allow the fabric to roll easily and not be stretched widthways. Work in stocking stitch with the right side of the work facing you. When you have worked sufficient depth, allowing for enough turnover, cast off loosely. The rouleau can be left to roll back on itself, leaving the cast off edge free, or alternatively, this edge can be slip-stitched down around the neckline to create a fixed roll. Stitching does, however, tend to have a slight flattening effect.

Knitted separately If this is to be a fairly long edging, it is best knitted vertically so that you do not have to cast on an enormous number of stitches. Working this way will give a stocking stitch appearance. It also means that the length can be adjusted as you go along. Cast on enough stitches to give you approximately three times the width of the rouleau you want, to make allowance for doubling over, rolling and stitching. Don't make it too deep, or it will flatten out after stitching.

Work in stocking stitch for the required length and cast off. To attach, divide the rouleau into equal portions and pin it to the main work, edge to edge, with the right sides together. Work a backstitch along the edge, leaving a very small seam

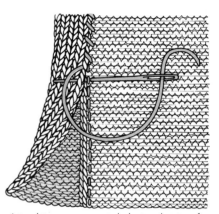

Attaching a separately knitted strip of stocking stitch to a selvedge to form a rouleau effect.

allowance. Allow the edging to roll around the edge on to the wrong side. Pin and then slip-stitch down along the line of backstitching, avoiding any twisting. This should produce a fat rouleau with a small edge seam inside. Padding can be added to emphasize the effect but as this makes the rouleau quite heavy, it is only suitable on sturdy knitted fabrics which can provide the support.

Fancy edgings

There are numerous edging patterns, using lace and filet knitting techniques, which are not listed here since this is not a stitch directory. Many of the lacy edgings which you see on old linens are not in fact true lace but knitted edgings, worked in fine cotton. These can be used as trimmings as you would add any other type of braid, ribbon or lace.

Edgings are yet another example of a finishing detail which, when poorly executed, can ruin a beautifully worked garment. Take the time to work them with care for the best results.

ELASTIC

Shirring elastic/Elastic thread

When working ribbing in a yarn with little or no natural elasticity, the addition of shirring elastic will keep the work in shape. This may also be useful on areas of a garment which are in danger of becoming stretched – sweater cuffs, which are habitually pulled up the forearm, are an obvious example.

If you can obtain the transparent type of shirring elastic, or can achieve a good match with the coloured variety, then it can actually be knitted in with the yarn which you are using. The yarn and elastic are held together but the elastic should be pulled taut every once in a while. If the elastic is not transparent, or a poor colour match, it can be added by carrying it

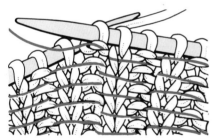

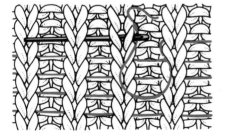

Shirring elastic can be added at the knitting stage, by stranding (above), or after completion, using a tapestry needle.

at the back of the work. This can be achieved on k1 p1 rib by weaving the elastic in behind every knit stitch on the right side rows and in front of every purl stitch on the wrong side rows (see the section on stranding and weaving in *Fairisle*).

If you are using a stitch which makes weaving in either on every or on every alternate stitch difficult – k2 p2 rib, for example – the elastic can be threaded through the backs of the stitches, using a tapestry needle, after the work has been completed. This same method can also be used to rescue garments which have already gone out of shape due to wear, bad washing or too loose a tension (gauge) in the first place.

Whichever method you use to add shirring elastic to your work, the tension must be regulated very accurately. Ideally it should create a natural-looking tension in the work. Drawn too tightly, it will make its presence obvious, too loosely and the whole object of the exercise will be lost.

Elastic is by far the best method of keeping cotton ribs or welts (finishing borders) in shape and can give extra 'guts' to stress points in garments made from delicate fibres such as mohair and silk mixes. It can be used not only over welts but also any areas liable to stretch, such as round a loosely finished neck or across the bottom of an extra long sweater prone to 'posterior pouch'.

Ribbon elastic

When using wide elastic, such as around the waistband of a skirt, there are two methods of encasing it.

Knitting a tube This can be done using a method of hemming – see

A turned tube, stitched down, leaving a gap for the ribbon elastic.

Hems – but leaving one side seam open so that the elastic can be threaded through, and then the two sides sewn together. If you are using this method, it is advisable to secure the elastic to the knitting at a couple of points around the circumference, preferably on the side seams. This will prevent it from twisting within the hem while the garment is being worn.

Stitched encasing This is preferable if the minimum of bulk is required since it does not involve two layers of knitting. Instead, the elastic is sewn into a circle and placed in position, on the wrong side of the knitting. A criss-cross (zigzag) stitch is then worked in self (matching) yarn to keep it in place. Once again, it is advisable to catch the elastic down to avoid later twisting.

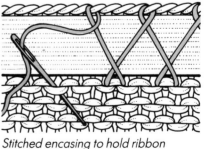

Stitched encasing to hold ribbon elastic in place.

EMBROIDERY

See *Swiss Darning.*

ENDS

Besides being a time-consuming bore to fasten, ends produce unlimited opportunities for untidy finishing, and if they are not dealt with properly, can produce weak spots in both the main fabric and the seams.

Avoiding ends should be uppermost in the knitter's mind at all times. Here are a few helpful tips.

1. When beginning a piece of work which is to be seamed after knitting always leave an end of yarn which is long enough to complete a practical section of the seam. After a few rows,

An ample end left at the start of the knitting for seaming yarn.

roll the end up and safety pin it to the work to avoid tangles. Leaving a tiny end and then joining in another one to work the seam is illogical, and particularly silly at a stress point on a garment, such as a sweater welt (finishing border).

2. Any ends which have been left at the edges of a piece of work, where new yarn has been joined in, can be used for seaming where the original end is not long enough to complete the entire seam, or where a different colour is preferred on multicolour work.

3. Ends still left can be secured by the needle actually working the seam if a backstitch is being worked, since these will not show on the right side. If working a flat seam, spare ends should be left until after the seaming is completed and then secured through the seam thread for extra strength.

4. Minimize the number of ends produced on colour knitting by following the hints in *Colour Knitting, Fairisle* and *Intarsia.*

5. If working a one-colour garment, try to buy your yarn in as large a unit as possible – large balls, hanks, even cones if you can obtain them – since they will frequently hold enough yarn to complete an entire garment. Theoretically, this can mean a garment without a single join although there are usually knots and faults in the yarn. If you only have a part ball left, put it aside to be used for something small like a pocket, don't use it to begin a large piece of work – start with a full ball so that you can get as far as possible before joining in the next end.

6. When securing ends *always* use a pointed needle. Even if you have been using a blunt tapestry needle for seaming, leave the end and come back to it with a sharp needle. Go back through a couple of the seam stitches, and then double back through the stitches just formed. Each time, the needle will split the yarn it is passing through, making it virtually impossible for the end to work itself loose.

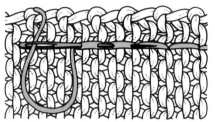

Securing an end with a pointed needle to split the previously worked seam stitches.

Even when you are not securing an end into a seam, use the doubling back procedure so that if the end should be pulled it becomes even more secure. If any end is merely woven in and around the stitches, for whatever distance, it will work its way straight back out again as soon as the knitting is subjected to any movement. Taking the yarn back to split itself, once or twice, will ensure a permanent fastening.

ENTRELACS

Entrelac knitting – from the French *entrelacer,* meaning to interlace or intertwine – results in a woven, crisscross (zigzag) effect although it is, in fact, knitted in one piece.

The patchwork effect emerges by turning the work, decreasing, working held stitches and picking up new ones. It can be worked in one colour, simply for its slight bubble texture, or in two or more colours for greater effect.

It is one of the best examples of a method which looks and sounds incredibly complicated in pattern form but which is plain sailing (if not addictive), once started. The instructions below for a small sampler show how easy it can be.

Entrelac sampler

Stitch numbers are suitable for a medium-weight yarn, and the instructions are for two colours only to avoid confusion.

Note: See *Knitting/Picking Up Stitches* for details of this technique.

Cast on 30sts. Start by forming the base triangles in colour A:

Row 1: (WS) P2, turn.
Row 2: K2, turn.
Row 3: P3, purling the extra st from LH needle, turn.
Row 4: K3, turn.
Row 5: P4, purling the extra st from LH needle, turn.
Row 6: K4, turn.

Cont as set, adding an extra st on every purl row, until you have 10sts on the RH needle, ending with a purl row.

This forms the first base triangle. Work two more in the same way, so that all 30sts are now on the RH needle.

* Now join in colour B and work the selvedge triangle.

Row 1: K2, turn.
Row 2: P2, turn.
Row 3: Inc into first st, sl 1, k1, psso, turn.
Row 4: P3, turn.
Row 5: K1, inc into next st, sl 1, k1, psso, turn.
Row 6: P4, turn.
Row 7: K1, inc into next st, k1, sl 1, psso, turn.
Row 8: P5, turn.
Row 9: K1, inc into next st, k2, sl 1, k1, psso, turn.

Cont as set, inc into the second st on every knit row until you have 10sts, ending on a knit row.

Now work the first rectangle from the second side of the first base triangle (see direction arrows on the photograph if this makes no sense).

Knit up 10sts along this edge, top to bottom.

Row 2: P10, turn.
Row 3: K9, sl 1, k next st from LH needle (this is in colour A), psso, turn.
Row 4: P10, turn.

Keep repeating these last two rows until all the stitches from the second base triangle are worked.

Work another rectangle from second side of the second base triangle. Now pick up and knit the 10sts from the second side of the last triangle and work another selvedge triangle thus:

Row 1: P2 tog, p8, turn.
Row 2: K9.
Row 3: P2 tog, p7, turn.

Cont as set, until 1st remains from selvedge triangle.

Now change back to colour A and work the second set of rectangles, worked in the opposite direction. With the right side of the work facing, knit up 10sts from triangle just completed, from left to right.

Row 1: K10, turn.
Row 2: P9, p2 tog (last st from triangle and first st of next rectangle) turn.
Row 3: K10, turn.

Rep last two rows until all the sts from first rectangle have been incorporated.

Now knit up 10sts from next rectangle and work in the same manner. Finally knit up from last rectangle and incorporate sts from selvedge triangle. *

* to * forms the complete pattern which can be repeated however many times you require.

To finish with a straight edge, a row of triangles must be worked.

Row 1: K2, turn.
Row 2: P2, turn.
Row 3: Inc into first st, sl 1, k1, psso, turn.
Row 4: P3, turn.
Row 5: K1, inc into next st, sl 1, k1, psso, turn.

Entrelac sampler showing the criss-cross patchwork effect created.

Row 6: P4, turn.
Row 7: K1, inc into next st, k1, sl 1, k1, psso, turn.
Row 8: P5, turn.
Row 9: K1, inc into next st, k2, sl 1, k1, psso, turn.
Row 10: P6, turn.
Row 11: K2 tog, k3, sl 1, k1, psso, turn.
Row 12: P5, turn.
Row 13: K2 tog, k2, sl 1, k1, psso, turn.
Cont as set until triangle is complete and 1st remains.

Now knit up 10sts along the other side of the first rectangle, top to bottom, right side facing.
Row 2: P9, p2 tog.
Row 3: Sl 1, k1, psso, k7, sl 1, k1 (from next rectangle), psso, turn.
Row 4: P9.
Row 5: Sl 1, k1, psso, k6, sl 1, k1, psso, turn.
Row 6: P8.
Continue as set until 2sts remain.
Row 18: P2.
Row 19: K1, sl 1, k1, psso, k1, turn.
Row 20: Sl 1, p2 tog, psso.

Now work another triangle from the next rectangle in the same manner. Finally work the last selvedge triangle. Knit up 10sts, as before.

Row 2: P9, p2 tog.
Row 3: Sl 1, k1, psso, k6, k2 tog.
Row 4: P8.
Row 5: Sl 1, k1, psso, k4, k2 tog.
Row 6: P6.
Row 7: Sl 1, k1, psso, k2, k2 tog.
Row 8: P4.
Row 9: Sl 1, k1, psso, k2 tog.
Row 10: P2.
Row 11: K2 tog, fasten off.

EYELETS/ROUNDS

See *Buttonholes*.

▪ FACINGS

It is a great mistake, and one which was common in the past, to equate dressmaking techniques with those in knitting. Facings are a perfect example of a tailoring feature which should be translated into knitting terms, not duplicated using a knitted fabric. Any one of the numerous bands, borders and edgings which are covered in this book can be used to finish an area of knitting. If that area needs strengthening, in addition, this can still be achieved within the knitting, by using smaller needles for a tighter tension (gauge), a different stitch for a firmer fabric, or double yarn for extra thickness.

The only place where a true facing is necessary is to back the fronts of an edge-to-edge jacket, worked in one stitch where bands of another stitch are not desirable. The facings should be knitted up from along the front edges, at right angles to the main work, and using smaller needles (as in hemming, see *Hems*). Facings should always be worked in stocking (stock-inette) stitch since this provides the smoothest, flattest fabric. If the jacket has hems, mitred cornering should be used where the facing and hem meet (see *Corners*). Make the facing as narrow as possible to cut down on unnecessary bulk, and when stitching down take great care that the line of stitching is not visible on the right side of the work.

Fabric facings should only be used as a last resort when the yarn and stitch which you have used are really too fragile or floppy.

▪ FAIRISLE

Before considering the technique of fairisle knitting, it is necessary to distinguish it from the traditional style of knitting which originated on Fair Isle.

Fair Isle

Situated in the Shetland Isles, off the north coast of Scotland, this tiny island is closer to Norway than to the Scottish mainland, and its cultural heritage, not surprisingly, has far more in common with Scandinavia and the Baltic circle, than with the rest of Britain. In this context, it is easy to see where the brightly coloured, repetitive geometric motifs of Fair Isle knitting came from, although the islanders have adapted and developed these influences over the years to make the style very much their own.

Romantic theories about shipwrecked Spanish sailors from the Armada swapping knitting designs with the islanders have never been substantiated. In fact, there do not appear to be any documented examples of Fair Isle knitting before the middle of the 19th century, when stockings and caps were made. The commercial production of multicoloured sweaters on Fair Isle and in the Shetland Isles did not emerge until the turn of the century. This was probably due to the increased sophistication of factory-produced knitwear, which priced plain hand knits out of the market. Since the islanders had relied on knitting as an integral part of their economy for centuries, they had to turn their hands to work which could not, at that time, be mass produced.

By the 1920s, Fair Isle sweaters had become a fashion garment, their most famous publicist being the Prince of Wales. Since then, they have been in and out of fashion with such regularity that although shapes, colourways (colour schemes) and yarns may change, fairisle will never die out.

Although fairisle work often appears to have more colours than you can count, there are never more than two colours per row. The secret in getting the maximum variation out of a colour scheme lies in the colour changeover from row to row. While working a simple geometric motif, such as a star, the colours of both the base and contrast may change almost every row while still keeping the continuity of the design. Even with a limited range of colours, the permutations are almost endless.

Since Fair Isle knitting was an industry, albeit a cottage one, it resulted in the knitters perfecting the fastest techniques possible for colour knitting, many of which are still in use. Everything is knitted in the round, even cardigans, which have openings cut after working (see *Cutting*). The work is done on sets of double-pointed needles (sometimes three, not four), the right-hand working needle often being stuck into a knitting belt, leaving the right hand free to move the yarn. Besides being quicker than flat knitting, since no purl rows are worked, circular knitting also allows the knitter to keep track of the design far more easily.

Most importantly, it means that each colour is always ready to use at the beginning of a round and the knitter does not have to worry about which side of the work the yarn was left on, as with two-needle knitting where yarns frequently have to be

broken off and rejoined to bring them to the correct side.

Another aid to speed is the simultaneous use of the regular and continental methods of knitting. This enables the knitter to hold one colour in the left hand and one colour in the right (see *Continental Knitting*). The time saved by not having to drop one colour and pick up the other all across a row is considerable.

Fairisle method

Although experts differ, here the term fairisle is used to denote any colour knitting where only two colours are used per row, and the one not in use is carried at the back of the work.

Before you start any fairisle work, take a good look at the graph which shows the colour pattern to see if you can help yourself by simplifying it. Many traditional patterns originated from circular working, and in modifying them for flat knitting, no account has been taken of which side of the work the yarns not in use have been left. If you are working with two needles it is in your interest to cut down the number of times the yarns have to be broken off.

Take one colour at a time, and work up through the graph ensuring that an even number of rows lies between each use of that colour. For instance, if you have just completed a band of red and must then work four rows using white and green before another band of red, your yarn will be at the correct side of the work. If you work five rows using white and green, however, your red yarn will be at the wrong end of the work when you next need it. To rectify this, odd rows can be removed or added or a colour can be shifted a row to even up the row numbers.

Sometimes, especially through the centre of a motif, an odd number of rows cannot be avoided, without spoiling the design. If the colour or colours that you need for the next row are at the other end of the work you can cheat by slipping all the stitches from one needle to the other and working from the other end. Since, in effect, you are working the same method as in the round, if you have just completed a knit row then you knit the next, if it was a purl row then you purl the next. After this, continue in stocking (stockinette) stitch as before. Naturally, as it is rather time-consuming, the number of times you do this over the entire repeat should be limited.

Unless you are going to weave in the colour not in use (see below), also check the graph for the numbers of stitches between colours, since the colour carried at the back of the work will have to be stranded across these areas, forming 'floats'. If these floats are too long, they will catch when the garment is being put on. Ideally, they should span a maximum of four or five stitches, but if in doubt do the fingernail test. If you can hook your finger through them with ease, they're too long.

Most traditional fairisles have small, regular repeats of colour which have been custom-made for easy stranding and various designs can be analysed from this point of view. Consider Scandinavian ski sweaters which use the deer motif, for instance. The snowflake-covered backgrounds are not only decorative but carry the contrast yarn from one deer on to the next. A snowflake, a bird's eye, a tiny cross or cube can all be used to cut down float length, but do mark any alterations on the graph before you start to make sure that the whole thing will work out.

If the design demands larger gaps between colours, the yarn not in use can be woven intermittently, say every three or four stitches, or you can leave long floats which can be stitched down after completion.

Fairisle tension/gauge

Incorrectly handled stranding and weaving is one of the most trouble-some problems in knitting. The main difficulty is that it is quite possible to get the stitch tension accurate but then work the floats so tightly that they completely destroy the original measurement. The yarn being carried *must* be woven or stranded loosely enough to have the same degree of 'give' as the knitting itself. Unless you achieve this, the resulting fabric will have no elasticity whatsoever and, in extreme examples, very tight floats will buckle the stitches so much that the front of the work looks puckered when finished.

Stranding This is the method whereby the yarn not in use is simply left hanging at the back of the work (or held in the left hand if you are using both hands to hold the yarn), until it is next needed. The yarn in use is then left at the back of the work and the carried yarn taken up. Before using it to work the next stitch, make sure that the float which you are creating is sufficiently loose to allow the stitches in front of it to stretch. It is better to leave a small loop at the back of the work rather than pull the float too tightly.

Weaving With this method the yarn being carried is looped over or under the working yarn on every stitch, creating an up-and-down woven effect on the wrong side of the work. Some knitters find this method easier for

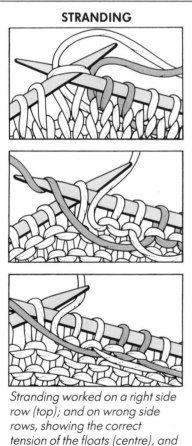

Stranding worked on a right side row (top); and on wrong side rows, showing the correct tension of the floats (centre), and floats stranded far too tightly (above).

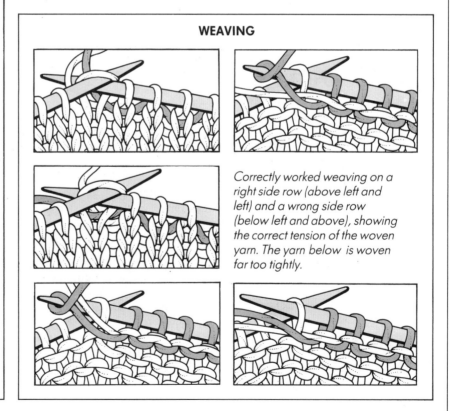

WEAVING

Correctly worked weaving on a right side row (above left and left) and a wrong side row (below left and above), showing the correct tension of the woven yarn. The yarn below is woven far too tightly.

producing the correct tension in the non-working yarn since the fingers do not have to regulate the size of any floats. It tends to produce a far more dense fabric, however, and unless it is worked very carefully the woven colour may show through on the right side of the work.

Stranding and weaving The combination of methods is the most common technique for working fairisle since most designs have, at some point, gaps between colours which are too wide for floats. The way to deal with these is to strand for so many stitches, weave the carried yarn behind the stitch at the mid-point (or every three or four stitches if the gap is large), then strand to the point where the carried yarn is next required.

FAROE KNITTING

Faroe knitting comes from the Faroe Islands, which lie northwest of Scotland and southeast of Iceland, but are actually Danish territory. It is similar to fairisle knitting in that it uses two colours per row, but is far less complicated and uses fewer colours. The patterns themselves are simple geometric repeats, on a very small scale. These are worked in horizontal bands divided by rows of the base colour, which is traditionally natural or off-white.

FELTING

Felting (or fulling) is the name given to any one of the processes which result in the matting of woollen fibres.

When felting occurs accidentally, it is irreversible and this matting is always accompanied by shrinkage. If it is to be used as an intentional finishing process, you must make allowances at the knitting stage for the shrinkage.

In the days of the craftsmen knitters, felting was frequently used to turn knitting into extra-thick, waterproof fabric which, when densely matted, could be cut without fear of the stitches running. This was particularly useful for the production of headgear which could be shaped during the knitting stage and then weather-proofed by fulling. The pancake-shaped hats of Tudor England and the original versions of both the beret and the fez were all made in this way.

As a technique for experiment, fulling can be extremely difficult to control. Even when a swatch is subjected to the intended treatment on a test run, there is no guarantee that a whole garment will behave in precisely the same manner. The safest method is to concentrate on one particular aspect of the process such as using chemicals alone – soaking the garment in strong detergent – rather than a combination of treatments which may cause unexpected interaction.

The degree of shrinkage can then be calculated, within a certain margin, and the garment knitted that much larger. If you are attempting to size a garment accurately, however, do not be tempted to try felting.

A dense, fluffy fabric can be produced far more easily by knitting a garment at a tight tension (gauge), which can be precisely calculated, and then brushing the finished fabric with a stiff bristle brush.

FISHERMAN KNITTING

See *Guernseys*.

FLARES

A flared or fluted effect can be produced in knitting by working regular lines of shapings within the fabric. Although this can be done by starting at the widest part of the work and decreasing to reach the narrowest, it is better to start with the fewest stitches and increase, since increases can be worked almost invisibly using the strand between the stitches method.

The technique is illustrated using a flared skirt, knitted from the waist down. Using your tension (gauge) measurements, calculate how many stitches you will need at the waistline and at the hemline. The difference between the two will be the number of stitches which will have to be increased. Now, decide how many increase lines or flares you wish to have across the width of the skirt. Divide the number of increase stitches by the number of flares; this will tell you how many stitches have to be increased down each flare. Lastly, divide the number of rows in the entire skirt by the number of stitches in each flare.

Fairisle technique. A geometric design worked in cotton from a colour graph. The swatches illustrate the right side of the work and then the wrong side; the one on the left shows the stranding method, the one on the right the weaving method of carrying the yarn at the back of the work when not in use.

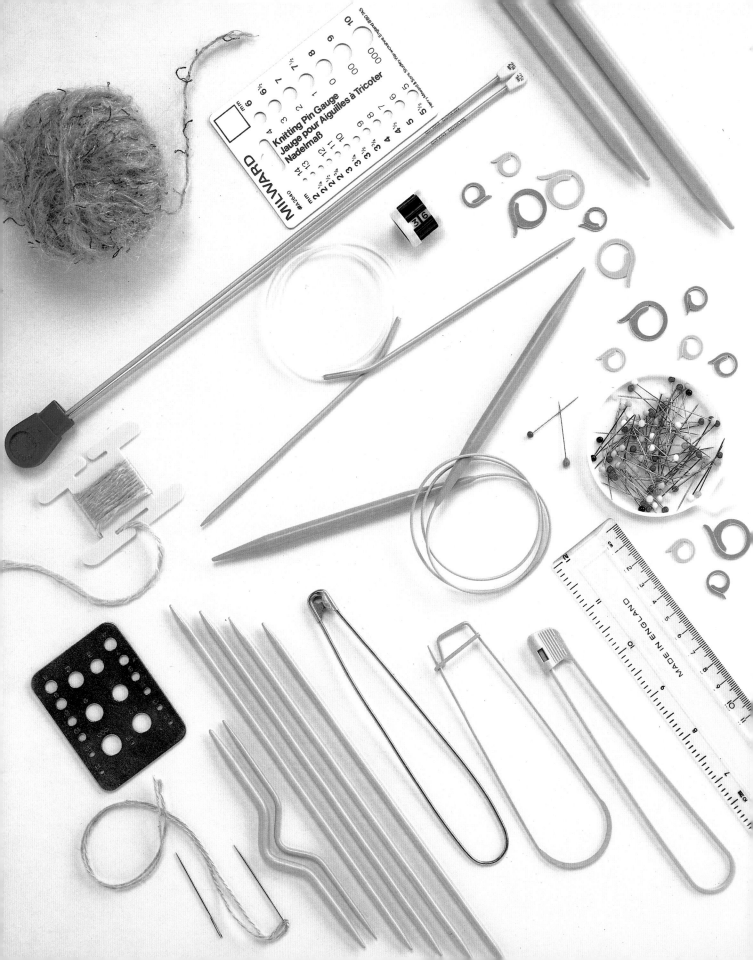

This will tell you on which rows to increase the flares. For example:

the waistline = 150sts
the hemline = 450sts
sts to be inc = 300sts (the difference between 450 and 150)
no. of flares = 6
sts per flare = 50sts (300 divided by 6)
rows in skirt = 250
Therefore, one st must be increased at each flare point on every fifth row (250 divided by 50).

Don't worry if the divisions don't work out equally. Any leftover stitches can be increased at the flares on the second row. You can then work increasings in a uniform progression

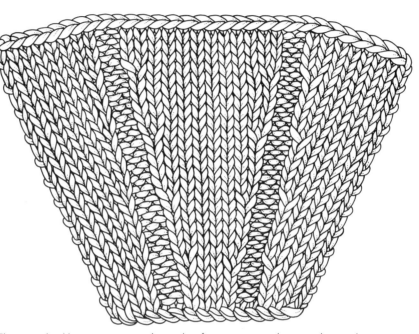

Flare worked by increasing either side of a reverse stocking stitch panel.

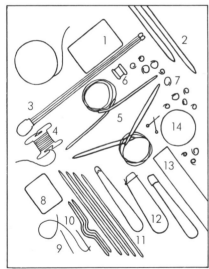

Knitting equipment.
1. Needle gauge; 2. jumbo needles;
3. needles with needle stops attached to the ends; 4. a bobbin; 5. circular needles; 6. row counter; 7. markers;
8. needle gauge; 9. tapestry needles;
10. curved cable needles; 11. double-pointed needles; 12. stitch holders;
13. clear plastic ruler; 14. pins with coloured plastic ends.

throughout the remainder of the work.

A marker loop can be used to identify the flare stitches and by working the increasings one stitch before and then one stitch after the marker, alternately, the line will be kept central. If the number of stitches allows, an easier way to keep track of shapings is to pair them, working one either side of an axial stitch at each flare point.

Flares can also be worked on either side of panels of different stitches, to give a mock pleat effect. For instance, panels of reverse stocking (stockinette) stitch, six stitches wide, could be used at the flare points on a stocking stitch skirt. The increases would be worked at either side of the panels, without affecting the width of the reverse stocking stitch.

With techniques such as flaring, don't think solely in terms of current fashion. Experiment with flaring; by thinking three-dimensionally you can sculpt virtually any shape you care to imagine.

FLOATS

See *Fairisle*.

FLORENTINE KNITTING

This is an incredibly ornate type of knitting which originated in Florence in the 16th century. It used purl stitch relief, intarsia colour work and embroidered outlines to create floral and zoological motifs in the manner of the brocade fabrics of the time, and is sometimes referred to as 'brocade knitting'. Most of the surviving examples are short men's tunics which would have been worn over tights.

FOUR PLY YARN

This is a lighter weight yarn than double knitting (worsted) and was the yarn used for nearly all the fine sweaters and cardigans of the thirties and forties, when fashion dictated a perfect fit. In recent years, with the advent of more loose-fitting styles, chunky (bulky) weight yarns have become far more popular since they are far quicker to knit. Very few knitters seem to have the patience to tackle 4-ply work these days with the result that most fashion patterns are produced for heavier yarns.

A standard 4-ply tension (gauge) is approximately 28sts and 40 rows to 10cm (4in.), measured over stocking (stockinette) stitch on 3.25mm (size 3) needles. There are variations, however, since the term '4-ply' can be used arbitrarily (see *Ply*).

FRILLS

These can be worked as separate edgings, plain or ornate according to the style of the garment, and stitched to the main work at the finishing stage. Worked sideways, they utilize the turning technique to achieve the frill effect – more rows being worked at one side than the other (see *Turning*). Alternatively, they can be worked at the beginning or end of a piece, using an extreme form of gathering (see *Gathers*).

GADGETS

As with any gadgetry, there are the good and time-saving knitting aids, and the ones designed solely to take up counter space. Those discussed here are among the more useful (see also the photograph on page 86).

Stitch holders

Although stitches which are not being worked can have a piece of yarn slipped through them to stop them from dropping, the stitches will tend to shrink in size, and prove more difficult to pick up and put back on a needle. Having to thread up a tapestry needle and pass the yarn through the stitches is also more time-consuming than simply slipping them on to a purpose-made holder.

There are many different designs on the market, varying from giant safety pins to odd springed devices. The holder which you choose must be long enough to take the required number of stitches, as it is absolutely essential not to stretch those at either end of a set being held. It should also be as lightweight as possible, for the same reason. (See *Holding Stitches*.)

Row counters

These fit on to the end of the needle, and are extremely useful since they do away with pencil and paper when you are keeping track of your row count. If you are fond of knitting on the move, a row counter is essential.

Needle gauges

These are not necessary if you buy a complete set of brand new needles every time, but if, like most people, you have inherited or acquired a fascinating bunch of mismatched, unmarked needles over the years, an identification gauge is essential. It should have both metric and old-fashioned needle sizes marked so that conversion from one to the other can be done at a glance, allowing you to use old needles with new patterns and old patterns with new needles.

Knitting belts

These are usually made of leather, and have a small padded area with holes punched in it which will hold needle ends (the double-pointed variety), leaving the right hand totally free to control the yarn. The old contract knitters invariably used such belts, or primitive versions of them, since speed was of the essence. With the needle attached to one side of a belt, the finished work hooked up and held towards the back and the yarn in a pocket, the knitters could go about their daily chores, dropping and picking up their work at will.

GARTER STITCH

Garter stitch or 'plain knitting' is the most basic stitch, formed when every row is worked as a knit row, making both right and wrong sides of the fabric identical (see *The Knit Stitch*). It produces a thicker, looser fabric than that made by stocking (stockinette) stitch, and produces raised ridges on both sides of the work. This means that it takes more yarn than stocking stitch and has a greater degree of vertical springiness.

When worked on two needles, that is, in the flat, it is quicker to knit than stocking stitch, since the necessity of working a purl row on every alternate row is avoided. If worked in the round, however, it is slower because

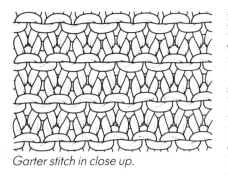

Garter stitch in close up.

the work is not turned, and every alternate row must be purled.

Garter stitch fabric does not have a tendency to curl, so it is frequently used for borders and bands. Always use needles one or two sizes smaller than those used for the main work when you are working separate bands/borders. If they are to be knitted as part of the main work, make an effort to regulate your tension (gauge) over the garter stitch section, making it as firm and neat as possible. Indeed, if you are working a garment in all-over stitch, start out with smaller needles than those you would normally use to work stocking stitch with the same yarn. This will compensate for the stitches' lateral 'give'.

As with so many other aspects of knitting, garter stitch may be directly traced back to one of the earliest uses of the craft – the production of hand-knitted hosiery. While stocking stitch was used for the main section of the hose, garter stitch was used, as the name suggests, for the garters.

GATHERS

Gathers should always be knitted, rather than stitched, into a fabric, since stitching, as in dressmaking,

results in too many thicknesses of knitted fabric. Always think in terms of knitting before resorting to tailoring techniques.

If you find yourself with a knitted selvedge which has to be gathered because it is far wider than the piece to which it is to be attached – a collar larger than a neckline, for instance – do not start pleating it into great lumps. Instead, measure the length of the selvedge and then calculate how much of it you must get rid of. Convert both measurements into numbers of stitches, according to the tension (gauge) of the work, subtract the second number from the first and you will be left with the number of stitches which should then be evenly knitted (picked) up along the selvedge (see *Knitting/Picking Up Stitches*). Once this has been done, cast (bind) off, keeping the tension the same as the work. The new selvedge will be the correct length to attach directly, without any tucks or pleats.

A gathered effect across a knitted fabric can be produced by either increasing or decreasing across one row so that the width of the fabric is either widened or reduced. The variation in the number of stitches depends on how extreme you want the gather

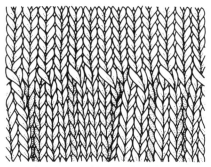

A gather created by working k1, k2 tbl all along a row.

to appear. For example, if you are increasing, and the effect you want is a deep gather which will look almost frill-like, then increase into every alternate stitch. Increasing into every third stitch will produce a medium gather, and so on.

When increasing or decreasing across a row, always use invisible methods (see *Decreasing* and *Increasing*). If you need a great variation in stitches, always try to work decreases if the direction of the work allows – a large number of increases will put a strain on the row in question and may pull the stitches out of shape. Gathers can also be worked over two rows to spread the shaping.

Gathers can be used at waistlines, cuffs, welts (finishing borders), puff sleeves, necklines, yokes – in fact, almost anywhere. Double gathers (that is, where a gather is worked and after a few rows another is worked in reverse to bring you to the original number of stitches) may be worked to create an intentional puckered effect across the work.

GAUGE

See *Tension/Gauge*.

GORES

Gores are triangular insets of fabric, cut as a separate piece in tailoring but worked into the fabric in knitting. In effect extreme flares, they can be calculated using the same method (see *Flares*). As for flares, use decreases if the garment is being worked from the bottom up, and increases if the gar-

A gore or triangular inset created by increasing either side of a triangular wedge.

ment is being worked from the top down. The shapings are far more frequent than in a flare, however – for a gore, they are worked each side of the triangular wedge on every alternate, or even every, row to produce a fluted fabric.

The technique can also be used to shape the hemlines of skirts and jackets and the interesting angles produced by the direction of the knitted fabric are comparable to the effect created by entrelac knitting.

◼ GRAFTING

Grafting is the technique used to join two pieces of the same knitted fabric together by exactly replicating a row of knitting using a tapestry needle and thread. It can, therefore, only be used on basic stitches – stocking (stockinette), garter, and single rib – since more complicated stitches become too difficult to reproduce with only a needle and thread. When worked properly, a grafted join should be invisible and should not be confused with any of the methods of joining

open rows of stitches which produce an obvious line where the two edges meet.

Many knitters find grafting skills very difficult to acquire, since the path of the grafting thread is not the obvious one which you would automatically use to bring two open stitches together. Written grafting instructions can appear mind-bogglingly difficult, so here they are represented diagrammatically. The coloured thread represents the one that is used to execute the graft, and the arrows denote the direction in which the needle must travel. The golden rule to remember is that the route which your needle takes exactly traces the path of the yarn in a normal knitted row. Never deviate from this path.

Always use a blunt needle to avoid splitting stitches and only pull the grafting thread as tight as the tension (gauge) of the knitted stitches themselves. A slight variation in tension will work itself out but a very tight thread or one not pulled firmly enough will produce a noticeable line on the finished work. Because the thread must pass easily in and out of the knitted stitches, *grafting should not be attempted with any heavily textured yarns.*

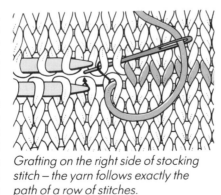

Grafting on the right side of stocking stitch – the yarn follows exactly the path of a row of stitches.

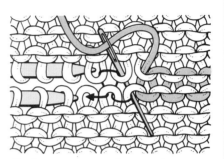

Grafting reverse stocking stitch (above) and garter stitch (below); the yarn follows a different path.

Stitches can be grafted together by placing the two rows of open loops one above the other on a flat surface, but with this method you risk dropped and twisted stitches. It is far safer to lay the work on a flat surface but to leave the stitches on the needles, slipping them off one or two at a time, as required.

Although stocking and garter stitch fabrics can be grafted together regardless of the direction in which they have been knitted, ribs can only be grafted together invisibly if they have both been worked in the same direction. Since both knit and purl stitches must be grafted alternately, this method is fiddly and not advisable unless you have already mastered stocking stitch and reverse stocking stitch.

Alternatively, regardless of which way it has been worked, single rib can be grafted by splitting up the stitches

Grafting k1 p1 rib, keeping the stitches in pattern.

of each piece; this entails four needles in all.

1. Divide the stitches so that the knit stitches are on one needle and the purl stitches on another. It is far easier to divide the stitches if you use double-pointed needles.

2. With the right side facing, graft the knit stitches.

3. Then, turn the work and graft the remaining stitches in the same manner, that is, as for stocking stitch.

Grafting can be used anywhere on a garment where a horizontal seam would be unsightly or uncomfortable, provided that each piece to be joined has the same number of stitches. It is equally suitable for delicate garments which are to be worn next to the skin or on extremely chunky garments where a seam would look clumsy or bulky. Grafts are frequently used on shoulder seams, either non-shaped, or those which have been shaped by turning rather than casting off, as they avoid creating any ridge at all on the shoulder line. Focal points on a garment, such as the tops of rectangular hoods and cardigan border joins, are also perfect positions for grafting.

The most rewarding use for grafting techniques, however, is in mending and alterations. When an area of a fabric has been damaged or removed for some reason, expert grafting can produce invisible mends. This makes mastery of the methods worth while.

GRAFTING

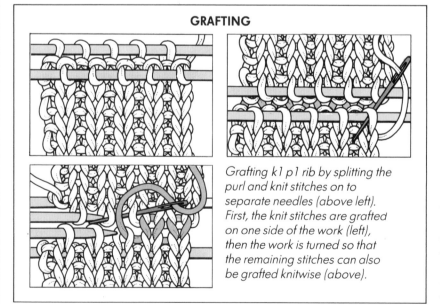

Grafting k1 p1 rib by splitting the purl and knit stitches on to separate needles (above left). First, the knit stitches are grafted on one side of the work (left), then the work is turned so that the remaining stitches can also be grafted knitwise (above).

GUERNSEYS

Guernseys or 'ganseys', as they are also known, are the seamless sweaters traditionally worn by British fishermen. Far from originating specifically on the isle of Guernsey, they can be traced in the photographic archives of virtually every fishing port in the British Isles, from Cornwall to the Orkneys.

Essentially work garments, they are knitted in a 5-ply wool, similar to a double knitting (worsted) but denser. Worked at a tight tension (gauge), in the round, the fabric produced is virtually water- and windproof and so tough that it has been dubbed 'seaman's iron'. Ganseys are traditionally worked in dark blue for dirt resistance, and since preserving the natural oils in the wool was extremely important, it is unlikely that a real gansey saw the inside of a wash tub very many times in its life, if at all. As they were often knitted by women on the quayside, during a lull in the herring gutting, ganseys must have had a fairly distinctive aroma.

Although stitches may vary, the basic straight-bodied, drop shoulder structure of a gansey is standard. The body is worked from the welt (finishing border) up to the armholes in the round on anything from five to ten needles. The work is then divided for the armholes and continued to the shoulder seams which are knitted together, often in a very decorative manner. The sleeve stitches are then knitted (picked) up from around the armholes and the sleeves are worked from top to bottom, making whole or partial sleeve replacement a simple task. Judging by the old photographs, the extreme wear and tear to which they were subjected must have made

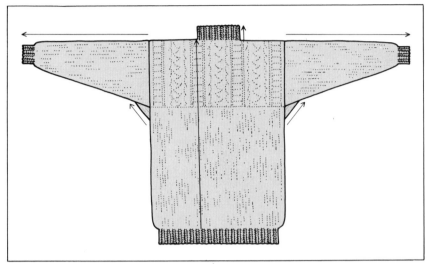

A traditional guernsey showing the direction of working.

such repairs common, since the line where new blue yarn joins the faded grey of the well-worn original is frequently obvious.

The neck was also knitted up in the round, forming a standing collar, deep enough to keep the wind out but not chafe the neck. The roll-neck (turtle-neck) version is a recent innovation. A gusset for ease of movement was worked under the arm, as part of the body and sleeve, since ganseys were meant to fit snugly for perfect insulation. Thus the entire garment was seamless and could take whatever the elements threw at it.

The stitch patterns used aided warmth and durability since they increased the thickness of the fabric, but their use probably also had a lot to do with both the wearer's and the knitter's pride. Some patterns were family 'heirlooms' handed down from generation to generation. On his travels, Michael Pearson, author of *Traditional Knitting*, found a lady with photographs showing the same style of gansey, worn by five generations of her family. Although there was a certain amount of pattern exchange, especially among the women who travelled from port to port following the migration of the herring – which they would gut, salt and pack on the spot – in many areas it was possible to tell which town a fisherman came from by the pattern on his gansey. Fine ganseys were often given as gifts on special occasions such as birthdays and weddings, and 'Sunday best' ones would be worn as just that. Some ganseys were called 'bridal shirts', and knitted by a bride for her groom.

The texture patterns are made by using purl stitches on a stocking (stockinette) stitch ground, with the addition of small cables and some rib. The raised designs can be simple bands, columns and zigzags or more elaborate motifs such as diamonds, trees, hearts and anchors. Sometimes they are combinations of any number of these, but they are always formed by areas of moss (seed) stitch, double moss stitch, garter stitch or reverse stocking stitch with small cables used as repeat breaks. The designs, always on a small scale, can be worked all over a garment, just on the body or, most commonly, on the yoke area and upper sleeves. Some ganseys use just one stitch, such as double moss stitch, to form the yoke area, while others are completely plain, as are the modern, machine-knit copies.

If two graphs were drawn to represent the decline of Britain's fisheries and the decline in the art of gansey knitting they would probably follow the same line. Other important factors in the decline of the gansey include the advent of mass-produced industrial knitwear, even in remote fishing communities previously cut off from the rest of Britain, and changing social attitudes. The elaborate ganseys that their grandfathers had been proud to wear were no longer so important to the modern fishermen and they passed from the work world into the realms of rural museums or 'olde worlde gift shoppes'.

GUSSETS

Like the flare and the dart, the gusset is a tailoring feature, not, strictly speaking, a knitting technique. The positioning of the shaping required to produce a gusset within the knitted fabric does, however, need explanation.

The function of a gusset is to give extra strength to a part of a garment or to enlarge the fabric available at a particular point for ease of movement, as at the crotch of a pair of tights or the underarm of a traditional gansey (guernsey) sweater. When laid flat, the shape of a gusset is that of an elongated diamond.

A gusset to be inserted into a garment which is being knitted in the round is formed in the same way as a gore. Shapings are worked on either side of a triangular wedge, and then reversed out to form the diamond shape. On a gansey, for example, the gusset would be started at the side seam point of the body, approximately 7.5cm (3in.) from the point where the work is divided to form the armholes. Stitches are then increased each side of the seam marker (remember that there is no real seam since the garment is being knitted in the round) on every so many rows, according to how many stitches are to be gained over the 7.5cm (3in.). If the gusset is to be 20 stitches at the widest point and the garment is being worked at a fairly standard tension (gauge), this would involve increasing one stitch each side

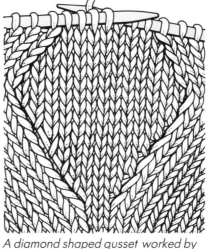

A diamond shaped gusset worked by increasing and then decreasing.

on every alternate row. When the body is divided, the gusset stitches are left on a holder while the back and front are completed.

When the sleeve stitches are knit-ted (picked) up from round the armhole, the gusset stitches are put back on to the working needle at the point which corresponds to the sleeve seam. As the sleeve is worked down-wards, stitches are decreased on either side of the gusset to reverse out the increases which were worked at the beginning. When no gusset stitches remain, the diamond shape is com-pleted and the sleeve may be con-tinued as usual.

If a garment is not being worked in the round, gussets can be knitted as separate pieces and then sewn in at the making up (assembly) stage, as they would be in tailoring. However, since they are usually situated where ease of movement is required, un-wanted bulk has to be avoided; for this reason, they should only be used on garments which will be assembled using flat, rather than backstitched, seams.

HEMS

Hems are essential on garments knitted in a curling stitch which are to fall in a straight line, without a welt (finishing border) or obvious border. On something like a skirt or coat, the extra weight of the hem also improves the way the fabric hangs. The same methods can be used on any part of a garment which needs finishing or where a tube is required, as when a casing is worked to hold elastic at a waistline.

Most stitches, with a few obvious exceptions, will take a hem. It is not advisable to include a hem on lace or openwork patterns, however, since a turned hem will be visible on the right side. Stitches which have a lot of bias 'give' are also unsuitable as they make producing a straight, flat hem virtually impossible. With stitches which produce a heavy fabric, such as cables, it is down to personal preference how much heavier you are prepared to make the garment by the addition of a hem.

Since it is all too easy to work a hem which will not lie flat, the following rules should be noted:

1. Whatever stitch is used for the garment, the section of the hem to be turned under should be worked in stocking (stockinette) stitch as this produces the flattest fabric.

2. The section to turn under should always be worked at a tighter tension (gauge) than the main work. If the whole garment is being worked in stocking stitch, this merely involves using smaller needles, but if you are working a stocking stitch turn-under on to another stitch, you must compare the tension of the two stitches to ensure that the turn-under is slightly narrower than the main fabric.

If the knitting is already being worked at a rather firm tension, and making it any tighter would not be advisable, the entire hem can be worked across fewer stitches. On a fairly wide dress hem, for instance, approximately 2cm (⅞in.) can be removed. If the hem is worked at the beginning of the work, this will involve casting on fewer stitches; if it is worked at the end, the few unwanted stitches should be decreased, evenly, over the first row of the hem.

3. Whichever method you choose to secure the turned-under hem, it should never produce a visible line on the right side of the work.

4. If hemmed knitted pieces have to be joined, a flat seam should be worked. A backstitch will produce too much bulk within the seam. If one hemmed edge is to meet another at right angles, the turn-under must be mitred (see *Corners*).

To simplify the following instructions, the methods described assume that it will not be necessary to increase or decrease any stitches for the turn-under sections, and that the hems are being worked on stocking stitch garments.

Stitched hems

If the hem is being worked at the beginning of the knitting, the stitches should be cast on using a non-bulky method such as simple thumb/one needle (see *Casting On*). The size of needle which you use depends on personal tension variation between needle sizes. They should always be at least one size smaller, but two or three sizes difference may be needed to produce a turn-under which will lie flat neatly. Work the number of rows which corresponds to the depth of the hem required. To create a 'sharp' fold line, form a ridge by knitting into the backs of the stitches on the next wrong side row, that is, a row which would normally be purled. This will mark the fold row and helps prevent a twisted hem. If a ridge is not required, continue in stocking stitch, change to the correct size needle for the main work and complete the piece.

When the knitting is finished, turn up the hem and carefully pin it into position so that the lines of stitches on the main turn-under correspond exactly to the lines of the stitches on the main work. The cast on edge can then be slip-stitched down, stitch for stitch to avoid a bias twist. Use a blunt tapestry needle, taking it through a cast on loop and then the stitch in a line, directly above it, at the top of the hem. Mark the top hem row so that the stitching is worked in a straight line and the hem is not secured to the row above or below. The stitching should not be pulled up tightly as this will produce a puckered line on the right side of the work.

If you are working a hem at the end of a piece of knitting, follow the instructions above but turn them upside-down and attach the cast (bound) off edge, rather than the cast on one. This should either be an

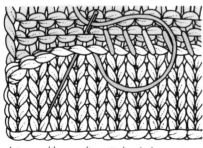

A turned hem, slip-stitched down into position.

elastic (suspended) cast off edge or, alternatively, when you have reached the depth required for the turn-under, leave the stitches on the needle and slip-stitch them directly to the main work, as around a double neck band (see *Crew Necks*).

Knitted hems

When working a knitted hem at the beginning of a piece of work, cast on using the open (looped) method (see *Casting On*) so that the loops can be picked up easily.

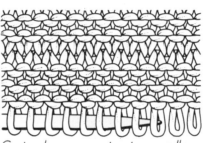

Cast on loops are put on to a needle, ready to knit a hem in place (above). The hem is then knitted together.

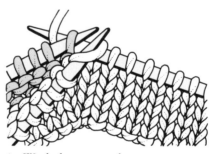

1. Work the turn-under section to the required depth but work the top part of the hem two rows short, ending on a right side row. Purl the next row on a size larger needle than the main work. Using another needle of the same size, pick up the row of cast on loops so that both needles are pointing in the same direction.

2. Using a third needle of the same size, knit the working row and the cast on loop row together. Keep the tension correct so that this row has as much 'give' as the actual fabric (see *Knitting Stitches Together*). If it is worked too tightly, the finished hem will stick out, exhibiting the 'shelf effect'.

Now change back to the size needles required for the main work and continue working up the garment.

If the hem is to be worked in the opposite direction, that is, at the end of the piece of knitting, work the first row of the hem on the larger size needle and the turn-under section one row short. Pick up the stitches along the enlarged row on to an extra needle and knit them together with the working row of stitches to form the turned hem.

Picot hems

A hem with a picot edge can be worked by following the basic hem instructions, according to the direction in which the hem is to be knitted and whether it is to be knitted or stitched up. When the fold line row is reached, instead of working a ridge, work a row of eyelets (rounds) to create a row of picot points when the hem is turned under. (See *Edgings* for details of the picot technique.)

Naturally, all hems require pressing, but if the hem lies really badly when you have completed the knitting, it is unlikely that any amount of pressing will remedy the fault, especially if there is a bias pull, a 'shelf effect' or a puckered row where the hem has been secured. As this will ruin the hang of the garment, the hem must be undone and re-turned to produce a perfectly flat finish.

HOLDING STITCHES

Whichever way you choose to hold stitches which are not being worked, the most important thing is to safeguard against letting those stitches get out of shape for any reason. When they are returned to the working needles, there should be no visible signs that the held stitches have been treated any differently from the rest.

If a whole piece of knitting has to be put aside, by far the best idea is to leave it on the needle which you have been using or, if you do not have a spare one of the correct size, use one as near the size as possible. Place a stitch stopper or cork on the needle point to prevent the stitches from slipping off. Leave the yarn attached in case it can be used when you return to these stitches.

When only part of the row of stitches is to be held while you continue to work over the remainder, a purpose-made stitch holder must be used. Before choosing which type of holder to buy, see *Gadgets*. Take care

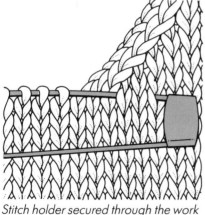

Stitch holder secured through the work to avoid stretched stitches.

not to twist the stitches when they are slipped on to the holder or when they are returned to the working needle. Rather than let the stitches support the weight of the holder, place the holder through the actual knitted fabric at either end of the set of held stitches. Avoid splitting any of the fabric stitches with the point of the holder. This method prevents the strands between the working stitches and the first and last held stitches becoming badly stretched.

Should you need to hold only one or two stitches, as at the point of a 'V' neck, for example, do not use a large holder as it will slide back and forth as the work is moved. Slip a safety pin through the stitch/stitches and then through the fabric to keep it in place.

In emergencies, when no spare needles, holders or pins are available, a length of yarn may be used to hold stitches. This should be either the same yarn as being worked or, if you prefer a contrast, use a smooth yarn with a tight twist, such as polyester rayon. A soft yarn will leave traces of the contrast colour clinging to the held stitches when it is removed. Use a blunt needle to thread it through the stitches and leave enough yarn to tie loosely at either end to hold the stitches securely.

Since stitches held on a thread or a very thin holder will shrink from their

original size, it may be advisable to work one extra row before putting the stitches on hold. When the work is resumed, slip the stitches from the previous row on to the working needle in order to avoid a noticeable line of smaller stitches. Naturally, if the stitches are only being held before knitting together a seam or continuing in another stitch or colour, this will not be necessary because the line will not be visible.

HOLES

Intentional

Holes are the basis of all lace and openwork stitches, the permutations of which are endless. Nearly all are made by a simple yarn over the needle procedure. This strand is then treated as a new stitch, and a decrease made at some point to bring the stitches back to the original number. A stitch made in this way will form a hole, the size of which will depend upon the stitches around it, and the size of the yarn and needles which are being used.

The most basic hole is an eyelet (round), made by 'yarn over needle,

Eyelet holes divided by two knit stitches.

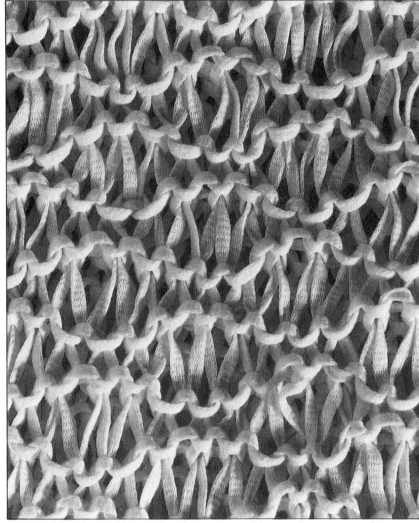

A holey fabric formed by winding the yarn round the needle a number of times.

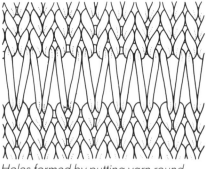

Holes formed by putting yarn round needle twice before working a stitch.

work two together'. This is made at intervals over a solid fabric, usually stocking stitch, so that the eyelet shows up. It can be used for practical purposes such as buttonholes and threading holes, or simply as part of a pattern in itself. Larger holes are made by casting (binding) off stitches, see *Buttonholes*.

Another variety of hole which is, strictly speaking, only an enlarged stitch, can be made by working a stitch normally but winding the yarn around the needle more than once. When the next row is worked these 'wraps' are then treated as one stitch so that when it is slipped off the needle the extra yarn forms an elon-gated stitch. The number of times that the yarn is wrapped around the needle regulates the size of the loop. Some very effective patterns are created in this way, worked over both plain stocking stitch and garter stitch.

Unintentional

For hints on the prevention of and cure for accidental holes, see *Dropped Stitches* and *Uneven Knitting*. There is, however, no substitute for keeping a constant eye on your knitting in order to catch mistakes before they become irretrievable. Any variety of sloppily worked stitches can produce an un-wanted hole in your work if you are aiming for speed at the expense of care and attention. The most common faults in careless stocking (stocki-nette) stitch are split stitches and stitches worked from the previous row.

Split stitches occur when the work-ing needle divides the yarn of the stitch rather than working cleanly through the loop to form a new stitch. It is as serious as a dropped stitch since the strand which has been split will be much weaker than the surrounding stitches and likely to break sooner or later, resulting in a stitch which will run. Split stitches should be dealt with in the same way as dropped stitches and never ignored in the hopes that they will hold out.

Another common mistake, when the knitter's attention wanders, is for the loop from the previous row, rather than the next stitch in the current row, to be worked. Since the stitch which should have been worked is slipped off the needle at the same time, it forms a very noticeable flaw in the finished work. Once again, such a mistake should be remedied as a dropped stitch would be.

Holes in intarsia colour knitting can be easily avoided by twisting the yarns around one another every time that the colour is changed (see *Intarsia*).

For ways of dealing with holes which are made accidentally, after the garment is completed, see *Mending*.

HORIZONTAL KNITTING

Horizontal knitting is worked from side to side, rather than, as in vertical knitting, from bottom to top. This means that it is the stitch tension (gauge) which governs how long the garment is to be, and the row tension

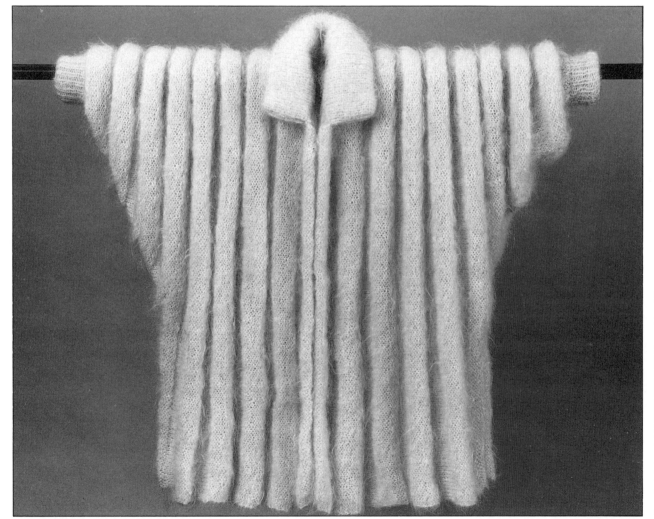

A jacket worked horizontally – from cuff to cuff.

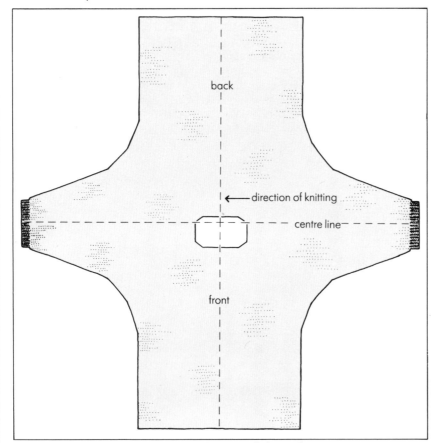

The shape of the fabric produced in a horizontally knitted sweater.

which governs the width, rather than the other way round as in conventional knitting. Thus, it is even more vital to get your tension absolutely accurate when knitting in this way.

Designers use this method of knitting for a variety of reasons. It is possible to produce numerous vertical colour patterns simply by changing colour in horizontal bands while working from side to side. This avoids using the intarsia or fairisle colour methods which would be necessary if you were knitting the garment from bottom to top. This means that even beginners can produce quite intricate patterns, using very simple methods.

Certain shapes – most notably dolman and batwing sweaters – lend themselves naturally to horizontal knitting. When these are worked from cuff to cuff, in one piece, sleeve and shoulder seams are completely eliminated. The line of the finished garment is not interrupted, giving it far more fluidity to hang in its natural folds.

There are also pattern effects which utilize the natural qualities of a stitch when worked sideways. Even plain stocking (stockinette) stitch may be used with dramatic effect in horizontally worked bands.

When choosing a pattern for a horizontally worked garment, always try to find one which has a clear diagram of how the garment will appear when laid flat, since written instructions only can shroud a garment shape in mystery. Shapings which may be quite familiar on a vertically worked garment often become unrecognizable in horizontal instructions. If you are truly in doubt as to how the work will turn out and no diagram or clear picture is to hand, take some graph paper and draw the shapings out.

INCREASING

Increases are used to widen knitting by adding new stitches to those already on the needle. The same structural rules apply to both decreasing and increasing, see *Shaping*.

Note: When a large number of increases are required, extra stitches should be cast on at the beginning or end of rows (see *Casting On*).

There are two major categories of increased stitches – those which are formed out of the previously knitted stitches and those which are produced by putting the working yarn over the needle to form a new loop. Since the former group involves using stitches or loops from the existing knitted fabric, they take up yarn from around the increased stitch and cannot be used repeatedly over consecutive rows without an inevitable loss of elasticity in this area. If many increases are to be worked across a row, this will also put a strain on the previous row by stretching the work laterally, which may be undesirable when working something like a ribbed cuff. If you have to increase the number of stitches for the width of the sleeve, it is far

better to work a few of them across the row immediately after the ribbing and then divide the rest over the following rows. This will avoid pulling the rib stitches out of shape, so that the elasticity of the cuff will remain un-affected. Many patterns which have been lazily drafted will incorrectly use increases in this manner so do not hesitate to alter them if you require a well-fitting cuff.

Yarn over needle increases

1. When you reach the point for an increase, place the yarn over the RH needle.
2. Work the next st normally.

This method produces a strand

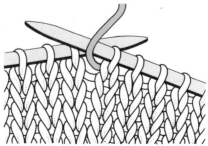

Place yarn to front of work, under needle.

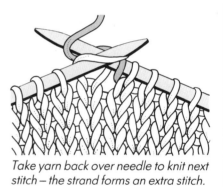

Take yarn back over needle to knit next stitch – the strand forms an extra stitch.

which is then treated as a proper stitch on the following row. It does, however, leave a hole in the fabric and is more commonly used to form eyelets (rounds) and lace patterns where it is paired with a decrease to bring the stitches back to the original number. It can be used as an increase where decorative holes are desired.

Working into a stitch twice/ Simple increase

1. When you reach the point for an increase, work into the front of the st.
2. Then, without slipping the strand off the LH needle, work into the back of the same st. Slip the strand off the LH needle and work next st as normal.

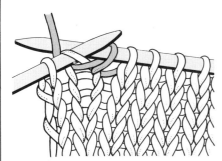

Increasing by working into a stitch twice, once into the front (above), and then into the back (below).

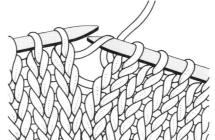

Picking up the strand between stitches (above), and then working into the back of it (below).

This method may also be called invisible since it produces the neatest finish of all. When the stitch to be increased is reached, the loop below it, that is, the stitch directly below it on the previous row, is worked without slipping the stitch off the left-hand needle. The stitch itself is then worked in the usual way and slipped off the left-hand needle. On stocking stitch, it is virtually impossible to spot where the increase has been worked without very close examination.

Decorative increases

If the work calls for an ornamental line of increases, worked at very regular row intervals, the stitch to be increased may be worked into twice, varying the stitch used. When increasing a stitch on the right side of stocking stitch, knit, then purl, into the same stitch. This will produce a row of purl stitch bumps on the finished work.

Double increases

To produce a double increase, increases may be worked, one next to another, using any of the above methods, according to the finished effect you require. To create a neat, symmetrical effect, they should be divided by, and worked either side of, an axial or central stitch.

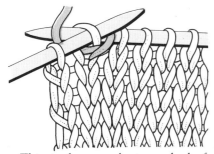

This is the most basic method of increasing, but when worked on stocking (stockinette) stitch it does, in fact, produce a most untidy finish since it results in a bar effect across the stitch where the increase is made. It can, however, be neatly worked on garter stitch. Although undesirable on areas where they will be visible, the bars of this increase may be useful in keeping track of the number of increases which have been worked. If worked close to the edge on work which is to be seamed using a backstitch, the increased stitches can then be taken into the seam so that they will not show on the finished garment.

Working the strand between stitches/Raised increase
1. With the RH needle, lift the strand which runs between the sts.
2. Put strand on to the LH needle and

then work it as a normal st. Since this tends to form a small hole, the lifted stitch is usually twisted by working into the back of it.

As the lifted strand pulls spare yarn from the stitches on either side of it, this method is not recommended for work at a very firm tension (gauge).

Working the stitch below/ Lifted increase

Working into the stitch from the previous row.

A traditional type guernsey sweater which has been knitted in the round. It illustrates various texture patterns, has a patterned shoulder panel and buttoning stand-up collar, intended to keep out cold sea breezes. Such sweaters were originally fishermen's work garments, and examples can be seen in the photographic archives of almost all of Britain's fishing ports.

INSTRUCTIONS

The instructions contained within each knitting pattern will vary slightly. Always check the points highlighted below before making your choice, and investing in the necessary yarn (see *Patterns*).

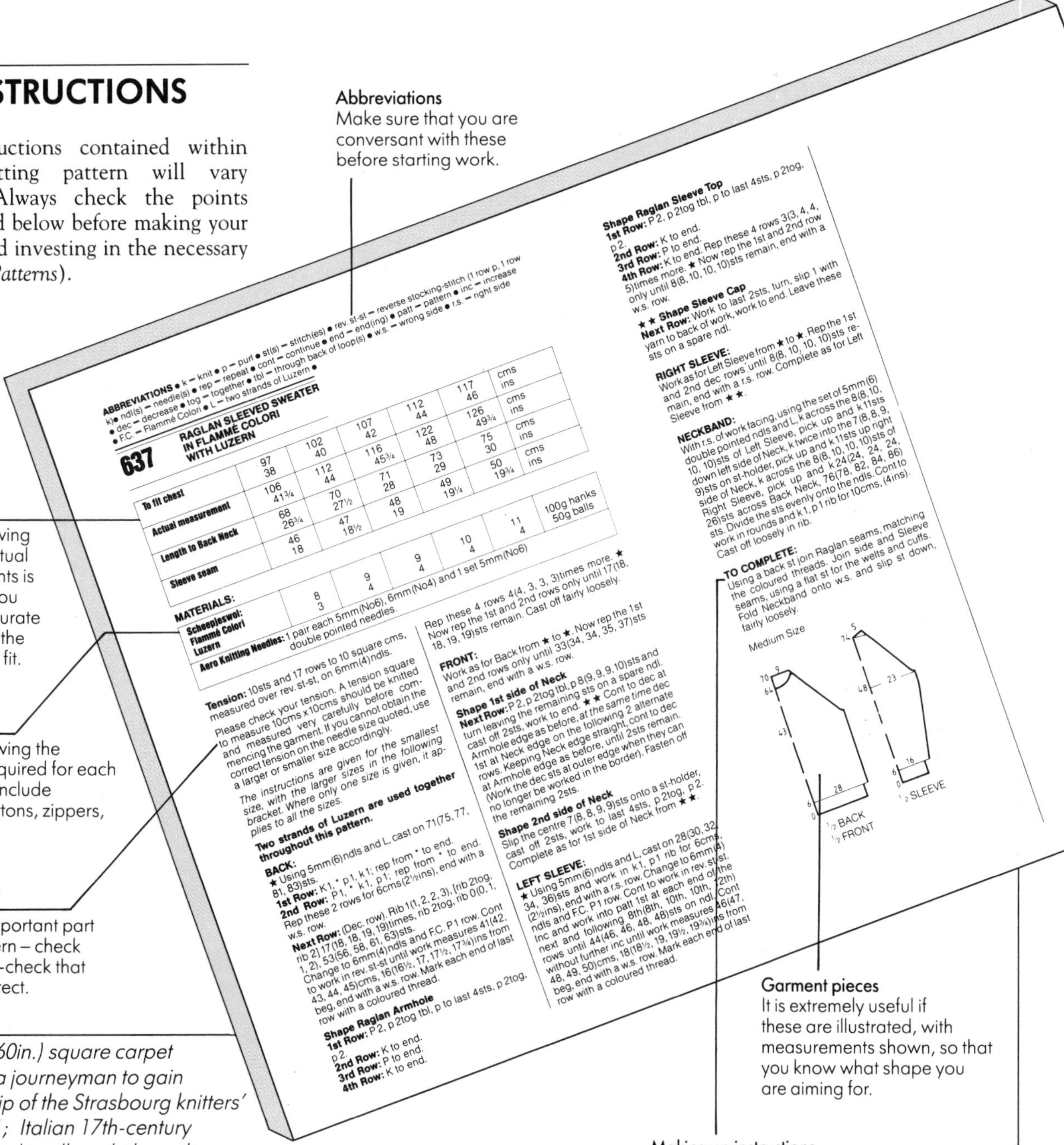
ABBREVIATIONS • k – knit • p – purl • st(s) – stitch(es) • rev. st-st – reverse stocking-stitch (1 row p, 1 row k) • ndl(s) – needle(s) • rep – repeat • cont – continue • end – end(ing) • patt – pattern • inc – increase • dec – decrease • tog – together • tbl – through back of loop(s) • w.s. – wrong side • r.s. – right side • F.C. – Flammé Colori • L – two strands of Luzern •

637 RAGLAN SLEEVED SWEATER IN FLAMMÉ COLORI WITH LUZERN

To fit chest	97 38	102 40	107 42	112 44	117 46	cms ins
Actual measurement	106 41¾	112 44	116 45¾	122 48	126 49¾	cms ins
Length to Back Neck	68 26¾	70 27½	71 28	73 29	75 30	cms ins
Sleeve seam	46 18	47 18½	48 19	49 19¼	50 19¾	cms ins
MATERIALS:						
Scheepjeswol: Flammé Colori	8	9	9	10	11	100g hanks
Luzern	3	4	4	4	4	50g balls
Aero Knitting Needles: 1 pair each 5mm(No6), 6mm(No4) and 1 set 5mm(No6) double pointed needles.						

Tension: 10sts and 17 rows to 10 square cms, measured over rev. st-st, on 6mm(4)ndls.
Please check your tension. A tension square to measure 10cms x 10cms should be knitted and measured very carefully before commencing the garment. If you cannot obtain the correct tension on the needle size quoted, use a larger or smaller size accordingly.
The instructions are given for the smallest size, with the larger sizes in the following bracket. Where only one size is given, it applies to all the sizes.
Two strands of Luzern are used together throughout this pattern.

BACK:
★ Using 5mm(6)ndls and L, cast on 71(75, 77, 81, 83)sts.
1st Row: K1, * p1, k1; rep from * to end.
2nd Row: P1, * k1, p1; rep from * to end.
Rep these 2 rows for 6cms(2½ins), end with a w.s. row.
Next Row: (Dec. row). Rib 1(1, 2, 2, 3), [rib 2tog, rib 2] 17(18, 18, 19, 19)times, rib 2tog, rib 0(0, 1, 1, 2). 53(56, 58, 61, 63)sts.
Change to 6mm(4)ndls and F.C. P1 row. Cont to work in rev. st-st until work measures 41(42, 43, 44, 45)cms, 16(16½, 17, 17½, 17¾)ins from beg, end with a w.s. row. Mark each end of last row with a coloured thread.
Shape Raglan Armhole
1st Row: P2, p2tog tbl, p to last 4sts, p2tog, p2.
2nd Row: K to end.
3rd Row: P to end.
4th Row: K to end.
Rep these 4 rows 4(4, 3, 3, 3)times more. ★ Now rep the 1st and 2nd rows only until 17(18, 18, 19, 19)sts remain. Cast off fairly loosely.

FRONT:
Work as for Back from ★ to ★. Now rep the 1st and 2nd rows only until 33(34, 34, 35, 37)sts remain, end with a w.s. row.
Shape 1st side of Neck
Next Row: P2, p2tog tbl, p8(9, 9, 9, 10)sts and turn leaving the remaining sts on a spare ndl. cast off 2sts, work to end. ★★ Cont to dec at Armhole edge as before, *at the same time* dec 1st at Neck edge on the following 2 alternate rows. Keeping Neck edge straight, cont to dec at Armhole edge as before, until 2sts remain. (Work the dec sts at outer edge when they can no longer be worked in the border). Fasten off the remaining 2sts.
Shape 2nd side of Neck
Slip the centre 7(8, 8, 9, 9)sts onto a st-holder, cast off 2sts, work to last 4sts, p2tog, p2. Complete as for 1st side of Neck from ★★.

LEFT SLEEVE:
★ Using 5mm(6)ndls and L, cast on 28(30, 32, 34, 36)sts and work in k1, p1 rib for 6cms (2½ins), end with a r.s. row. Change to 6mm(4) ndls and F.C. P1 row. Cont to work in rev. st-st. Inc and work into patt 1st at each end of the next and following 8th(8th, 10th, 10th, 12th) rows until 44(46, 46, 48, 48)sts on ndl. Cont without further inc until work measures 46(47, 48, 49, 50)cms, 18(18½, 19, 19½, 19¾)ins from beg, end with a w.s. row. Mark each end of last row with a coloured thread.
Shape Raglan Sleeve Top
1st Row: P2, p2tog tbl, p to last 4sts, p2tog, p2.
2nd Row: K to end.
3rd Row: P to end.
4th Row: K to end. Rep these 4 rows 3(3, 4, 4, 5)times more. ★ Now rep the 1st and 2nd row only until 8(8, 10, 10, 10)sts remain, end with a w.s. row.
★★ **Shape Sleeve Cap**
Next Row: Work to last 2sts, turn, slip 1 with yarn to back of work, work to end. Leave these sts on a spare ndl.

RIGHT SLEEVE:
Work as for Left Sleeve from ★ to ★. Rep the 1st and 2nd dec rows until 8(8, 10, 10, 10)sts remain, end with a r.s. row. Complete as for Left Sleeve from ★★.

NECKBAND:
With r.s. of work facing, using the set of 5mm(6) double pointed ndls and L, k across the 8(8, 10, 10, 10)sts of Left Sleeve, pick up and k11sts down left side of Neck, k twice into the 7(8, 8, 9, 9)sts on st-holder, pick up and k11sts up right side of Neck, k across the 8(8, 10, 10, 10)sts of Right Sleeve, pick up and k24(24, 24, 24, 26)sts across Back Neck. 76(78, 82, 84, 86)sts. Divide the sts evenly onto the ndls. Cont to work in rounds and k1, p1 rib for 10cms, (4ins). Cast off loosely in rib.

TO COMPLETE:
Using a back st join Raglan seams, matching the coloured threads. Join side and Sleeve seams, using a flat st for the welts and cuffs. Fold Neckband onto w.s. and slip st down, fairly loosely.

Medium Size
70
9
64
43
28
6
0
½ BACK
½ FRONT
5
74
48
23
16
6
0
½ SLEEVE

Abbreviations
Make sure that you are conversant with these before starting work.

Size
A chart showing sizes *and* actual measurements is essential if you want an accurate idea of how the garment will fit.

Materials
A table showing the materials required for each size should include needles, buttons, zippers, and so on.

Tension
The most important part of any pattern – check and double-check that yours is correct.

Garment pieces
It is extremely useful if these are illustrated, with measurements shown, so that you know what shape you are aiming for.

Making up instructions
Always check this section in case it involves a technique, such as crochet, with which you are unfamiliar.

A 163cm (60in.) square carpet knitted by a journeyman to gain membership of the Strasbourg knitters' guild, 1781; Italian 17th-century jacket knitted in silk and silver gilt thread; Multicoloured socks from Iraq, circa 1930; Beaded bag from the mid-19th century.

■ IN-THE-ROUND KNITTING

See *Circular Knitting*.

■ INTARSIA

Intarsia knitting is colour knitting in which separate balls of yarn are used for each individual area of colour. No colours are carried at the back of the work as in the fairisle method. Any design which involves large blocks of colour should be worked in this way.

There are no limitations as to how many colours can be used on any one row, other than those imposed by lack of patience and/or dexterity. If you are planning your own design or using one that was intended for another craft, such as embroidery or rug-making, work out the maximum number of colour areas on any one row before deciding upon its suitability. As with any other knitting project, make life as easy for yourself as possible. If you find that shifting an area of colour up or down a few rows will cut down the number of balls you will have in use at a time, without spoiling the design, then do so.

Bobbins can be used to hold the yarn for each separate area, greatly reducing the potential number of tangles (see *Bobbins*).

Always leave a reasonably sized piece of yarn at the beginning and end of every area since, as they are within the work, it is very important that they are secured extremely carefully (see *Ends*).

The most important part of intarsia knitting, however, is securing the changeover points between the different colours. Every time you move from one colour to the next, the yarns must be firmly twisted around one another before you drop the old and start the new. If this is not done, you will simply be knitting numerous quite separate areas of work. If it is done too loosely, untidy gaps will form between the colours and ruin the overall effect of the garment.

JACQUARD

J. M. Jacquard of Lyons invented an apparatus to facilitate colour weaving in the late 18th century. Since then, however, his name has passed into common usage to denote any sort of colour pattern. It is a term which more properly belongs to the realms of textiles and machine knitting; when used with regard to hand knitting, it is a vague, imprecise term which does not describe any specific technique. For colour knitting methods, see *Fairisle* and *Intarsia*.

JOINS

Unless you are joining in colours for individual intarsia areas, are desperately short of yarn, or are working in the round, you should never make joins within the work. Not only is a join unsightly, it will always be a weak spot in the garment.

Splicing

If you are knitting in the round or using a yarn which is too precious to waste, then splicing the old and new ends together is the only answer. (You can also allow it when an unforeseen

Spliced yarn which has been trimmed back and rolled.

break or fault occurs in the yarn near the end of a row with an enormous number of stitches.) On smooth yarns, this can never be completely disguised, but on fluffy yarns it can be quite acceptable.

Make the splice over as large a length as possible – at least 10cm (4in.). Try to avoid splicing plied yarn, but if it is essential, separate the ply and trim half of it away on each end. Put the two ends together and roll them between your palms to simulate the ply. Knit as normal, trimming any visible ends when you have finished. If the yarn is not plied or is very fluffy, the splice has to be made over a shorter length since the yarns can only be carefully plucked at to produce fibres which will then stick to one another when rolled.

Perfect joins

These should always be made at the edge of the work. Simply start working the row with the new end of yarn and after a few stitches tie the old and new ends in a loose knot at the side of the work. These can be further secured when seaming, or better still, use the ends to work the seam.

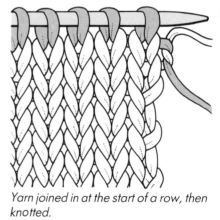

Yarn joined in at the start of a row, then knotted.

Running out of yarn mid-row

There is nothing more annoying than running out of yarn after working most of your row. To avoid this, when you are unsure whether you have enough yarn to complete an entire row, lay the yarn which you have left across the width of the work. If it will reach across at least three times, you will have enough yarn to finish a stocking (stockinette) stitch row. If you are working a yarn-greedy stitch, however, it is a case of trial and error, but it is well worth working it out and making a note for future reference.

Other methods

Knots Not only should knots never be made, but they should always be removed from any yarn in which you find them. Then make a proper join.

Knitting two ends together Since you are using two thicknesses of yarn this will always look lumpy and the ends can easily work themselves loose.

Both knots and ends will almost always insinuate themselves through to the right side of the work, however careful you may be – avoid them.

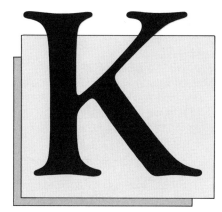

THE KNIT STITCH

The knit stitch is the most basic stitch in knitting and the most important since it forms the basis of so many other stitches. It should always be the first stage of knitting to be mastered by the beginner.

Using the non-continental method of knitting, the knit stitch is worked as follows:

1. Insert the RH needle diagonally into the st on the LH needle – under the LH needle – from the front to the back.

2. Bring the yarn, held in your right hand at the back of the work, under and around the point of the RH needle.

3. With the RH needle, pull this yarn through the st on the LH needle to form a loop on the RH needle.

4. Drop the old st off the LH needle.

To carry out these steps with minimal strain on the stitches being worked, it is essential to keep sliding the stitches on the left-hand needle up towards the point without crowding them so that they drop off. At the same time, the stitches on the right-hand needle should be gradually pushed down the needle to allow room for the new stitches being formed.

It is very much down to personal preference how each knitter chooses to hold the yarn but try, right from the very beginning, to hold it in a way that allows you to put it round the point without your right hand leaving

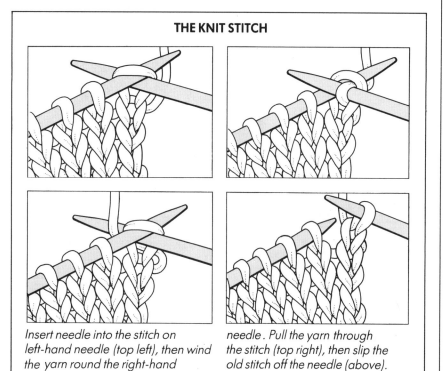

THE KNIT STITCH

Insert needle into the stitch on left-hand needle (top left), then wind the yarn round the right-hand

needle. Pull the yarn through the stitch (top right), then slip the old stitch off the needle (above).

the needle. The best way to achieve this is to control the movement of the yarn with the index finger of your right hand, but actually hold the yarn with your remaining fingers, curled into your palm. With the thumb of the right hand under the right-hand needle, supporting it, only the index finger needs to be moved up to the needle point each time the yarn is placed round it. This positioning of the thumb feels almost impossible at first as the natural span of the hand seems over-extended, but by careful regulation of the stitches close to the points of both needles, the stretch required is minimized. The hand soon becomes accustomed to sliding up and down the right-hand needle rather than dropping it, moving the yarn, and then picking the needle up again, which is an unnecessarily time-wasting action.

When you first learn to knit, don't worry about speed, that will come with practice. The true indication that a stitch has been mastered is when you are able to hold the work in a relaxed way without any tension or strain in either your hands or the knitting.

KNITTING STITCHES TOGETHER

For the purposes of this section, knitting stitches together does not refer to decreases where two or three stitches are worked together to form one. Here, it means working across a whole row of stitches from more than one needle so that two or three fabrics are joined by that row.

> HINT
> If you are learning to knit from scratch, start with the knit stitch, if you can find a willing volunteer to cast on for you. Master casting on at a later date – when you are familiar with the knit stitch.

A classic example of two sets of stitches being joined is on a knitted hem being worked up from the bottom. When the hem is the required depth it is turned up and the loops from the cast on edge put on to a spare needle (see *Hems*).

1. Make sure that the two needles hold exactly the same number of sts. Hold both in your left hand, one directly in front of the other.

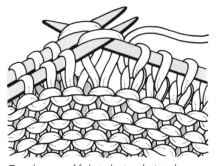

Two layers of fabric being knitted together simultaneously off the left-hand needles.

2. The right hand is used to knit in the normal way, but put the point of the RH needle simultaneously through both the first st on the front and the first st on the back needle.
3. Pull the loop through both sts, forming a single st on the RH needle. Then slip both old sts off the LH needles.

Repeat steps 2 and 3 across the row

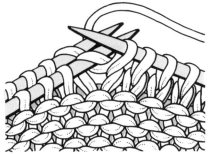

One stitch is made on the right-hand needle; from this row, work can be continued as normal.

so that the two fabrics are joined, leaving a single row of stitches on the RH needle from which the work can be continued as normal.

The same method can be used to join the tops or bottoms of knitted pleats, but here the stitches are held on three needles in the left hand (see *Pleats*). Holding a number of needles in one hand is not easy, even after practice, and three is the maximum number which is practical.

This technique of knitting stitches together can be used in virtually any situation where a horizontal seam would normally be made. The stitches of a pocket flap, for instance, may be knitted together with the stitches directly above the pocket opening before the main garment is continued. This method frequently provides an efficient and effective alternative to attaching two pieces of work using a sewn seam and is commonly used in conjunction with simple casting (binding) off to form knitted seams (see *Seams*).

Before casting off any piece of work which is to be attached to another, always consider if it might be suitable for knitting together, as this always saves time, and produces a neater finish.

KNITTING/ PICKING UP STITCHES

Since stitches usually have to be picked up at the focal points on a garment – around the neckline, or on the fronts of a cardigan – the techniques involved rate among the most important for any knitter who wishes to produce a professional-looking finish.

First and foremost, the edge which is to form the basis for the picked up stitches must be as neat and firm as possible. On straight edges, take great care to form a suitable selvedge (see *Selvedges*). When shapings are required, they should be worked at least one or two stitches in from the edge, unless the stitch being used prevents you from doing so. If a colour pattern is being worked on a base colour, stop the pattern short so that the last one or two stitches of the row are worked in the base colour. Ideally, you should have an even, single-colour edge, ready to work from.

When you complete a piece of work which is to have stitches picked up at a later stage, leave the yarn attached so that it may be used as and when required.

If stitches are going to be knitted up from a cast (bound) off edge, cast off in a suitably elastic method (see *Casting/Binding Off*). If you are going to use held stitches with knitted up stitches, make sure that they have not been stretched while being held, especially at either end, and place them on the needle in the correct way, without twisting.

The number of stitches to be knitted up depends on whether you are picking up along a row or down a line of edge stitches. It also depends upon which stitch is to be used to work the knitted up stitches. Cast off or held stitches may usually be counted stitch for stitch, unless there is a very great difference in tension (gauge) between the cast off stitch and the one to be worked up from it. When knitting up along edge stitches, if the knitted up portion is to be worked in the same stitch as the main work, then it will not work out one stitch per row, as a row tension is almost always greater than a stitch tension. On stocking (stockinette) stitch, for example, about one row in four should be left without knitting up a stitch. If the knitted up stitches are to be worked in rib, as is so often the case for most borders, the rib stitches and row tension will be more or less equal, so a stitch may be knitted up from each row on a small area such as the side of a crew neck. Over a longer edge, as when picking up for horizontal cardigan bands, for example, a row should be skipped every so often, depending on needle size, personal tension, number of buttonholes, and so on. With practice, it becomes second nature to know when you have just the right number of knitted up stitches.

Even when a pattern states exactly how many stitches should be knitted up, if you are going to work them in a stitch for which you have not worked a separate tension sample – in rib, for example, when the pattern has only required you to work a tension sample over stocking stitch – it is worthwhile working a few knitted up stitches as a test piece before launching into the knitting up proper.

Note: Rib is notoriously variable in tension, see *Ribbing*.

When you have calculated the correct number of stitches to be knitted up, divide your work into halves and then quarters (and then eighths if you are working over a long edge), and mark these points with pins. Divide the number of stitches equally between these sections. If they don't divide equally, use any extras where they might be needed, at either end or around convex curves, for example. Never distribute the stitches as you go along; it isn't worth risking all the time and effort involved to find that the stitches are bunched in parts and then horribly stretched over others to compensate.

Many beginners make the mistake of thinking that knitted up stitches are simply loops from the edge of the work itself which are pulled out and put straight on to the needle. This is why it is more accurate to refer to the method as 'knitting up stitches' rather than 'picking up stitches', since the latter implies that the stitches are picked out rather than knitted up from scratch. By actually making a new stitch by pulling a loop of the new yarn through a stitch on the edge of the main work, an even row of stitches from which to continue working can be created. This is impossible by simply picking up strands from the knitting – loops created in such a manner will sit at odd angles to one another, be of varying length and give an unacceptably irregular result.

Whether you use the needle or the crochet hook method of pulling the loops through, the holding needle – that is, the needle which they are first slipped on to – should be at least two sizes smaller than the ones quoted for the knitting up: the smaller the stitch on the first row, the neater the line. Change to the correct needle size on your second row. If the knitted up stitches are to be worked in a contrast colour to the main work, knitting up the stitches in the same colour as the main work, and then changing to the contrast on the second row will make a far neater dividing line between the colours.

With the right side of the main work facing you and the needle/crochet hook in whichever hand feels most comfortable, pull through one stitch at a time and slip each, in turn, on to the holding needle, which may rest on the work without being held. Although some knitters like to pull the loops through with the holding needle itself, with a slippery yarn this can make keeping the stitches firmly in place quite difficult. The second needle, used as the crochet hook would be, is more satisfactory. In this way each individual stitch can be pulled tight on the holding needle, where it stays undisturbed until the next loop joins it.

When knitting up through cast off stitches, take the loop through under the entire cast off stitch rather than just one side of the loop. If the cast on edge really is too tight to achieve this, it should be re-cast off.

When knitting up through edge stitches, always pull the new stitch

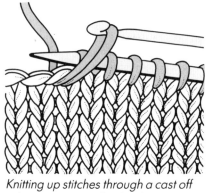

Knitting up stitches through a cast off edge, using a crochet hook.

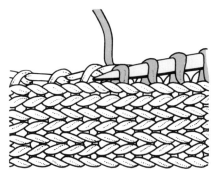

Knitting up stitches through a side selvedge.

through the knot, rather than the loop, of the stitch – the loop will be too stretchy to form a good base stitch.

If held stitches come in between two areas of knitted up stitches, as they often do at the centre front edge of a crew neck, slip them on to another needle and then knit them on to the holding needle. This saves having to break the yarn, slip the held stitches on to the holding needle and then join in the yarn again to knit up further stitches. It is also helpful to knit up a stitch from the loop between the stitches at the beginning and the end of the set of held or cast off stitches, as this will prevent holes forming at these points – a common feature on many a badly knitted up crew neck.

Once all the stitches are on the needle (or set of needles if you are knitting up something like a polo neck, in the round), the first row can be started. If the knitted up stitches are to be worked in rib, moss (seed), or any fancy stitch which involves moving the yarn forward and back, purl the first row if you have knitted up from right to left, that is, with the wrong side facing, and knit it if you have knitted up from left to right, with the right side facing. This avoids

the stitches of the first row becoming stretched as the yarn is moved back and forth. If the knit up line still appears a little untidy or if you want a small decorative ridge along this line, work the first row the other way round – knit a wrong side row and purl a right side one. Naturally, this will not disguise large unsightly loops, but it does provide an effective finish for a slightly uneven knit up. After this row, continue in the appropriate stitch, with the correct sized needles.

KNOTS AND YARN FAULTS

However careful spinners are in setting quality control standards, knots and faults always slip through from time to time. The fact that they are the responsibility of the spinner, however, does not mean that knots and faults may be ignored. Some knitters seem to think that faults in a branded knitting yarn should not be tampered with. *Anything* which will mar the finished knitting must be removed (see *Joins*). Knots are fairly easy to spot and deal with, but if a length of thin, lumpy or badly dyed yarn appears, keep unwinding the yarn until the quality returns to normal. If this leads to considerable wastage, keep the offending piece and return it to the spinner along with the ball band and your complaint. The same thing applies if an inordinate number of knots are found in a single ball of yarn. This is another good reason why you should allow extra yarn when calculating the amount needed.

As with any job of work, it is pointless to blame your tools. A yarn is what a knitter makes of it.

LACE

Many knitters are unnecessarily intimidated by lace stitches, under the false impression that they all fall into an 'experts only' category. The truth is that, just as with any other type of stitch, a great variety of lace effects is available – from beginners' basics to dedicated 'state of the craft' masterpieces.

All true lace stitches are made up from the simple 'yarn over the needle' method of making a hole. The pattern produced depends on exactly how the hole is made, how many are made and in what configuration. The way to gauge the complexity of a lace pattern is to look at how many rows go to make up a repeat. Within reason the intricacy of each row is fairly unimportant if it is regularly repeated every few rows. You will soon begin to recognize a pattern as it grows off the needles. A stitch which varies over a considerable number of rows, however, will mean you must pay constant attention to the pattern as its progression will be nowhere near as obvious. A design which involves an 18 or 32 row repeat, for instance, needs solid con-

> **HINT**
> *If you are working a lace stitch with a clear-cut design, such as a leaf, rather than a regularly repeated overall open stitch, it is not advisable to use textured yarns since the stitch definition will be lost. Fluffy yarns will have the same effect, unless the lace design is a very bold one. Cotton-type yarns are ideal for modern lace designs, as they give the stitch the required crispness.*

centration! There are even larger lace patterns which never repeat but take up the whole area of a garment. Any image may be created, using holes rather than colour or texture to build up your picture. There is only one attitude suitable for such an undertaking, however – single-minded attention.

When working any lace pattern, the manner in which the finished fabric will behave must be taken into account. A garment worked entirely in lace will have far more elasticity

and be more fragile than one worked in any other type of stitch. If this is not practical, lace panels used in conjunction with a more robust stitch may be more suitable.

Lace selvedges often turn out to look rather untidy with a slight frill effect because of their elasticity. To counteract this, where the garment design will allow, leave a narrow border of a firmer stitch, such as garter stitch. This will act as a solid base for seaming.

Remember that any features such as hems and inset pockets will show through to the right side of a delicate lace fabric.

Lace shawls
The Shetland Isles were once famous for the quality of the lace knitting produced there, and most notably for the shawls. In the days of home-spun yarns these were made from the finest of Shetland wool, plucked from the necks of the local sheep and spun into yarn so delicate that it resembled cobwebs.

From this yarn the most beautiful lace shawls were produced. The various stitches were traditionally

An example of fine Shetland lace knitting from the 19th century.

learned by heart or invented as the work progressed; there were no written patterns until well into this century. The finished items were then blocked or 'dressed' on large wooden frames, adding yet another laborious task to the totally hand-made product. The delicacy of the work was second to none, however, and it was even used as bridal veiling.

Because of the method of working the square shawls – creating the borders from just a couple of cast on stitches, working them sideways and then building up the rest of the shawl by knitting (picking) up stitches – there were no heavy cast on or cast (bound) off edges. The overall effect was so fine that these shawls were known as 'wedding ring shawls' since 2m (6ft) square ones could easily be pulled through the circumference of a wedding ring.

Although there are machine-spun 2-ply (fingering) Shetland wools, called 'lace weights', on the market today, it is rare to find someone putting in the time and patience required to produce shawls of a traditional quality.

LEFT-HANDED KNITTING

To the left-handed person, 'normal' knitting can be painfully awkward. It is a great mistake to assume that it is necessary to reverse out the work completely, however, knitting a row left to right rather than right to left. This sort of approach involves having to 'translate' every single pattern so that it can be worked back to front, and on a garment with complicated patterning or shaping it can become a nightmare.

A far simpler solution is to adopt the continental method of knitting. With this technique, the left hand, rather than the right, controls the yarn. It is ideal for the left-handed knitter, who can feel comfortable with this method of working, and means that you do not have to go to the length of rewriting every pattern you want to use. See *Continental Knitting*.

LINEN

Linen is a natural cellulose fibre obtained from the flax plant. Linseed oil is also produced from the seed of the plant but, as this involves harvesting when over-ripe, flax plants cannot be cultivated for both crops.

The plant can be grown in any region which can provide a rich soil and fairly damp climate, but the quality of the linen varies a great deal, according to how it is processed. The linen fibres are loosened from the stem by water or chemical decomposition. The finest grades are said to come from Belgium, where the purest water is used for this 'retting' process.

When made into clothing, linen, like cotton, allows the body heat to escape and absorbs a great deal of moisture, which will evaporate at an even faster rate than from cotton. Linen also shrinks less than cotton and is more resistant to the effects of light, although it does not take dyes so well.

From archaeological evidence – most notably the burial cloths of the Ancient Egyptians – it appears that linen was one of the earliest fibres to be spun by man, and many examples have survived, virtually intact, for thousands of years. One of the most robust natural fibres known, it is two or three times stronger than cotton.

Linen, however, has almost no elasticity, which causes even more problems than cotton in hand knitting. Unless you are making something totally shapeless, such as a bedspread, a pure linen yarn is not to be recommended as it has a particularly 'dead' quality when knitted up. Also, since it tends to be spun into medium- to heavyweight yarns, using shirring elastic (elastic thread) to give ribbing some shape will have almost no effect. Most branded linen yarns are mixed with various other fibres to counteract this tendency and, when you are selecting, look for one mixed with more elastic fibres such as wool.

LOOP KNITTING

Loop knitting is the technique whereby either clusters of, or individual, loops are produced on a stocking (stockinette) stitch or reverse stocking stitch background. This gives a fake fur appearance which can be used as an all-over fabric or to create fancy borders.

Single loops

Although single loops do not form such a dense 'fur' effect, they have the advantage that they can be cut after working without allowing any stitches to become unravelled. If worked in a fluffy yarn such as mohair, the finished strands may then be gently brushed for a furry effect.

Start with the side of the work in which you want the finished loops facing you.

1. Work to st requiring a loop. K into this st but do not slip the loop off the LH needle.
2. Bring the yarn forward, between the two needles and over the partly worked st.
3. Form a loop around your left thumb, held at the front of the work (a ruler or a piece of card/cardboard may be used if you want accurately measured loops). The loops should be a minimum of 4cm (1½in.) in length.
4. Put the yarn back through the needles and knit into the st still on the LH needle (making 2sts from the original).
5. Place both sts back on to the LH needle and k tog.

Loop clusters

Forming three loops at a time makes a denser fabric but means they cannot be cut, since the loops are actually knitted as a stitch rather than being formed between two stitches.

Start with the opposite side of the

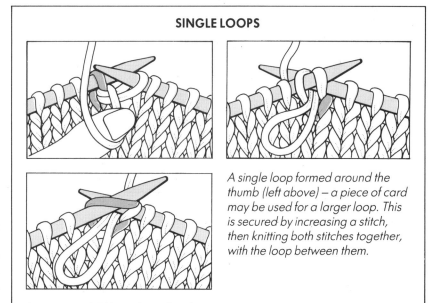

SINGLE LOOPS

A single loop formed around the thumb (left above) – a piece of card may be used for a larger loop. This is secured by increasing a stitch, then knitting both stitches together, with the loop between them.

LOOP CLUSTER

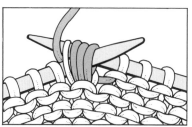

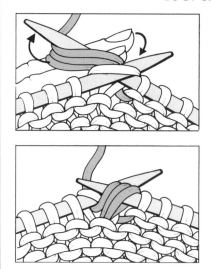

A cluster of loops formed around the fingers, worked as a stitch and then worked together with the loop of the original stitch. Worked on the wrong side, the loops hang on the right side.

---

work to the one where the loops are to appear facing you (that is, the purl side of stocking stitch if the loops are to hang from the knit side).

1 Work to the st where a loop is to be formed. Place the RH needle into this st, k wise.

2 Put one or two fingers of your left hand (depending on how large you wish the loops to be), behind the RH needle and pass the yarn around both needle and finger(s) three times in the direction indicated.

3 Using the RH needle, pull these loops through the st as if they were a

normal st but do not slip the loop off the LH needle.

4 Slip the loops back on to the LH needle and knit them together with the loop of the original st, through the backs of the loops.

Whichever method is used, the length of the loops can be varied to form an uneven effect. Worked on every stitch, the loops will form a thick fabric suitable for items such as rugs or fake fur jackets. Worked spasmodically with plain stitches worked in between loop stitches and plain rows separating looped rows, the effect

will be much flatter and is useful in creating fringe effects.

Looped edging

Loops for edging are not formed during the knitting stage, although an extra border of stitches should be worked up the edge that is to have the loops. When the work is completed, these extra stitches are slipped off the needle and pulled out so that a loop is formed at the end of every row by the unravelled stitches. The length of the loops varies according to how many stitches are dropped to form them.

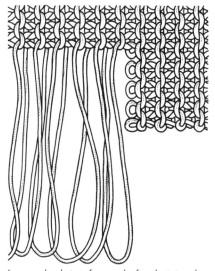

Looped edging formed after knitting by dropping five stitches and then letting them run down the work.

MAKING UP/ ASSEMBLING

'Making up' is the blanket phrase which covers all aspects of the finishing of a garment and, as such, is a most important stage in the whole process of making a piece of knitwear. Unfortunately, most knitting patterns do not emphasize this point. Even though the knitting instructions may be written out row for row, stitch for stitch, the making up instructions often consist of as little as two sentences: 'Sew side and sleeve seams. Press.' It is not surprising that most knitters, unless they have already learned the rudiments of dressmaking, are left holding the pieces and panicking.

By following the steps laid out below, taking all the advice detailed here, and referring to all the relevant sections elsewhere in the book, making up can become as enjoyable and, perhaps, even more satisfying than the knitting itself. It is not necessary to be an excellent tailor – with the addition of a few professional tips a high-quality garment can be produced even by a beginner.

Measuring

Double check all your measurements and make sure that each piece of the garment has been knitted to the same size specification – on a pattern quoting several sizes it is easy to misread the instructions. Place all the pieces together to check that they fit as they should – back and front armholes are exactly the same depth, cardigan bands are long enough, and so on.

If the sizing or type of knitting requires blocking, consult the ball band or label and decide what method to use (see *Blocking*).

Checking

Take the time to go over every piece before you start sewing: it is better to spot mistakes now rather than after hours of careful finishing. In knitwear factories, garments are slipped on to an illuminated dummy and a light shone through the knitted fabric to reveal any flaws. You can reproduce this procedure at home by simply holding each piece of knitting in front of a window or any other strong source of light – this cannot be done after making up since the light will not shine through two layers of knitting.

Mark any trouble spots, such as dropped stitches, with a safety pin so that when you have checked the whole garment, you can return to each problem and decide upon the best course of action. Naturally, if you end up with one sleeve holding six separate pins, you will have to reknit. For remedying less drastic mistakes, see *Dropped Stitches*, *Holes*, *Mending*, *Knots* and *Yarn Faults*.

Prepare for knitting/picking up stitches

Join the pieces of the work which are necessary before you knit up stitches (see *Bands or Borders*). On a crew neck, for instance, one shoulder seam will have to be joined if the border is to be knitted on two needles, but both shoulder seams if the border is to be worked in the round. Choose the most suitable method of seaming, grafting or knitting the pieces together (see *Seams* and *Grafting*). Also, see *Knitting/Picking Up Stitches* before you start knitting up stitches.

Pinning

Use long, thin pins with coloured plastic heads so that they will not

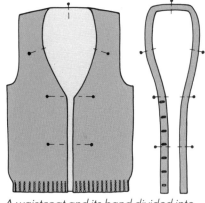

A waistcoat and its band divided into equal sections using pins.

disappear into the knitted fabric. If you are still nervous about seaming or the yarn with which you are working is particularly bulky or slippery, thread a tapestry needle with contrast yarn and tack the pieces together using long, loose running stitches. It is a waste of time to start sewing before pinning to ensure that both pieces are equally distributed – bunched or overstretched seams will completely destroy the way a garment will hang.

When attaching pieces such as collars and separately worked bands to the main work, it is essential to divide them into sections before pinning. This will avoid coming to the bottom of a cardigan front, for example, and still having 5cm (2in.) of buttonband to dispose of, or attaching most of a collar and then realizing that the remaining part will only reach halfway down the side of the neck. Take both of the pieces which are to be joined together, in turn, and divide them in half. Place a pin at the halfway point, divide into quarters, and so on, according to the length of the seam. Then place the two pieces together and pin them so that the pin markers correspond to one another. Make sure

that they stay in position when you start seaming.

This same method can be used to centre pieces such as the back neck seam on a cardigan band, or a collar opening. You may safely assume that such seams should be centred, unless the instructions specifically state otherwise. If your finished garment is lopsided, you have made a mistake. Always think symmetrically.

Main seams

Before working the main seams and making the garment bulky to handle, attach small pieces such as pockets and collars wherever possible. Working embroidery, fringing, crochet edging, and so on, is also easier when the garment is still partially in pieces, so that access to the back of the work is quicker and the weight of the entire garment is not on your hands.

Before you begin to seam, see *Seams*. Decide which is the most suitable method for the type of work which you are making up. Do not work a seam blindly but continually check what you are doing, as you should when knitting. Open out the pieces every so often to confirm that all is going according to plan and that colour or stitch areas are still aligned. Knitted fabrics are flexible and elastic, they do not stay rigid.

Securing ends

Any ends which have not been secured during seaming should be dealt with after all seaming has been completed (see *Ends*). Turn the garment inside out and check that you have dealt with every last one.

Pressing

This is a separate procedure from blocking and the two should not be

confused. Blocking is carried out while the garment is still in pieces, pressing is done after the making up has been completed. Only press if the type of yarn allows and if the garment really needs it. Many patterns automatically include the instruction to press, even though in most cases it is not necessary. Cardigan bands which have been stitched on will often need a light press since, if they have been worked correctly, they will be a little shorter than the cardigan fronts to allow for dropping. This results in a slightly puckered seam which can be easily pressed out.

Note: Only apply the edge of the iron to the seam itself. Do not press the actual band as this will stretch it unnecessarily.

Finally, try it on. This is the only way to see if a garment really works. Remember that you do not have to be an experienced dressmaker to make up a knitted garment competently – all that is required is common sense. If a collar will not fit around a neck by its cast (bound) off edge, for instance, turn it around and attach it by the more elastic cast on edge. Use your eyes as well as your brain.

■ MARKERS

In order to keep track of shaping, locate seam points in circular knitting, position pattern panels, and so on, it is vital to use markers in your knitting. They are also useful in making up (assembling) – marking the depth of the armhole on a garment without armhole shaping, for instance.

There are two basic types of marker – stitch, and row.

Row marking

It is often necessary to mark the row where shaping starts or finishes so that other parts of the garment can be lined up correctly at a later stage. The start of the neck shaping on a 'V'-necked cardigan, for example, will need to be marked if a collar is to be attached from this point, or if the last buttonhole on the buttonhole band needs to be aligned to this position.

Markers may also be needed to mark a depth measurement if the length of a garment is being quoted in rows or pattern repeats rather than centimetres (or inches). On a large, complicated lace or cable stitched garment this is essential since it is often impossible to count the rows after knitting as they do not appear clearly defined.

Use safety pins for marking or, if these will get in the way of the knitting or the making up, take a small length of contrast yarn and tie a loose knot through the edge stitch on the row to be marked.

Stitch markers

Mark a point between stitches on a working needle with a loop of yarn in a contrast colour or a small plastic ring. Such rings, specially made for the purpose, are available in yarn shops. If this same point is to be marked on every row, then every time that the marker is reached it should simply be slipped from the left-hand needle to the right-hand needle and the work carried on as normal. When the marker is no longer required you can take it off the needle without affecting the work since it has never become an actual part of it.

This device is often used on aran patterns. When several sizes are quoted within the same set of instruc-

Plastic markers used to denote the pattern panel in aran knitting.

tions, the main design will be worked as a panel of stitches, the number of which remains constant. It is the border stitches on either side of the panel which will vary, according to sizing. Markers can be introduced at particular points on the first row of the pattern, denoting the beginning and end of the panel stitches on every row of that particular piece of knitting, regardless of how the border stitches may vary.

Another common use for stitch markers is in circular knitting, where they are used to show where each round finishes. They are also used when it is necessary to indicate where

seams would occur if the knitting was being worked on two needles so that the work may be divided accurately when need be, as, for example, for the armholes on a sweater. Sometimes the seam points are marked by a line of stitches within the knitting but if this interferes with the design then separate markers should be used.

If the line of shapings within the piece has to be kept vertically aligned, as when working flares on plain stocking (stockinette) stitch, markers should be used to indicate the increase or decrease points on the next row where shapings are to be worked. Trying to align shapings by eye is

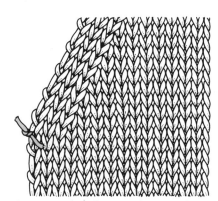

A yarn marker showing the row where shaping commences.

time-consuming and difficult to do accurately.

There are some instances, as when measuring the tension (gauge) of a heavily textured yarn (see *Tension/Gauge*), when a marker has to be placed around a stitch rather than just being slipped between stitches. Make a loop, as above, but slip it right over the next stitch on the LH needle, put it back and then work it as normal. If you make the loop sufficiently loosely, the end of the loop can be pulled out of the work when it is no longer needed. This method may be used if absolute accuracy is required when positioning pieces such as symmetrical pockets on either side of a jacket, or marking the position where decora-

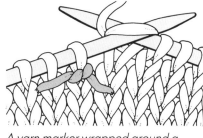

A yarn marker wrapped around a specific stitch.

tion, such as Swiss darning, is to be worked at the finishing stage.

Never cut corners when it comes to such seemingly minor techniques as using markers. Guesswork often means 'more haste, less speed', and can waste more time than it saves.

MEASURING

The importance of accurate measurements seems so obvious that no further mention should be necessary, but, in fact, failure to measure properly is the cause of innumerable knitted rejects. Haste, boredom, or over-eagerness to complete a garment often make it all too tempting to stretch that extra couple of centimetres or extra inch or so out of your knitting so that it reaches the required point on the ruler. When you come to sew up a back and a front without any hope of the lengths matching, however, it does not seem such a good idea. Take time and trouble over every measurement, and if, when you think you have finished, you find that ten more rows are required, just take a deep breath and plod on.

The basic rules of measurement are detailed under *Tension/Gauge*. If you are measuring a large piece of work use a long ruler rather than a tape measure since it is essential to measure on the straight, that is, parallel to the line produced if you follow the same stitch all the way up the work. The work must be laid flat so that there is no bias pull. When a pattern gives instructions to measure something always assume that this measurement is to be taken on the straight, unless otherwise stated. An armhole depth measurement, for instance, is always taken

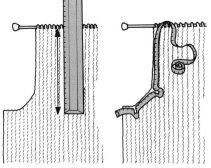

The right (left) and wrong (right) ways to measure an armhole.

along the stitch line and not around the curve that has been created by shaping.

To make sure that two sleeves are exactly the same length and that all shapings correspond, they may be worked simultaneously on the same needle, using two balls of yarn. Before starting, however, consider the suitability of the type of work – two lots of intarsia would make life much more difficult, for instance -- and make sure that the needles you are using will be long enough to take the total number of stitches after any increases have been worked.

If measurements must be echoed on two sides of a garment, such as the depth of unshaped armholes or the positioning of pockets, take each measurement individually, then fold the work and make sure that they are identical. This will ensure symmetry.

A child's sweater worked in cotton using four colours and the intarsia technique. The front is complete, the back, still being worked, shows, on the wrong side, how one colour has been twisted around the next, each time the colour changes.

MEDALLION KNITTING

Round, square, octagonal and hexagonal medallions may all be knitted in one piece using sets of double-pointed needles. They are useful for household items such as table (place) mats and coasters, or may be sewn together to form patchworks.

If the medallion is to be worked from the centre outwards, a few stitches are cast on which are then divided between the number of double-pointed needles which are required for the shape that you wish to produce. As the rounds are worked, increases are made at specific intervals until a medallion of the required shape and size has been completed. Cast (bind) off very loosely to avoid the outer edge curling up. The end left at the centre of the medallion may be used to draw up any slight hole which still remains.

When working a medallion from the outer edge inwards, a very loose cast on edge (see *Casting On*) should be worked – again, to avoid curling. The stitches are then divided between the number of double-pointed needles, but the medallion shape is formed by decreasing rather than increasing. After the final round has been worked, the stitches may either be cast off (see *Casting/Binding Off* for suitable methods) or the end of yarn threaded on to a needle and passed through the remaining stitches. The stitches should then be pulled all together into the centre and secured there.

Traditional lace. A cardigan, sweater and shawl knitted in very fine weight Shetland wool.

Medallions – round, triangular, hexagonal and square – all worked from the centre out.

MENDING

Mending is something which often appears to be rather out of step with the technological age in which we live. But if someone has taken the time and trouble to create a hand knit, often with tender loving care, it seems only right to extend the life of that garment for as long as possible.

Whenever an accident happens, don't panic. Try to remember where you have stored any leftover yarn or the original tension (gauge) swatch, which should be on file. If nothing else is available, this swatch may be unravelled to provide the yarn required for a professional-looking mend. If new yarn must be bought, then take the garment with you when you start the search. This may sound like ridiculously obvious advice, but one can leave the house knowing *exactly* which shade of grey is required only to become totally confused when confronted with a choice of a dozen different greys. There are even numerous different blacks and whites.

Caught or pulled thread

If the yarn which has been pulled has not been broken, it should be possible to work it back into the fabric of the knitting. Since it usually creates a very obvious pulled line, it should not be left or fastened off just as it is.

A short pull can usually be dealt with simply by giving the surrounding knitting a really good pull and tug. The strain put on the surrounding stitches by this rough treatment will pull any spare thread back into its rightful position.

Even after a bout of tug-of-war, a longer thread may need some very careful assistance with a tapestry needle. Starting from the end of the row that is furthest away from the offending thread, work your way back along the row, easing a little yarn over from one stitch to another as you go, so that you finally arrive at whatever is left of the thread. After another good tug, if only a small loop remains, pull it through to the wrong side of the work if it is not there already, and leave it. With any luck it will work its way back into the knitting during normal wear. If the loop is still too long, break it, then secure the two ends individually, using a sharp needle. Do this very neatly, using the minimum of stitches to avoid a great lump on the work, and carefully so that the ends will not work free (see *Ends*).

If the pulled loop has already been broken, pull the ends through to the wrong side of the work and tie them in a knot so that they will not disappear into the garment, resulting in dropped stitches. Now subject the work to the same tug-of-war treatment. When as much spare yarn has been taken up as is going to be, undo the knot and secure the ends at the back of the work, as before. But, again, don't just leave the knot as it is (see *Knots and Yarn Faults*).

Broken stitch

Here it is necessary to do the reverse of the above cure. Since there will not be enough yarn available to secure a single stitch effectively, a little extra yarn must be pulled from the surrounding stitches. Use a tapestry needle to ease the yarn across the row so that no visible line of tightness remains. When sufficient yarn is available, secure as above.

Small holes

Even the tiniest cigarette burn or moth hole can completely ruin a knitted garment. One way to disguise this is to cover the blemish in embroidery, making it a design feature (see *Swiss Darning*). However, this can only be done on knitting where the position of the hole and the style of the garment allow.

If the work is in a plain stitch and the hole only affects one row, the problem can be remedied by grafting. First remove the line of stitches as far as necessary so that any discoloured or weakened yarn has been discarded. Provided that your spare yarn is still a reasonable match with the knitted yarn, you can make a virtually invisible graft within the work. Leave a long enough end at each side of the original hole to secure neatly along with the yarn used for grafting (see *Grafting*).

Large holes

These present a problem as far as invisible mending is concerned since each row that has been destroyed creates ends at either side which must be secured. Mary Thomas quotes a method whereby strands are created upon which new stitches may be built up. The technique involves a great deal of patience, which is not always justified by the finished result. The only practical solution is a patch or partial patch.

For a partial patch, remove any damaged yarn so that there is a clean rectangular or square hole to work from with open loops at the top and bottom and loosely knotted ends down both sides. Using the same size needle as for the original work (do a test swatch if you cannot remember the size), pick up the row of loops from the bottom edge of the hole and then knit up exactly the same number of rows as are missing. It is important to get the correct tension and right number of rows so that the new knitting fits the hole perfectly. The final row can then be grafted to the row of loops at the top edge of the hole.

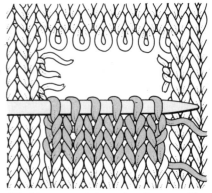

Working a partial patch – the top will be grafted, leaving only the sides to be sewn.

This still leaves the sides open. These must be stitched down afterwards extremely carefully, using a flat seam and securing the broken yarn ends on every row as you go. Provided that the yarn is a reasonable match this method can give a surprisingly good finish. It is not, however, recommended for areas which will take strain, such as on the elbows of a sweater, since the side joins will always have a weak point.

Where extra strength is required, where a non-graftable stitch has been used or where none of the original yarn is available, a true patch should be used, either knitted or cut from fabric. Before applying the patch it is important to strengthen the area to which it is being attached, especially if a weakened area is still in position – for example, an elbow which has worn thin but where the stitches are not yet broken, or are broken but still in place. A line of stitching, hand or machine, should be worked in the shape of the patch but 1cm (½in.) smaller so that it will not show afterwards. Then work a few crisscross lines of stitching over the area to form a foundation for the patch.

If the hole has already worn right through, do not try pulling it together before patching as this will create a lumpy, puckered finish. Simply stitch around the hole edges to prevent it from getting bigger. After patching, stitch the untidy edges of the hole carefully to the back of the patch.

Replacing sections

If an accident occurs on an easily replaceable section of a garment, such as a buttonband, collar or pocket, and sufficient yarn is available for a reknit then simply replace the whole section. This may also be done if such sections have become stretched and baggy after wearing. Welts (finishing borders) which have suffered the same fate can easily be reknitted to give an old, tired-looking garment a new lease of life (see *Alterations to Finished Garments*). Never throw away the old yarn that has been removed but unravel it and put it aside for any further emergencies which may occur in the life of the garment. Since it has already been subjected to a certain amount of wear and tear it will provide a better match than unused yarn.

Where the direction of the working and the yarn match allow, a part section of knitting may be replaced – for example, traditional ganseys (guernseys), which have the sleeves worked from armhole down to cuff, may have the entire elbow and forearm section reknitted (see *Guernseys*).

Drop stitch

If a break in the yarn causes a stitch to drop, remedy this as described in *Dropped Stitches*. Secure the broken ends on the wrong side of work, using a separate strand of yarn and a sharp needle.

Darning

Although this is the traditional solution for holes which form in a knitted fabric it should be avoided if another technique is available. Darning will always create a very obviously different finish from that of the knitted fabric since the path that the darning needle takes is a weaving one, not one creating interlocking loops.

It is quite extraordinary how attached some people become to their sweaters. Rather like teddy bears, the older and tattier they become, so their sentimental value increases in proportion. If you can master the arts of sweater mending, you can have friends for life.

MITRE

See *Corners*.

MOHAIR

This lovely fluffy yarn, in fact, comes from the angora goat, which has absolutely nothing to do with angora yarn. Angora (Ankara) is simply the province in Turkey first renowned for rearing these mop-headed creatures, and the word mohair is from the Arabic *mukayyar*, meaning 'choice' or 'select'. The main areas of production today are South Africa, Lesotho and Texas. Spinning, however, is carried on all over the world, most notably in the United Kingdom.

Mohair is a very delicate fibre (kid mohair, the finest and softest, comes from the young animals), and so it is very rarely spun by itself. Although pure mohair yarn can be obtained,

Angora goats – mohair is produced from their luxuriant coats.

what is normally referred to as mohair contains a certain percentage of wool and a very small amount of nylon 'binder' to strengthen the yarn. Naturally, the percentages used in the blend vary considerably and both economics and fashion have dictated an enormous range of different mixes, including all manner of synthetic fibres. When buying a yarn, always check the actual fibre content – all that's fluffy is not necessarily mohair!

The structure of moss stitch, formed by k1 p1, in close up.

MOSS/SEED STITCH

Single moss stitch is the most basic texture stitch. Made up of alternate knit and purl stitches, as in single rib, rather than being kept in vertical lines, the stitches in moss stitch are worked at odds to those on the previous row. Thus a stitch which has been knitted on the first row will also be knitted on the second row. This breaks up the surface of the knitted fabric, making its appearance quite different from that of single rib, although each incorporates rows which read k1 p1. Both sides of the work are identical.

Using an even number of stitches, moss stitch is worked as follows:
Row 1: * K1, p1, rep from * to end.
Row 2: * P1, k1, rep from * to end.
These two rows form the pattern.

Double moss stitch is formed in the same way but working k2 p2.

Since it is non-curling like garter stitch, moss stitch is often used for borders. If these are being worked on a stocking (stockinette) stitch garment, use smaller needles for the moss stitch since the backward and forward passage of the yarn makes the stitch spread. It is ideal for borders where the pull-in effect of ribbing is not desirable, such as on wide turn-back cuffs or shawl collars, since it lies quite flat. Although inevitably slower to knit, moss stitch has the advantage over garter stitch in forming a firmer fabric without so much lateral give.

Where no borders are required, moss stitch can be used as an all-over stitch to create a flat fabric which needs no edging. It is the most independent of stitches, being self-finishing, and so gives the designer a great deal of freedom to experiment with shapes alone. Remember, however, that a moss stitch fabric is thicker than a stocking stitch one and will take more yarn, as would an all-over rib garment.

You can use the simple yet effective texture created by moss stitch to great effect in conjunction with other stitches. It is often worked for border areas on either side of cabled panels on aran knits. Moss stitch fill-in areas are also used within the shapes formed by cables, such as diamonds and lozenges.

Narrow colour stripes worked in moss stitch look far more interesting than those worked over stocking stitch or even reverse stocking stitch since the change in stitch breaks up the bands of colour, creating a far softer, graded, striped effect.

MOTIFS

Colour motifs are isolated designs which appear on an otherwise plain background. In many cases, two totally different knitting methods are used. As these are worked at different tensions (gauges) great care and attention must be taken.

Motifs are nearly always charted so that when you reach the position of the motif within the written instructions of a pattern it will read 'now work from graph' (see *Charts*).

Large designs present relatively few problems since they are usually worked using the intarsia technique. For this reason, the tension of the motif should not differ greatly from the tension of the rest of the work (see *Intarsia*).

Small or intricate motifs which require the fairisle technique for colour work are those which present the problems. Every effort must be made to regulate the tension of the stitches and the weaving or stranding used since the tightening effect which can happen when working fairisle – especially if you are a beginner – will result in an extremely noticeable puckering around the motif. Unfortunately there are no specific techniques for avoiding this, other than following the hints in *Fairisle*. Just slow down and take your time over each individual stitch and each individual float. Also do not hesitate to substitute very small colour areas with Swiss darning rather than knitting them in. It is not the coward's escape, rather the thinking knitter's alternative.

NECKBANDS

For all the general rules that cover neckbands, see *Bands or Borders*. This section on 'neckbands' refers specifically to those neck borders which have no opening. These may be worked in two basic ways. If one of the shoulder seams only is completed the band can be knitted using two needles (see *Knitting/Picking Up Stitches*); the ends of the band are then stitched together when the second shoulder seam is completed. The other method is to join both shoulder seams and then work the band in the round on a circular needle or set of double-pointed needles.

Some patterns give instructions to work the neckband separately, but this is not advisable unless a very out of the ordinary design is being worked since it produces an unnecessary seam at a focal point on the garment.

Crew neck

The basic shaping which must be executed within the main work to create a 'crew'-shaped neck opening is covered in *Crew Necks*.

This shape of neck is best finished

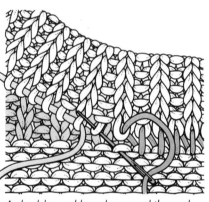

A double neckband secured through open stitches, rather than cast off.

with a ribbed border. Its curves are too deep for a garter stitch or moss (seed) stitch border to be used without shaping. These stitches are best used on a more scooped neckline. The depth of the band to be worked depends upon the depth of the opening. An average neck 'drop' – that is, the measurement from the shoulder line to the lowest part of the shaping – of 7cm (3in.) will allow for a band approximately 3cm (1¼in.) deep.

When casting (binding) off the neck border always use an elastic method (see *Casting/Binding Off*), and

do the 'head test'. If you can get the garment over your head without too much difficulty, the neckband is big enough.

If you are working a double neckband which is to be turned and stitched down inside the neck, it is not necessary to cast off at all. Work the band to twice the required finished depth, plus an extra row for turning. Put the working stitches on to a thread – if you leave them on a circular needle or set of double-pointed needles, you will have problems – and instead of casting off, thread up a tapestry needle with the working end of yarn and slip-stitch, through each open stitch, down to the corresponding stitch on the first row of the border. It is essential to do this stitch for stitch to avoid the neckband becoming twisted. This is such a common problem which totally ruins the look of the neckline that the correct method cannot be stressed enough. Take a stitch on your tapestry needle, find its counterpart on the first row, and secure it there and only there – and do be careful to catch every stitch, leaving none to drop. This provides the most flexible neckband.

'V' neck

For the basic shaping which creates a 'V' shape in the work see 'V' *Necks*. The depth of the neckband can vary a great deal since shaping is easy to incorporate.

Crossover 'V' If the garment is being worked in the round, an opening is left at the very bottom of the 'V' shape.

Normally worked on two needles, the neckband is worked in two sections. Since no shaping is worked at the point of the 'V' to take up any fullness, there is a limit to how deep the band can be worked. When completed and crossed over, the two edges of the band must be stitched down to correspond to the angle of the neckline shaping. This method is not, therefore, suitable for necks which have been shaped with a very sharp 'V'. When stitched correctly, a diamond shape of double fabric is produced.

A crossover 'V', slip-stitched down along the row edges.

Seamed 'V' This is worked in exactly the same way as the crossover 'V' but, instead of crossing over and stitching

A seamed 'V', the excess band fabric is turned back and stitched on the wrong side.

down, the two pieces are joined at the point of the 'V' with a straight seam down the centre. The triangular-shaped pieces which are left are then stitched down at the back of the work.

Shaped 'V' These are formed by working decreases either side of a central stitch; there is therefore no opening at the point of the 'V'. If the stitches being worked for the front make an odd number, this centre stitch may be left on a pin when they

A shaped 'V' – stitches are decreased on either side of the axial stitch.

are divided at the beginning of the neck shaping. If the stitches make an even number then, when the neckband is worked, a centre stitch may be knitted (picked) up from the strand left between the two halves. This then forms the axial stitch.

After knitting up the required number of stitches around the neck, the band is worked with a double decrease at the point of the 'V', one decrease being worked each side of the axial stitch (see *Decreasing*). Any method may be used, but the neatest appearance is created by keeping the axial stitch in stocking stitch throughout, that is, knitting it on a right side row and purling it on a wrong side row. The frequency of decreasing is determined by the angle of the 'V'. Work a decrease on every row for an angle of less than 45 degrees and on every alternate row for a wider angle. When working in rib, keep in pattern, regardless of shapings. Continue the shaping, even on the cast off row.

Slash neck

A slash neckline is worked in a completely straight line and requires no shaping. This lack of shaping makes no allowance for putting the garment over the head, however, so the neckline must be wide enough to compensate for its lack of depth. Since the neckline is straight, the neckband must be inset. Any one of the non-curling stitches can be used, either worked as one with the main work or, more properly, worked after completing the main garment, on smaller needles. For an inset neckband see *Designing*.

Scoop or boat neck

This is a widened, deeper version of a crew neck; laid flat it forms a half-oval

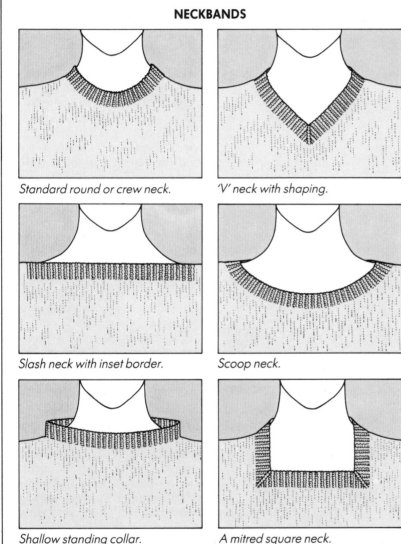

NECKBANDS

Standard round or crew neck.

'V' neck with shaping.

Slash neck with inset border.

Scoop neck.

Shallow standing collar.

A mitred square neck.

either end to work a side border which corresponds in width to the depth of the rows already worked. When the side borders are long enough, cast on the previously cast off stitches and work across all the stitches to form a complete square or oblong with a hole in the middle.

If the bottom and sides of the neckband are to be worked at right angles to one another, however, it will involve four sets of mitres, one for each corner (see *Corners*).

A standing collar

This type of neckband is best worked from a straight, or only slightly scooped, neckline. It is knitted up in the same way as a crew neckband but, because no shaping has been worked to allow for it, the finished band will stand up rather than lie flat. It is worked only to a depth of approximately 4cm (1½in.) – any deeper and it would become a type of turtle or roll neck.

Naturally, this is not a comprehensive list of all neckbands – that would be impossible. Those described and illustrated here are the most common shapes which may be used as a basis for further experiment.

NEEDLES

Over the centuries knitting needles or 'pins', as they are sometimes called, have been made from almost any material which lends itself to their manufacture. Natural substances as diverse as whalebone and bamboo have been used to make needles as effective as those produced in the metals and plastics of today. Whatever

rather than the semi-circle of a crew neck. The neckband is worked in the same way, single or double.

Square necks

Although the neckline shaping is one of the easiest to work, the neckband for a square neck can be one of the most complicated. If worked in garter or moss stitch, as one piece, however, the neckband is relatively easy. Work a certain number of rows for the bottom edge, then cast off the central stitches, leaving enough stitches at

KNITTING NEEDLE CONVERSION CHART

	Metric	English	American
	2mm	14	0
	2¼mm	13	1
	2¾mm	12	2
	3mm	11	
	3¼mm	10	3
	3¾mm	9	5
	4mm	8	6
	4½mm	7	7
	5mm	6	8
	5½mm	5	9
	6mm	4	10
	6½mm	3	10½
	7mm	2	
	7½mm	1	
	8mm	0	11
	9mm	00	13
	10mm	000	15

type you choose is a matter of personal preference and ease of handling, since the composition of the needle makes no difference to the knitting.

The size or circumference of the needle is of supreme importance, however (see *Tension/Gauge*). The length, provided it is suitable for the number of stitches which the needle is to hold, is again a matter of preference. Some knitters always like to use long needles so that the right-hand needle may be supported by tucking the end of it under the right arm. If you do not use this technique, however, extra long needles can often be a nuisance, making the handling of the knitting far more difficult than is necessary. When a great number of stitches must be accommodated it is often easier to use a circular needle as if it was a set of two needles, that is, not working in the round.

The choice of length becomes crucial when circular needles are being used for knitting in the round (see *Circular Knitting*). By the same rule, so does the number of double-pointed needles which are to be used.

Modern plastic or metal-covered plastic needles create very few problems when it comes to maintenance since they are so robust. Provided that they are washed occasionally to prevent them from becoming sticky and interfering with the smooth flow of stitches across them, they should last a lifetime. Do not use chipped or scratched needles, however, since a needle which is not completely smooth will slow up your knitting and can damage the yarn, catching on it as the stitches move back and forth. Bent needles also slow up your work as they are difficult to handle and prevent the work from being laid absolutely flat when measuring.

OPENINGS

Vertical openings

Straightforward vertical openings can be worked simply by dividing your knitting into two and continuing to work each section with a separate ball of yarn (see *Buttonholes*). This type of opening can be used on the back of a sweater with a very close-fitting neckline so that it is possible to get it over the wearer's head. A button may then be placed at the neckline with a loop

A vertical neck opening; extra stitches are added for the band after the work is divided.

on the other side to hold it in place.

To create an overlapping opening with a placket which will take buttons or buttonholes, extra stitches must be added after the work has been divided. First decide how many stitches wide the overlapping band is to be. If it is to be placed centrally, bear in mind that the centre line of the garment will divide this band in half – thus, if the band is eight stitches wide, for instance, when it comes to dividing the work for the beginning of the opening, the division must come four stitches short of the centre line. Continue with the greater number of stitches, working the first eight stitches in whatever border stitch you have chosen. This will form the band which will overlap. When this side of the work is complete, return to the smaller number of stitches, join the yarn in at the beginning of the opening, cast on eight stitches and work across all the stitches for this side of the garment. Work the new eight stitches as the band which will lie underneath the overlapping one, already worked. When this side is complete the eight-stitch cast-on edge may be stitched down inside the work.

Horizontal openings

One of the most commonly used horizontal openings is on the shoulder of sweaters, especially on babywear since a larger opening than the one supplied by the neckline is needed to pull the garment over the baby's head. A limited amount of extra opening can be provided by working the neckband on two needles rather than in the round and leaving the neckband seam unsewn. A few extra stitches can be added to one side of the neckband at the shoulder line if an overlap is

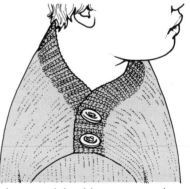

A horizontal shoulder opening – the front buttonhole border overlaps the back border.

required. One or two buttonholes can also be worked when knitting the neckband, or loops can be added afterwards.

If a wider opening is required, the shoulder must be left open, and an overlap worked. Without an overlap the weight of the garment will cause the opening to gape when it is worn. Rather than placing the opening directly on top of the shoulder, however, add the extra overlap rows to the front only, so that the buttons sit slightly to the back and do not look so obtrusive. This is straightforward on a non-shaped shoulder but on one with shaping the extra rows which incorporate buttonholes should be added after the shaping has been completed. This means that a shoulder with cast-off (bound-off) shaping cannot be used unless the shaping is worked by the turning method (see *Shoulders* and *Turning*).

PATCHES

See *Mending*.

PATCHWORK

True patchwork

Working each patchwork section as a separate piece does have its advantages. Besides being an excellent way of using up scraps of yarn, a garment or coverlet may be put together at a later date without the pre-knitting planning which is essential if you are knitting the 'patchwork' in one piece. Square sections are best worked corner to corner rather than on the straight so that you can control the exact dimensions, regardless of the tension to which you are working. By starting off with two stitches and increasing one stitch at each end of every alternate row, a right-angled triangle is formed. When the sides of this are as long as the side of the square you require, start decreasing in the same ratio. A perfect square will have been formed by the time you are left with

An English 19th-century white cotton coverlet, made of patchwork squares.

two stitches. These are then cast (bound) off. Each section may be worked in a different stitch, or you can incorporate patterns into the squares so that when they are joined, larger designs are formed.

Patchwork sections of other shapes can be knitted on double-pointed needles (see *Medallion Knitting*).

Mock patchwork

It is easy to create patchwork effects within a piece of knitting without having to go to the lengths of working small separate pieces and sewing them all together. By dividing the work into small sections, each worked in a different stitch, colour, or both, some lovely results can be produced, especially if you vary the shapes of the sections.

If you do vary the stitches it is advisable to keep them reasonably similar in structure so that there will not be a great difference in tension (gauge) between one section and another. For perfect results the whole design should be worked out on graph paper to make sure that each section has the correct number of stitches and rows to allow for whatever repeats are necessary to create each type of stitch. Although they may look as if knitted at random, well-executed patchwork effects have been planned in detail before the needles are even picked up.

When changing colour, as well as stitch, from one section to another, make sure that the yarn is changed on a *knit* row if you want to achieve clean dividing lines (see *Colour Knitting*). As patchwork sections are a reasonable size they may be worked using separate balls of yarn for each area of a different colour (see *Intarsia*).

The entrelac method of knitting, which is worked in one piece, will also create a criss-cross patchwork effect (see *Entrelacs*).

■ PATTERNS

Printed knitting patterns are a relatively modern invention. The publication of such instructions only became necessary when the craft of hand knitting changed from being the commercially viable industry that it had been, into a genteel pastime for the middle classes. Although pattern books had been produced since the middle of the 19th century, it was not until the turn of the century that yarn manufacturers began to publish pat-

> **HINT**
> *If you are fond of taking your knitting with you – on the train or on the beach – patchwork sections make nice little manageable work items, and you don't have to carry the whole project around with you.*

terns solely to promote their own yarns. Today, the major spinners still dominate the publication of patterns; even those reproduced in magazines and books are almost always sponsored by these companies.

This should always be borne in mind when choosing a pattern. If it has been produced by a spinner then it has been created to sell a yarn manufactured by that company. The solemn warnings often printed at the beginning of the instructions stating that the pattern cannot be executed in any other yarn than theirs may be ignored, provided that the quoted tension (gauge) measurement is taken seriously. When choosing the yarn suitable for the pattern you must match the advised tensions rather than the brand of yarn.

Most commercially available yarns will quote a suggested tension on the ball bands (labels) but, if in doubt, ask the advice of the sales assistant. If the tension on the yarn corresponds to the tension required for the pattern then you are unlikely to have problems, provided, of course, that the style of the yarn is compatible with that of the garment – a tweed sports wool would be unsuitable for a summer evening top, for instance. If you are happy with the styling, then feel free to chop and change. There is no reason at all why a cotton yarn may not be used for

a pattern intended for wool, or a fancy lurex fringe substituted for a mohair mix provided that the tensions tally (see *Tension/Gauge*).

Reading a pattern

Before deciding on a pattern, read it thoroughly to check that the techniques it requires are within your capabilities. The degree of complexity of a stitch may be gauged by the size of the repeat (see *Lace*). Colour work involving intarsia or fairisle methods will be obvious if the colours change across the row or if a chart is included within the pattern. Each company producing patterns has its own house style of writing, but any abbreviations or special techniques are normally explained at the beginning of the instructions.

If diagrams are included which give a plan of each piece of knitting involved these will give you a quick idea of how cumbersome or fiddly the garment may be. The greater the number of pieces the longer the making up (assembling) will take, especially if there are small items such as pocket flaps, epaulets, belts, and so on. If, however, a garment is knitted in one piece, the weight and bulk of the work may cause difficulties, especially for knitters with problems such as arthritis.

Unfortunately, diagrams are a fairly recent addition, and are so far used only by the more sophisticated spinners and publications. Many patterns still leave the knitter quite in the dark as to what shape they are attempting to produce. Work is always more enjoyable when you know what the finished product should look like. So, unless you have difficulty relating to graphic illustrations, always look for patterns with explanatory diagrams so that you can tell at a glance if you are on the right track or have made a ghastly mistake.

Patterns which have been drafted for more than one size will usually print one size outside parentheses and then quote the other size instructions within parentheses throughout the pattern. If the one you have chosen is designed for several sizes, it is well worth going through the pattern before starting work and identifying the set of figures which applies to the size you are working at each stage. Underline them as you go; it will save time and confusion once you have started knitting.

The other common use for parentheses which can sometimes be misleading is when a certain set of instructions need to be repeated as in:
'**Row 1:** * K4, (sl 1,k1, psso) 3 times, rep from * to end'.
Part of the instructions are placed within parentheses so that they will not be confused with the rest of the row. The instructions in the parentheses, and only those, should be worked three times.

When repeating anything always make sure that you are doing so for the correct number of times. For example:
K1 p1 twice = 4sts.
K1 p1, rep twice = 6sts.

If you put your knitting aside, always mark the stage of the pattern which you have reached. You may think you will remember where you were, but you don't know how long it may be before you pick it up again, and memory plays funny tricks.

When deciding which size you wish to work, do not get carried away by the photograph accompanying the instructions. Remember that the garments are displayed by models whose figures will not necessarily bear any relation to the shape and size of the wearer. Although the model may be a size 10 she could be wearing a size 14 garment if the stylist working with the photographer thinks it looks better. Rather than following the size number, check the *actual* measurements quoted instead. By checking the measurements of the finished garment you will see how much 'ease' has been allowed. Although you may be knitting a garment for someone with a 101cm (40in.) chest, if only a few extra centimetres or an extra inch have been allowed for 'ease', they may want a larger size to allow for a looser fit.

Finally, never be intimidated by a pattern or assume that it must be correct, even though your knitting is turning out wrong. Patterns are drafted by humans, and errors can creep in. Don't give up the moment you find a problem. Attempt to solve it yourself, look at it every possible way, and if it still makes no sense get in touch with the company that produced the pattern. Their trained staff will probably be able to help you out in thirty seconds flat, since they will already be aware of any mistakes that have gone into print.

See also *Instructions*.

PICKING UP STITCHES

See *Knitting/Picking Up Stitches*.

PICOT

From the French '*pic*' meaning peak, a picot edge is a series of little points (see *Edgings*).

PICTURE KNITS

In the seventies 'the sweater as a work of art' emerged as a high fashion garment. The term 'picture knit' was coined and has since been so widely used that whole books have been dedicated to nothing else, and many knitters have been left with the erroneous impression that picture knitting involves a special technique all of its own. However complicated a design may appear, be it landscape, still life or abstract, it only involves the two methods of colour knitting described in *Intarsia* and *Fairisle* – with possibly the addition of a little embroidery or Swiss darning.

To avoid reams of written colour change instructions, picture knit patterns are illustrated graphically with the aid of charts (see *Charts*). After referring to the relevant sections for guidance there is no reason why you cannot create your own original picture knit. Alternatively, a picture can be translated into a knitting chart with the aid of pencil, tracing paper and graph paper.

When you have found a picture which is suitable for conversion into a knitted design – make sure its size and structure are a practical proposition – trace the basic outlines with a very soft pencil. Now turn the tracing paper over, lay it on your graph paper and rub the reverse side vigorously with a rounded object such as the blunt end of a knitting needle. The lines which you have drawn will be transferred to the graph paper. This will be a mirror image of the original, however, so if you want an exact reproduction, trace the lines now on the graph paper with the same soft pencil and repeat the rubbing process on to another piece of graph paper.

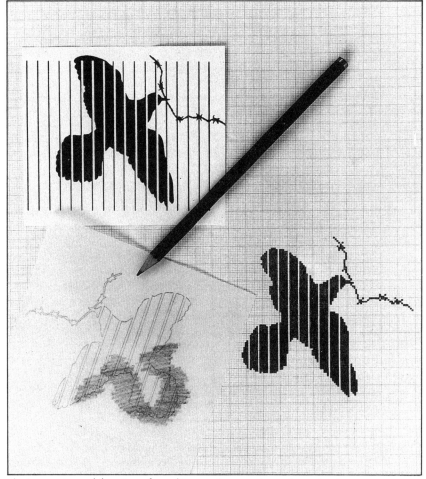

An image traced then transferred to graph paper to make a chart.

PILLING

Pilling occurs when friction causes small bobbles or 'pills' to appear on the surface of a knitted fabric. Unfortunately, unless it has been specially treated, the softer the yarn, the more likely it is to pill. The softness of the touch or 'handle' is due to short fibres being present in the yarn, and it is these which work free and congregate into little balls at points on the garment which are subject to rubbing, such as the underarm area on a sweater.

Nothing can be done to prevent pilling, but it is possible to remove the bobbles after they have formed. A very effective way of doing this is to run a razor very carefully across the surface of the knitting. This is fairly hazardous, however, since unless you hold the razor at exactly the right angle over a fabric which is completely flat you run the risk of nicking one or more of the stitches and ruining the garment.

Another method of removal is to use a length of very strong adhesive tape, wrapped around your hand sticky side out. This works if only slight pilling has occurred but it will not remove large bobbles on heavyweight yarns.

Small abrasive de-fuzzers which look like combs without teeth are available on the market. They remove bobbles but are very rough so tend to leave the surface of the knitting with an overall fluff, ready to form more 'pills' when rubbed.

The best method of all is to remove pilling by hand – an incredibly laborious task but something for those winter evenings when no knitting project craves attention.

Now that the design is superimposed on graph paper it must be 'squared up', each square representing a stitch across and a row down. A certain degree of trial and error is necessary here before the best result is achieved and you may have to alter the original design to a greater or lesser extent depending on how easily the shapes involved convert to a combination of squares. Remember, too, that these squares will be stitch size and shape when the knitting is worked.

Naturally, it is advisable to start by using an extremely basic design and gradually build your confidence until you feel able to tackle more adventurous subjects and create your own originals. Never feel limited to the hackneyed images which are readily available – with a little patience and ingenuity it is possible to produce real works of art with wit and style.

PLAIN KNITTING

See *Garter Stitch*.

PLEATS

Mock pleats

A pleated look can be achieved without actually involving the doubling over of any of the knitted fabric by using a number of wide rib variations. The most effective way to produce a mock pleat is with a wide purl or garter stitch section broken up with one knit stitch which gives the impression of being the fold line.

To produce this type of mock pleat, cast on a number of stitches divisible by 8.

Row 1: (RS) * K7, p1, rep from * to end.

Row 2: K4, * p1, k7, rep from * to last 4 sts, p1, k3.

These two rows form the pattern.

A narrower rib can be used to give a sun-ray pleat effect.

True pleats

True pleats involve folding the knitted fabric upon itself; this means that three layers will have to be joined together at the completion of the pleat. Extra stitches must be allowed for this when calculating the width of the fabric being worked and three times the actual number of stitches required cast on. If the pleats are to be worked as an inset, on the back of a knitted blouse, for instance, these extra stitches must be cast on at intervals along the row where the pleat is to commence. These cast on edges are stitched down at the finishing stage.

Since it produces a flat and smooth fabric, stocking (stockinette) stitch is the most suitable to use for pleating. Use a purl stitch to denote the under fold line and a stitch slipped purlwise to mark the upper fold line.

Cast on a number of stitches divisible by 12, plus 8. The two rows to be repeated would then read:

Row 1: (RS) * K8, p1, k2, s1 1 p wise, rep from * to last 8sts, k8.

Row 2: * P11, k1, rep from * to last 8sts, p8.

When the pleats have been completed, they may be cast (bound) off straight along the row, then folded and stitched down or, alternatively, they may be knitted together into the folded position. This method requires two extra double-pointed needles so that the extra pleat stitches can be divided between them, slipping the first four stitches on to one and the second four on to the other. These needles are then held in the left hand, along with the original needle holding the remaining stitches. By working through one stitch on each of the three needles, simultaneously, one stitch is made out of three and the three layers of fabric are joined (see *Knitting Stitches Together*). The four stitches left out of each 12-stitch group may then be used to continue with a waistband or yoke.

Pleats which fold to the left or right can be created by reversing the order in which the stitches are worked. By working a left fold followed by a right fold or vice versa, box pleats are formed.

Remember that three thicknesses of fabric are formed by any true pleat and so they should not be used where bulk is to be avoided – around the hips, for example. Here, the pleats should be closed lower down and a flat hip 'yoke' worked instead.

A mock pleat in garter stitch, the pleat line kept in stocking stitch.

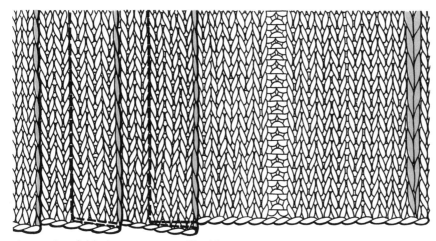

A true pleat folded in position, and laid flat.

Once pleats have been completed, they should have a tacking thread run through them to keep them in place while they are blocked, very thoroughly, into position (see *Blocking*). This process must be repeated after each wash or clean.

PLY

Although it is commonly accepted that 2-ply, 3-ply and 4-ply are specific thicknesses of yarn this is not an accurate use of the term 'ply', which simply means one of the strands within a yarn. A plied yarn is one with two or more strands twisted together, while a 'roving' yarn has only one strand. If the term is used in its strictest sense, then a 2-ply yarn, although generally accepted as an extremely fine lace-weight yarn, may also refer to any other weight of yarn which comprises only two strands.

Of the traditionally accepted plys, a 3-ply will knit up to an average tension (gauge) of approximately 16sts

and 22 rows to 5cm (2in.), while 4-ply is slightly thicker at around 14sts and 20 rows to 5cm (2in.). Never accept a yarn as a specific standard thickness without checking on the normal tension it will produce on the spinner's recommended needle size.

Plied yarns are usually far more resilient than non-plied ones, the direction of twist in each strand being varied to provide strength as each strand pulls in the opposite direction to the next. This makes them more difficult to break than a single roving yarn, which will pull apart when any force is applied. The tighter the twist, the firmer the yarn, as with cablé cottons and crêpe wools.

POCKETS

The first reaction most people have on trying on a cardigan, jacket or coat is to lunge at the sides of the garment to find the pockets. One wonders what on earth people did with their hands before pockets were invented.

There are endless varieties of pockets incorporating permutations of virtually every finishing technique. This section will enlarge upon and make clear the basic structures involved without going further into pattern detail, stitching, and so on, all of which may be found in other sections and applied to the creation of pockets.

If pockets may be categorized at all then they can be divided into those which may be added to a garment after completion, such as patch pockets or those which may be let into seams, and those which, like so many other aspects of expertly designed knitwear, *must* be planned well before the garment is started.

When adding pockets to finished garments or to patterns which do not include them in the instructions, make sure that the type of pocket suits

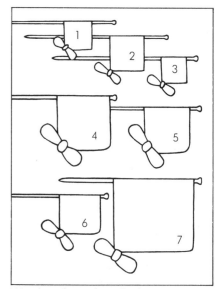

Weights of yarn from 2-ply to extra chunky. **1.** *3-ply;* **2.** *4-ply;* **3.** *2-ply;* **4.** *chunky;* **5.** *double knitting (worsted);* **6.** *aran;* **7.** *extra chunky.*

the style and stitch of the garment. If unsure about the size and placing of the pockets, cut out a paper replica and pin it to an existing garment to check that a hand will actually fit inside and that the positioning will not mean the wearer has to stoop.

Also ensure that the yarn is strong and thick enough for the garment to be able to support the pockets. The pockets themselves must be firm enough not to bag and pull the garment out of shape, but not be so bulky that they prevent the garment from hanging properly. Linings should be worked in the same yarn as the main work but at a very firm tension (gauge) and always in plain stocking (stockinette) stitch since this creates the flattest knitted fabric.

Whichever technique is being described, there are a number of basic rules which apply.

Most pockets require borders; details may be found in *Bands or Borders*. You should take even greater care when knitting (picking) up pocket border stitches to make sure that the correct number is being worked and that they are evenly spaced – a border which is too tight will pull the main work out of shape, while one which is too loose will allow the pocket to fall away from the main work and hang open. The tension of the casting (binding) off is extremely important for the same reasons. The border edge stitches must be perfectly neat as these will not be hidden within a seam.

When border edges, patch pockets or pocket flaps are stitched to the right side of the work this must be done

extremely neatly, using a slip-stitch seam (see *Seams*), following the right-angled lines made by the rows and stitches of the main work. Make sure that the points where the top of the pocket is attached to the main work are doubly secured as these are the major stress points when the pocket is in use.

Another way to strengthen these points on horizontally worked pockets is to cast on two extra stitches for the pocket lining. The extra stitches can then be knitted together with one stitch from the main work on either side of the pocket opening when the lining stitches are joined in. See the section on horizontal pockets below.

Any pocket lining edge which is left unattached should be slip-stitched down, inside the garment, at the final stage. The linings should be aligned to the main work just as carefully as when stitching on the right side of the work, taking the utmost care to ensure that the lining will lie absolutely flat and not bulge at the back of the work and pull at its stitching. When working the slip stitches it is a good idea to split the stitches of the main work since, if the whole stitch is used, the line of stitching becomes visible on the right side of the work.

When casting on for a lining always use a non-bulky method such as 'simple thumb'/'one needle' (see *Casting On*) so that this edge will be as unobtrusive as possible.

Patch pockets

Patch pockets are simply patches of knitting which may be worked in any shape or pattern and attached directly to the right side of the work. Although they are extremely simple from the planning point of view and may be placed on any flat part of the

garment where welts (finishing borders), hems, shaping, seams, and so on, will not interfere, many knitters steer clear of using them since they do require very careful stitching. But, provided that they are properly aligned to the main work in the first place, neatly pinned in the correctly measured position and then sewn with a flat seam (see *Seams*), they are far less daunting than most people imagine. They are most useful when the colour design or complicated stitch pattern of a piece of work would make working pockets as part of the garment too much of a problem. Conversely, the pockets themselves may be worked in a complicated design to give an otherwise plain garment some interest. Place patch pockets only on a very firm knitted fabric which can support the extra weight.

Pockets let into side seams

Since they do not affect the actual work itself, pockets let into side seams simply require the addition of a pocket lining; this may be single and attached to the inside of the front of the garment, or double and free-hanging.

Although pocket lining instructions are usually given for a square shape, in fact a triangular shape is far more appropriate for vertical pockets since the hand thrusts downwards into a pocket, not at right angles to the body.

If seam pockets are pre-planned, the linings may be knitted as part of the garment by casting on the required number of stitches where the pocket is to start and then decreasing to form the angle which finishes at the top of the pocket. Where a single lining is required the triangle is added to the back of the garment only. At the

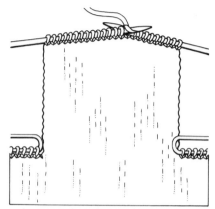

A horizontal pocket worked with a double lining. This need not be secured to the main work.

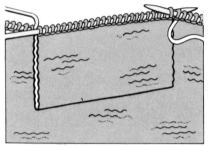

making-up (assembling) stage this will be turned in and stitched to the inside of the front of the garment.

If the garment is worked in a stitch which curls at the edge and the side seam is to be a flat one, work the front pocket selvedge with a narrow edging such as crochet or mock crochet (see *Edgings*). Should the side seam be a backstitch, this edge may be turned to the depth of the seam allowance and stitched inside.

A double pocket lining can be produced by working the triangle on both the front and back of the garment and then seaming them together before turning them into the inside of the work. If the garment is being

worked in stocking stitch the stitch which marks the fold line on the front triangle should be slipped purlwise on the right side rows to accentuate that line (see *Slipped Stitches*).

When opening up an existing seam to add vertical pockets, the linings can be knitted up from the selvedge produced or knitted separately and sewn in with a flat seam. Whichever method you use, the join should be very neat since it will be visible through the pocket opening.

Vertical pockets

To form a vertical pocket on the right-hand side of the garment, work to the row where the slit is to start, finishing on a right side row. Work across the row to the position where the opening is required but, instead of working across the remainder of the row, put these stitches on a holder and cast on a number of lining stitches. Ignore the stitches on the holder and continue to work across the stitches now on the working needle, including those for the lining. When you have worked the desired depth of pocket, work one more row over the lining stitches only and then cast these off loosely, leaving the remaining stitches on a holder. Return to the previously held stitches and work these to match

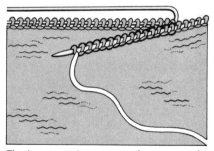

The lining stitches cast on for a vertical pocket.

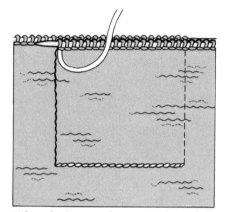

When the lining is the required depth, the stitches are worked together with the main work stitches.

the depth of the other held stitches. Now work across all the stitches, thus closing the top of the opening.

To finish the selvedge of the vertical opening, knit up a narrow border at right angles to the main work. Stitch the border edges to the right side. Stitch down the lining edges inside.

Reverse the above instructions to make a vertical pocket on the left-hand side of a garment.

Kangaroo or pouch pockets

A pouch pocket is made by working two vertical openings, one on the left-hand side and one on the right-hand side, with a single lining reaching from one to the other – so that the hands may be clasped while inside the pocket.

To produce a pouch pocket, follow the instructions for a vertical pocket to the right side row before the start of the openings. On the next (wrong side) row work to the right-hand slit and then put the central stitches which form the width of the front of the pocket on to a holder at the right

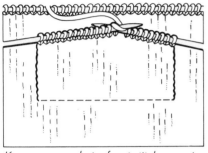

Kangaroo pocket – front stitches part worked, lining stitches at full depth.

side of the work. Cast on the lining stitches and then work across the stitches which remain on the left-hand side of the held stitches. Ignoring the stitches on the holder, work the stitches on the needle until the pocket is the required depth, ending on a wrong side row. Leave all these stitches on a holder or spare needle and return to the originally held stitches. Work these until they match the depth of the lining, ending on a wrong side row. Now place these stitches on top of the lining stitches and work across the whole row, knitting the central front pocket stitches together with the lining stitches, holding two needles in the left hand and working one stitch from each needle, simultaneously, so that the top edge of the pocket is closed (see *Knitting Stitches Together*).

Finish as for a vertical pocket.

Horizontal pockets

The basic structure of a knitted horizontal pocket is the same as that of a vertical one – the lining stitches which have been separately cast on are used to replace those which have been cast off or held to form an opening. This is the most commonly used pocket technique and, however complicated the written instructions may

appear, they are usually a version of this method.

Before starting the garment, cast on the number of stitches needed for the pocket lining. Work the entire pocket lining, then put it to one side and work the garment to the row where the pocket opening is to be positioned. Work to the start of the opening and then, depending on what type of pocket top border you will eventually work, either cast off or put on a holder the number of stitches required for the width of the pocket. On the next row, work to the pocket stitches and then take up the needle holding the lining stitches; work across these and then across the re-

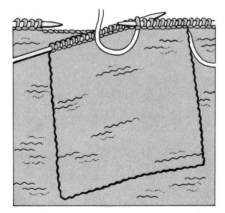

Horizontal pocket – cast off stitches from the top edge (above); lining stitches are then joined in.

maining stitches to the end of the row. Having completed the pocket, continue with the main work.

Work a border from the held or cast off stitches, stitch its edges on the right side of the work and the lining on the inside. Such separate borders are essential if a colour pattern is being used for the main work as the border will be worked in one colour only.

In some cases, however, it may be preferable to knit the border as part of the main work. Several rows before the required height of the pocket top, start working the pocket stitches in the border stitch you have chosen, while continuing to work the remaining stitches as normal. When the border is deep enough, cast off these stitches and replace them on the needle with the lining stitches, as before. This is not advisable, though, if the main work is already being worked on a large needle, since the border stitches will have to be worked at a firmer tension on a smaller needle.

There is an alternative method of working a lining for a horizontal pocket but this is suitable only for lightweight work or styles where extra bulk is not a problem – it involves three layers of knitted fabric, as the pocket lining is folded back on itself. When the row of the opening is reached (this should be a wrong side row), work to the start of the actual opening, but then knit into the backs of the pocket stitches so that a purl ridge is formed on the right side of the work. Now put the stitches on either side of the pocket on holders and continue, in stocking stitch, with the pocket stitches only. When this section is twice the height of the required pocket lining, ending on a wrong side row, double it over and complete the

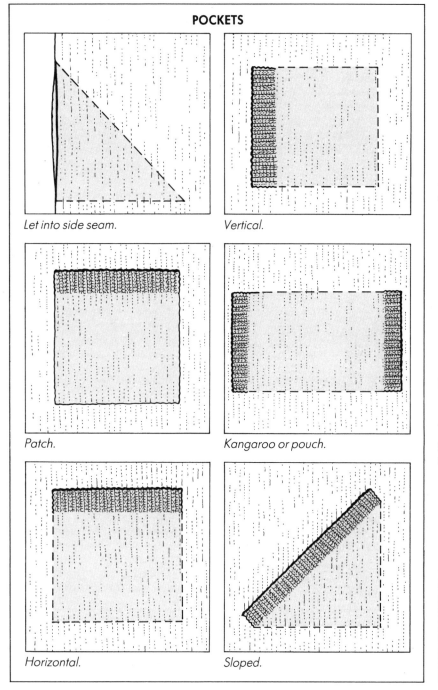

POCKETS

Let into side seam.

Vertical.

Patch.

Kangaroo or pouch.

Horizontal.

Sloped.

row of the opening which was started at the beginning by working across the second set of held stitches. All stitches are worked across on the next row, completing the pocket.

A separate border or edging may be worked on the pocket top after completion, as for the basic method. The sides of the lining are joined together using a flat seam.

Sloped pockets

Sloped pockets are knitted in the same direction as horizontal pockets and

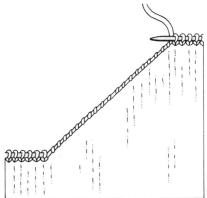

The front edge is formed by decreasing (above); the lining stitches are then worked on the wrong side (below).

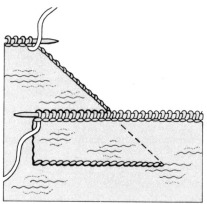

with a similar method – replace decreased stitches with lining stitches.

To produce a pocket which slants towards the left-hand side of a garment, work to the row where the opening is to begin, finishing with a wrong side row. Now work across the row to the pocket position, turn the work, place the unworked stitches on a holder and continue with the set of stitches just worked. Decrease one stitch at the turned edge on every alternate row if a steep slant is required and every row if a more acute angle is preferred, until you have the required depth of pocket. Place the remaining stitches on a holder.

Return to the original held stitches and cast on a pocket lining, with the number of stitches corresponding to those which have been cast off to create the slope. Work to the end of the row. Continue with this set of stitches until you have worked to the height of the pocket slope. Now work across these stitches and then the other held stitches to close the top of the pocket.

Pockets sloping in the opposite direction are worked by reversing the instructions, and two sloped openings may have a shared lining as for a pouch pocket. It is also possible to slope a pocket opening by turning the work rather than decreasing (see Turning).

When the pocket is completed, a diagonal border may be knitted up and stitched down at either end, as for a horizontal pocket. If the pocket is small, it is a good idea to make the lining larger than that produced by only casting on the same number of stitches as have been decreased. Also, you can work several rows of lining before joining it in to the main work in order to make the pocket deeper,

provided that the height of the welt/hem allows.

Pocket flaps

A tailored finish can be given to any one of the pockets described above by adding pocket flaps. They may be attached either to the main work above the pocket opening or attached to the front of the pocket itself, instead of working a border.

If the flap is knitted as a separate piece then it should be carefully slip-stitched into position. Alternatively, work it to the required depth and then knit it together with the stitches above the pocket opening before continuing with the main work.

Finally, when wearing a garment with knitted pockets do remember that a knitted fabric is elastic and will expand to accommodate the contents of the pocket. Overworked pockets containing ever-increasing amounts of loose change, keys, sweet (candy) wrappers, and so on will spell death to a garment – the fronts ending up considerably longer than the back.

◻ PRESSING

See *Blocking* and *Making Up/ Assembling*.

◻ THE PURL STITCH

After the knit stitch has been mastered the purl stitch is the next to learn. It is an essential stitch when

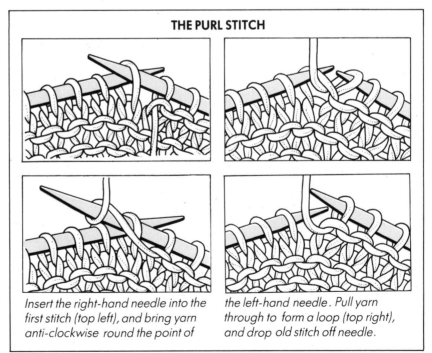

THE PURL STITCH

Insert the right-hand needle into the first stitch (top left), and bring yarn anti-clockwise round the point of the left-hand needle. Pull yarn through to form a loop (top right), and drop old stitch off needle.

145

working with two needles, that is, on the flat, as it forms part of stocking (stockinette) stitch, rib and moss (seed) stitch. The purl stitch is slightly slower to work than the knit stitch and some knitters tend to work their purl rows tighter than their knit rows when working in stocking stitch. For these reasons many expert knitters prefer to work in the round as this method allows every row to be worked as a knit row.

To produce the purl stitch when working in the regular or non-continental way, the yarn and needles are held as for a knit stitch with the exception that the yarn is held at the front of the work rather than at the back (see *The Knit Stitch*).

1. Insert the RH needle into the first st on the LH needle from the right to the left.

2. Bring the yarn anti-clockwise round the point of the RH needle.

3. Pull this yarn through the st on the LH needle to form a loop on the RH needle.

4. Drop the old st off the LH needle.

Besides being an integral part of many basic stitches, such as rib, the purl stitch is often used in its own right to provide a raised pattern on a stocking stitch background. An enormous variety of texture designs may be worked simply by reversing certain stitches in this way.

One line of purl on a stocking stitch ground, worked as a knit row on the wrong side of the work, is also very useful to clearly mark a line where the work will later be turned, as on a hem (see *Hems*).

▢ RAGLANS

A raglan-style garment has the armhole and sleeve top shaped at a diagonal slant so that, when joined, the top of the sleeve forms the shoulder of the garment. Since the shaping on the body cuts away right to the neckline, however, strictly speaking it does not form an armhole.

Because this diagonal shaping is so flexible, raglan sleeves lend themselves to an enormous variety of styles – the garment can be loose or fitted, as required.

When calculating the depth required for a raglan, measure on the straight, not along the diagonal of a seam, as the two measurements will not tally. If a very deep armhole is being worked in relation to the other proportions of the garment, remember to shorten the sleeve length as the underarm point will be that much lower.

Shaped in the normal way with a uniform progression of decreases producing a non-variable angle, a shallow raglan with a narrow sleeve will produce the effect of a rounded shoulder. If a more angular shoulder line is

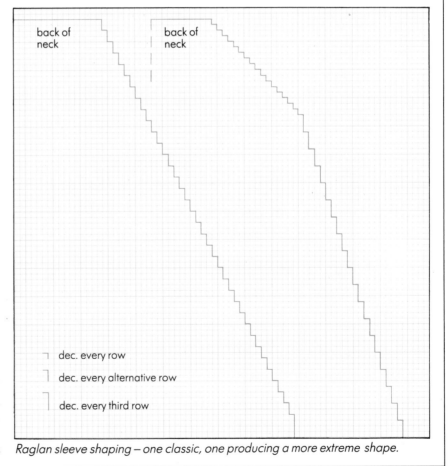

Raglan sleeve shaping – one classic, one producing a more extreme shape.

147

required, the angle of decreases should be varied, producing a sharper slope towards the shoulder top. Most of this variation should be carried out on the sleeve shaping, with the body shaping slightly echoing it. The sleeve should, therefore, be that much wider so that there are extra stitches to decrease.

To produce the same effect in another way, the extra sleeve stitches should still be added, but the raglan shaping remains uniform. The extra stitches may then be disposed of by working a dart into the centre of the sleeve top (see *Sleeves*). By combining both techniques the shoulder line is accentuated and raglan shoulder pads may be added to complete the look (see *Shoulder Pads*).

When you start a raglan shaping on a body or sleeve, if the garment is to have backstitched side seams, cast off a few stitches at the beginning of the first two rows – the exact number will depend on the depth of the seam allowance needed. On a garment which is to have flat seams this is not necessary and the raglan diagonal may be started straightaway. This should be worked with evenly spaced decreases. It is important to choose an appropriate pair to create the required finished effect (see *Decreasing*).

If worked in a smooth yarn and plain stitch so that the shapings are obvious, the line produced by the raglan may be accentuated to create a design feature. This is most commonly achieved by working the decreases a few stitches in from the edge of the work so that slanting bands of stitches are visible either side of the line of the seam. To make a really decorative feature out of the raglan, work lace-effect decreases or position cable patterns just inside the line of decreases so that they sit at the same angle as

the seam on the finished work.

When working out a neckline for a raglan sweater, allow enough room for all the neckline shapings since these must not be interrupted by the raglan shapings of the body. Also remember that the width of the sleeve top must be taken into account when working out the neck shaping as this will form part of the neckline at either side of the neck. Because of this, add half of the width of the sleeve top to the length of the front when calculating the overall length of the garment.

RIBBING

There is an enormous variety of rib stitches, from the very basic to the fancy, and as such they constitute whole sections in many stitch dictionaries. This section describes the most basic – k1 p1 – in detail and then goes on to discuss the broader subject of ribbing and its uses.

Single rib (k1 p1)
Worked over an even number of stitches.
Row 1: * K1, p1, rep from * to end.

Keep repeating this row to form the pattern.

If a stitch has been purled on the first row then on the next row, when the work has been turned around, it is

K1 p1 or single rib in close up.

knitted. This forms unbroken lines of alternate knit and purl stitches on each side of the work. If the lines break up then the pattern has been worked wrongly and, if kept up on every row, moss (seed) stitch will be formed instead of rib.

Continually changing from a knit stitch to a purl stitch right across every row means that the yarn is being moved from the front to the back and vice versa all the time. Take care that it goes between the needles and not over them or extra stitches will be formed by the resulting strands. It is important to keep the yarn under a tight tension (gauge) otherwise the continual to-ing and fro-ing will loosen up the work when compared to a row which is all knit or all purl. An inconsistent tension will produce a very untidy rib. That is why ribs are almost always worked on smaller sized needles than those for the main work. The usual difference is two sizes, although this may vary according to which stitch is being used for the main work, the elasticity of the recommended yarn, the position of the rib, and so on.

The different basic ribs are all combinations of varying numbers of knit and purl stitches. A double rib is k2 p2. The greater the number of stitches between each changeover, the

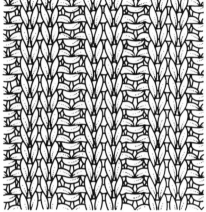

K2 p2 or double rib (above) and a
wide k4 p1 rib (below).

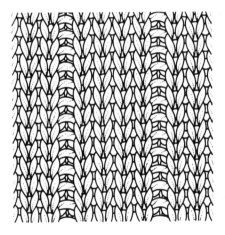

looser the rib will be, so that a really
wide rib of k8 p2 will have a tension
very similar to stocking (stockinette)
stitch.

Rib patterns that involve any
stitches other than straightforward
knit and purl are considered as fancy
ribs and as such are beyond the scope
of this book.

The uses of ribbing

As the most commonly used border
stitch, used for nine out of ten welts
(finishing borders), cuffs and neck
borders, it is essential to master and
then refine your basic rib technique
(see *Bands or Borders*).

Ribbing frequently causes the major
tension problems on a garment, either
by being too tight or too loose. The
main reason for this is that when the
main part of a garment is being worked
in another stitch, such as stocking
stitch, the pattern will only quote a
tension measurement for the stocking
stitch, with no mention of the rib.
Since the backward and forward action of ribbing means that the tension
is far less easy to control than with
stocking stitch, there is an even
greater variation in individual ribbing
tension from knitter to knitter. So,
even if a knitter has achieved a perfect
stocking stitch tension, the rib tension
may be way off that which the pattern
designer had in mind. The average
relationship of tensions means that a
rib will be calculated to be approximately two-thirds of the width of
stocking stitch. If you find that your
ribs become too loose or spoil the
shape of the garment by pulling in too
tightly, then it is worth checking your
rib tension as well as your main stitch
tension to ensure that you are achieving roughly this ratio.

If an entire garment is being worked
in rib, its 'pull in' effect must be taken
into account. Working a pattern
meant for stocking stitch in a rib will
create a drastically different garment,
since not only the stitch but also the
row tension of rib is much tighter than
that of stocking stitch. Also remember
that ribs take more yarn and more
time to work than stocking stitch.

ROLL NECKS

See *Collars*.

ROULEAUX

See *Edgings*.

RUCHING/
SHIRRING

Some very interesting ruched effects
may be created on plain stocking
(stockinette) stitch by slipping dif-

*A horizontal ruched effect created by
two lines of gathers.*

149

ferent combinations of stitches. Each time a stitch is slipped on a consecutive row it becomes tighter and tighter and will start to pull up the surrounding fabric, producing puckers. The spaces between the slipped stitches, the number of rows over which they are slipped and whether the yarn is at the back or front of the work when the stitches are slipped will all vary the appearance of the ruched fabric (see *Slipped Stitches*).

Ruched fabric is also formed by using rows of gathers (see *Gathers*).

A vertical ruched effect created with slipped stitches.

SCANDINAVIAN KNITTING

The tradition of colour knitting spreads over an area from the most northern isles of Scotland, through Scandinavia to the Baltic. Although the finished designs may vary, the knitwear of this area has the same origins and working techniques.

Comprising small, repetitive motifs, these designs all rely on the fairisle method of colour knitting, using two colours per row and carrying the colour not in use behind the work by stranding and weaving it (see *Fairisle*). It is in the type of motifs and use of colour that specific regional variations may be seen. Norway, for instance, has a tradition of using snowflake, reindeer and pine tree designs. These are often in black and white only, in contrast to Swedish knitting in which far brighter colour combinations tend to be used. This bold use of colour lacks the subtlety of the patterns from Fair Isle. The further east one travels, the more strictly geometric the patterning becomes, using very small design repeats and with very few recognizable representational motifs.

SEAMS

The word seams probably strikes the most terror in the hearts of knitters, and is the most common cause for abandoned work, even after hours of careful knitting. Rather than treating sewing up as a totally separate procedure, consider it as merely an extension of the knitting process. Careful preparations made during the knitting stage will guarantee neat and trouble-free seams.

The yarn used should have been left at the beginning of the piece of work specifically for that purpose, or should be the ends left when joining in new yarn – as such, they are already attached to the work and need no securing. If no ends are available and a new length of yarn has to be used, make sure the end is secure before starting. Do not use a knot; it is never secure enough and will look unsightly on the inside of the work, especially when using a heavy-weight yarn (see *Ends*).

If the garment has been worked in a heavily textured, uneven or fragile fancy yarn which is unsuitable for seaming, then use a finer, smoother yarn for the sewing, but check that it is compatible in terms of colour and fibre content. Try to find a yarn with washcare instructions identical to those for the main yarn, since one which reacts differently may cause puckered seams after washing or cleaning. When buying a novelty yarn, always consider the seaming as it may be possible to buy a perfectly matched yarn suitable for sewing from a co-ordinated colour range. This yarn may also be used to secure the ends of the main yarn if they really are difficult to thread through a needle.

Before starting any knitting, decide what type of seam you will eventually use as this will influence how you work the selvedges of each piece (see *Selvedges*). When choosing a suitable seam, consider the weight and type of yarn, along with the variety of knitted fabrics which are being joined, that is, the stitches which are to be used. A colour pattern which necessitates leaving numerous ends along the selvedge, for instance, will need a backstitched seam to hide any untidiness. The position that the seam will occupy on the finished garment is also very important. Collars and buttonbands, for example, always need a completely flat seam to avoid any obvious bulk.

Always carefully pin and, if necessary, tack each seam before you begin to sew (see *Making Up/Assembling*). Once the sewing starts, the real secret of a perfect finish is regularity and uniformity of stitch. Even using backstitch it is important to keep the line of stitching straight, and a specific number of stitches in from the edge, and then to make sure that the stitches themselves are formed to exactly the same length, and that there are no gaps between them.

On all the remaining open-type seams it is even more vital that each stitch looks exactly like its predecessor, is worked at the same angle and through exactly the same part of each stitch, every time. Always use a blunt tapestry needle to avoid splitting stitches. When joining two pieces worked in the same stitch they should be joined row for row so that the seam itself is barely visible.

Backstitch seam

With a backstitch seam it does not matter what type of selvedges the work to be seamed has, since a backstitch leaves a seam allowance of at least two or more stitches which will only be visible on the wrong side of the work. This type of seam should only be used for quite lightweight yarns – a DK (worsted) is the heaviest recommended, although it may be used on thicker yarns if specifically needed for neatness or extra strength. The heavier the yarn, the narrower the seam allowance should be, to minimize the bulk created by the two layers of fabric. Even on lightweight yarns the seam allowance should not exceed just over 1cm (⅜in.), especially if

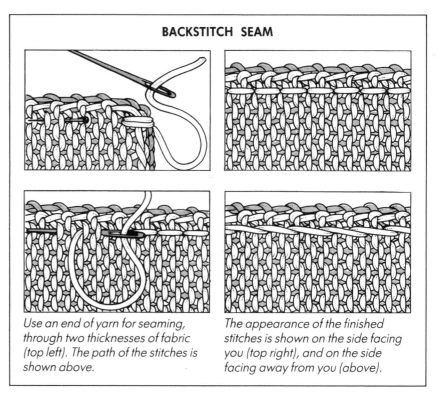

BACKSTITCH SEAM

Use an end of yarn for seaming, through two thicknesses of fabric (top left). The path of the stitches is shown above.

The appearance of the finished stitches is shown on the side facing you (top right), and on the side facing away from you (above).

stocking (stockinette) stitch has been used, since the edges will curl after seaming, making the seam even bulkier.

To work a backstitch seam first pin the two pieces, right sides together, making sure that the edges of each piece are absolutely flush. If the seam is to be started at the very edge of the work, take the needle around the two edges, closing the end of the seam with a double stitch for strength.

1. Take a running st a maximum of 1cm (⅜in.) long through both thicknesses of work. Pull the thread through.

2. Put needle back into work in exactly the same spot as before but make a st twice as long. Pull thread through.

3. Return needle to point where previous st ended on the side of the work facing and make another st the length of the previous one. Pull thread through.

Keep repeating stage 3 until the last stitch, which needs to be half as long to fill in the final gap left at the edge of the work.

With this method it is absolutely essential to keep the stitches a uniform length and to work them in an absolutely straight line. Wherever possible keep to a stitch line, say two and a half stitches in from the edge of the work, and use that as a guideline to keep the seam stitches straight. There should be no gaps between stitches, with one starting from exactly the point where the previous one has finished. On the side of the work facing you the stitches should appear as a continuous line, on the other side they should form a straight but overlapping line.

The thread should be pulled quite tightly after each stitch so that if the work is opened out and the seam pulled apart, no gaps appear.

Flat seam – oversewn/overcast

To many people the idea of oversewing to produce a flat finished seam appears to be a contradiction in terms. When worked properly, however, on two pieces of knitting which have neat, suitable selvedges, this method provides a speedy and professional-looking finished seam which, when opened out, is completely flat.

Pin the right sides of the work together, approximately 4cm (1½-1¾in.) in from the edge to allow room for your index finger between the two fabrics.

To work an oversewn flat seam on two stocking stitch edges where no special selvedge has been worked, place the needle behind the knot of

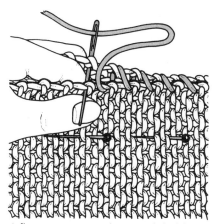

A flat seam on stocking stitch held ready for oversewing.

the edge stitch on one piece, and then through the same part of the stitch on the corresponding row on the other piece. Pull the thread through and repeat.

As this stitch involves an oversewing action many knitters are tempted to take a whole edge stitch or even two stitches into the seam, with the result that they produce an extremely lumpy, uneven seam which will not open out flat. The edge stitch knot alone must be used and not the looser strand that runs between the knots as this will not provide a firm enough base. By working behind the knot rather than through it, the seam is worked through the strongest part of the stitch without taking unnecessary fabric into the seam. When opened out and pulled apart no gaps caused by stretched knitted stitches should appear, provided that the original selvedge was firmly knitted (see *Selvedges*).

The same seam can be worked on two garter stitch edges but the needle should pass through the bottom of the knot on one edge and then the top of the knot on the corresponding row on the other edge. Thus the line of the garter row is not broken by the seam, which becomes barely visible once the thread is pulled up.

Flat seams can be used virtually anywhere other than very badly worked edges. This method is particularly suitable for attaching buttonbands and collars where flatness and neatness are essential.

Always use flat seams on ribbed parts of garments such as welts (finishing borders) and cuffs where the end of the seam will be visible at the edge. Even if the remainder of the garment is to have a different type of seam, start with a flat seam until the

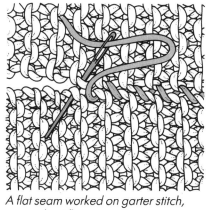

A flat seam worked on garter stitch, opened out flat.

rib is complete and then change over, taking in a tiny seam allowance at first and then smoothly widening it without making a sudden inroad into the work.

Invisible seaming

This seam is specifically used for stocking stitch and is worked on the right side of the work, with the two pieces to be joined laid flat edge to edge.

1. Take the needle across from the side where the thread is attached and under the strand between the edge st

An invisible seam, started using an end left for the purpose.

An invisible seam, partly completed and showing the lacing effect.

A slip-stitch seam worked along a selvedge and a line of stitches.

knot and the second st on the first row.

2. Returning to the other side, place the needle through the strand that corresponds exactly.

3. Keep repeating this zigzag action, pulling the thread tight as you go.

If the first two stitches of each row have been neatly worked and the seam is sewn row for row, the join created may be almost impossible to detect on the right side of the work unless it is pulled apart. On the wrong side, the small seam allowance made by the edge stitches will form a slight ridge.

Slip-stitch seams

When sewing down edges that need to lie completely flat, as on turned hems, patch pockets, double neckbands, and so on, use a slip stitch. By careful preparation in lining up the edge to be sewn on to the main work it should be possible to match the two pieces, stitch for stitch and row for row. If you find it difficult to keep track of a single row of stitches across the work, or column of stitches up the work, mark

them with a tacking thread or line of pins before starting. By working directly underneath the edge of the top piece of work and keeping a strict regularity of stitch this method may be worked on the right side of a garment to create a perfectly acceptable finish.

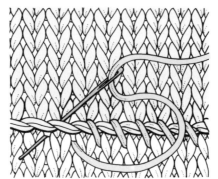

A slip-stitch seam formed along a row of stitches and a cast on edge.

Knitted seams

The technique involved in knitting seams together should not be confused with grafting since, although no needle and thread are used, a visible ridge

is formed. (A grafted join is undetectable.) A knitted seam is the neatest seam possible, however, and for those who dislike stitching (sewing) up a garment it is an essential alternative to have in your knitting repertoire. Since the two pieces to be joined must be worked stitch for stitch it is important that they both have exactly the same number of stitches. Even if they should have the same number of stitches, according to the pattern, double check the number which you actually have on your needle before you start your seam – it is all too easy to lose or gain the odd stitch.

A knitted seam is ideal for the shoulder seam of a sweater, provided that it is unshaped or has been shaped by turning rows rather than casting off. It will give a neat, flat finish but will provide a little more strength than a grafted join, which would tend to allow the shoulder stitches to stretch sideways when worn. If the back neck does not have to be shaped, all the back stitches may be left on a needle. The first shoulder seam is knitted together from the armhole edge to the neck, then the stitches for the back of the neck are cast off separately, and finally the second shoulder seam is knitted together from the neck edge to the armhole edge. As it is a continuous cast off row, the same end of yarn may be used straight across.

When knitting two rows of stitches together to form a seam at the end of two pieces of knitting, both sets of stitches are left on a needle rather than being cast (bound) off. The yarn is left attached to one set of stitches so that it can be used to work the seam. With both needle points in the same direction and the right sides of the work facing one another, hold the needles in the left hand.

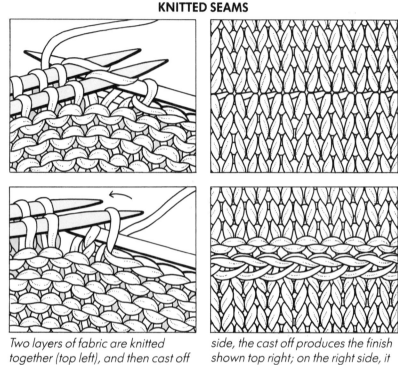

KNITTED SEAMS

Two layers of fabric are knitted together (top left), and then cast off (above). Worked on the wrong side, the cast off produces the finish shown top right; on the right side, it produces an ornamental ridge.

HINT
The use of knitted (picked) up stitches to create a seam need not be limited to selvedges. Stitches may be knitted or picked up directly from any part of a garment to create knitted joins so that pockets, borders, collars, and so on, can all be attached in this manner.

the strain of holding twice as much work inevitably tightens the working tension (gauge), however, it is always essential to have a third needle of a larger size to regulate the cast off tension.

SELVEDGES

The actual side edges of any piece of knitting are referred to as the selvedges. By altering the way in which the edge stitches are worked this edge may be neatened, enlarged or prepared specifically for another knitting stage.

All the following instructions for selvedges apply to work in stocking (stockinette) stitch or garter stitch. If you intend to add selvedge stitches to a patterned row then extra stitches should be added so that the pattern repeat is not altered. Such additions are frequently a good idea as many fancy patterns, especially those involving open-work stitches, produce very uneven edges which can cause problems if stitches are to be knitted (picked) up later or flat seams worked along them. If the pattern is continuous, then once the back and front have been joined by the side seams the selvedge stitches must be taken into

Now follow the instructions in *Knitting Stitches Together* until there are two stitches on the right-hand needle. Then cast off the first stitch using the basic method (see *Casting/Binding Off*). Continue by working another two stitches one from each needle in the left hand, to form one stitch on the right-hand needle. Cast off another stitch on the right-hand needle. Work across the row, alternating these steps until all the stitches have been joined and cast off.

The same basic technique may be used to join a row of stitches to a selvedge, the top of a straight sleeve and an unshaped armhole, for instance. Mark the beginning and end of the armhole and divide this into sections. Then evenly knit (pick) up the same number of stitches as at the top of the sleeve. The knitted-up stitches and those which were not cast off at the top of the sleeve can now be knitted together, as above.

Although a knitted seam is unobtrusive when worked on the wrong side of the work, it may be worked on the right side to create a very attractive decorative ridge. An extra knit row worked before casting off produces a more pronounced ridge.

This method seems rather awkward at first, but the clumsiness of holding two needles in one hand soon disappears with a little practice. Since

155

the seams to prevent a break in the pattern.

On plain stocking stitch the best selvedge is produced simply by working every edge stitch normally, but as tightly as possible. By placing only the tip of the needle into each edge stitch it can be worked without any unnecessary stretching. There is no reason why evenly worked stocking stitch should not provide a neat edge for most purposes.

If you have difficulty producing a neat edge, or if a specific effect is required, the following are the most useful basic selvedge techniques. With all methods involving slipped stitches, always slip knit stitches knitwise and purl stitches purlwise unless otherwise stated (see *Slipped Stitches*).

The edge produced by neat stocking stitch.

Stocking stitch selvedges

Simple slip stitch (Single chain edge) Slip the first st on every row but work all the others normally.

This creates a slightly enlarged chain effect selvedge which is very useful if the edge stitches are to be

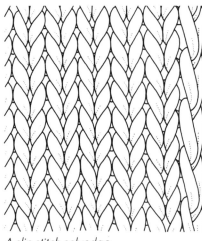

A slip stitch selvedge.

worked upon and are not large enough when worked normally as, for example, when knitting a border on to a selvedge (see *Bands or Borders*).

Alternative slipped stitch Slip the last stitch on every row.

This produces a finish as above.

Knitted 'pip' (Single garter) The first and last stitches on every row are knitted.

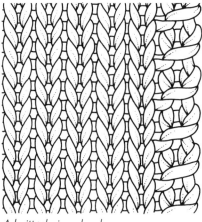

A knitted pip selvedge.

This creates a 'pip' ('seed') effect along the selvedge which may be used if you are having difficulty in knitting a tidy stocking stitch edge along which neat flat seams may be worked. The knitted 'pip' provides a very obvious guideline for the sewing needle so that you can create a regular stitch.

Double 'pip' (Double garter) Sl 1, k1, work to last 2sts, k2, on every row.

This forms a narrow garter stitch border which to some degree will prevent the selvedges curling and will assist in seaming.

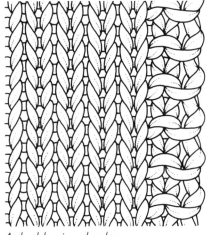

A double pip selvedge.

Garter stitch selvedge

Sl 1 p wise, yarn back, k to end on every row.

This produces a very neat chain selvedge which is well worth working if your garter stitch edge has a tendency to be uneven, as many do. It also

Knitting leaflets and books, showing changing styles from the thirties to the sixties; many of these spinners still produce patterns to this day.

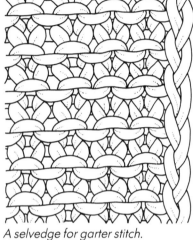

A selvedge for garter stitch.

makes a neat edge for knitting up stitches but it is too loopy for a selvedge which is to have a flat seam.

In addition to these basic methods a variety of decorative selvedges can be produced by varying the knit and purl stitches and the way in which stitches are slipped.

SHAPING

The blanket term 'shaping' not only covers the techniques of decreasing and increasing, where the number of stitches on the needle is actually

Yarn substitution. Exactly the same pattern, with the same number of stitches, knitted in three different yarns, all of which produce exactly the same tension and are therefore interchangeable. The purple one is tweed wool, the pink, cotton and the blue, mohair. All three garments are exactly the same size.

added to or reduced, but may also refer to the use of working short rows, that is, turning within the work (see *Turning*). It may even cover the basic principle of changing the size of needles you are using as the work progresses in order to make the work narrower or wider.

The techniques involved in shaping a knitted edge by increasing or decreasing are easy to grasp since the slope being formed is clearly visible. The angle of this slope may be varied by altering the frequency with which the shapings are worked – for example, decreasing one stitch at an edge on every row will create an angle of approximately 45 degrees with the line of the row, whereas decreasing at this edge only on alternate rows will produce a greater angle. Where the number of stitches to be added or subtracted is too large to be dealt with by methods of increasing and decreasing (see *Decreasing* and *Increasing*), groups of stitches are cast on or cast off. By using these variations in the angle being worked it is possible to work a piece of knitting with an outline of any shape, including smooth curves.

Working increases and decreases within the work rather than at the edges to shape the silhouette can be more difficult to visualize. These shapings are just as important to understand and master, however, since they represent one of the areas where the art of knitting really comes into its own (see *Darts*, *Flares* and *Gathers*).

Compared with dressmaking, knitted shapings offer a great deal, since the work never has to be cut and even when divided will immediately create its own selvedge. There are few garments that cannot be translated into knitting terms by the use of shaping.

SHETLAND

Since shetland sweaters became fashionable in the sixties, garments made in this particular type of wool have been referred to as 'shetlands', and it has become an erroneous generic term. A shetland is not a specific type of garment involving its own peculiar techniques, but merely a garment made from yarn which has been spun from the fleece of the Shetland sheep. A hardy breed, producing a coarse wool, these were once only to be found on the Isles of Shetland, but crossbreeds are now reared in New Zealand and the Falkland Islands.

SHOULDER PADS

Shoulder pads can add a new dimension to many sweaters and jackets, turning a shapeless, unflattering garment into one with shape and style. It is important to use the correct pad shape for the garment involved, however, and some styles are not suitable at all. Always remember that the pad must sit directly on top of the wearer's natural shoulder line or a fraction out from it if the sleeve head seam so demands.

A loose-fitting, drop shoulder style is not a good shape for pads since the sleeve head seam is situated off the shoulder, far too low down the arm to take a pad without making the wearer look deformed. Pads may be put in higher up, but this will result in a pad line across the actual shoulder and then another line at the seam point which can look rather odd unless the garment disguises it by the use of a textured stitch, for instance.

A tight-fitting garment with a set-in sleeve and shaped shoulder is equally unsuitable, as there will not be room enough to accommodate a pad without causing the garment to pull tightly under the arm.

Non-shaped shoulders with set-in armholes, loose raglans and styles knitted in one piece without any seams attaching sleeves to body, such as dolmans, are all ideal for pads, though the size, shape and thickness of them must be carefully chosen to suit the style of the garment.

Knitted pads

Since the fabric of a knitted garment is elastic, the best type of pad is a knitted one which will also have a certain degree of give. If it is knitted in the same yarn as the garment, it will not be visible through the work and the garment will look well finished on the wrong side – an important point to remember on a jacket, for example, where the inside may be visible when taking it on and off.

Pads should always be worked in garter stitch on the same size needles as for the main work, but using double yarn. This gives the right degree of firmness and bulk. Although exact

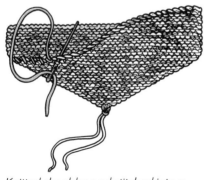

Knitted shoulder pad stitched into a triangular shape.

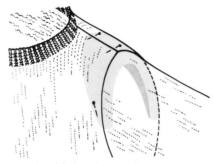

The shoulder pad pinned in place.

shapes may vary, the perfect straight-edged pad should be triangular to give the best effect, with a thicker edge along one side. This may be knitted by casting on two stitches and then increasing one stitch at each end of every alternate row until the required width is reached – approximately 17cm (6¾in.) for a medium-sized cardigan. Now work straight for approx 5cm (2in.), and then cast off loosely. Fold this cast (bound) off edge back on itself and slip-stitch down so that the part which was knitted straight is completely doubled over.

Carefully pin each pad into position before stitching, with the garment held up, as it would hang when worn. Place the pad into position inside the garment and pin through from the right side, aligning the centre of the pad along the shoulder seam and then pinning the points of the triangle to the armhole seam. Only now turn the garment inside out and stitch the pad, as pinned. If the pad is positioned with the garment turned inside out, it will not sit correctly when finished.

Only stitch a pad down at the points where it sits on a seam. If it is stitched directly to the fabric it will show on the right side as it pulls during wear. If you are putting pads into a garment which does not have

seams, they cannot be stitched in. Use strips of Velcro fastening instead. Take a length approximately 7cm (2¾in.) long of the hook side of the Velcro, and stitch it to the pad to correspond to an imaginary centre shoulder line. If the yarn you have used for the garment is fairly fluffy then the hooks will cling to the knitted fabric, holding the pad in place, without the fluffy side of the Velcro having to be attached to the garment. On a smoother yarn, heavy duty Velcro with larger hooks may be necessary to give a better grip. Both sides of Velcro can be used when a garment has a seam to which the fluffy side can be attached. The pads may then be removed quickly and easily for washing or cleaning.

Manufactured pads

There are certain instances where shop-bought pads are the best option for a garment. Raglan shoulders, although they can take straight-edged pads, should ideally have raglan pads, which are oval in plan and are moulded to fit the shoulder. Since this is a difficult shape to knit, it is best to buy pads ready covered and add Velcro if necessary.

Most straight-edged pads are made from moulded foam rubber which will give the extra body that heavyweight garments need and create a more extreme shoulder shape on any garment which requires it. Since they are rectangular, knitted covers are easily made – work them to size in the same yarn as the garment, using stocking (stockinette) stitch to give the smoothest finish. The covered pads can then be stitched into the garment, or attached with Velcro, as described for knitted pads.

When wearing a garment which has

shoulder pads, check that they are firmly in position when you first put it on. There is many a slip between shoulder and pad and it is all too easy to discover that, unknowingly, you resemble Quasimodo.

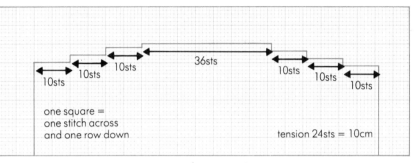

Classic step cast offs to shape shoulder slopes.

SHOULDERS

The human shoulder, unlike that of the shop window mannequin, does not usually make a right angle where it meets the neck but slopes to a greater or lesser degree depending on the individual. On a fitted garment this slope must be allowed for by the addition of shaping, which may be achieved in a number of ways. Loose-fitting, drop shoulder style garments may be worked without any shoulder shaping, the extra fabric being taken up in the loose folds under the arm. Shoulders which are to have pads added can also be worked without shaping since the pad will create a straight shoulder line underneath the garment.

Shaped shoulders

Most traditionally styled knitwear has set-in sleeves and shaped shoulders, creating a fairly close-fitting garment, the line of which corresponds to that of the body. If the shoulders were not shaped the shoulder line would droop, making the armhole bag out. The two exceptions are when the wearer possesses naturally square shoulders or when shoulder pads are to be attached inside the garment.

The shaping is worked over the final rows of the front and back of the garment. The greater the number of rows involved, the greater the slope of the shoulder seam will be.

At the point where the shaping is to start, the shoulder stitches are divided into more or less equal sections which are then either cast (bound) off or turned.

Casting off On an average-sized woman's sweater the shoulder stitches on each side will usually be divided into three, or maybe four, groups for the purposes of shaping. Instructions for shaping the back of such a sweater might read as follows:
Cast off 10sts at beg of next 6 rows.
Row 7: Cast off remaining 36sts.

Since the front has neck shaping, however, the shoulders must be worked one at a time so that the pattern for the left-hand shoulder would read:
Cast off 10sts at beg of next and every following RS row. This would then be reversed for the other shoulder, with the casting off at the beginning of WS rows.

If a sharper slope is required, the shoulder stitches are split into smaller groups – for example, five sets, each of six stitches, so that the shaping then occupies ten rows rather than six. This method creates marked 'steps' which are not advisable if the shoulder seams are to be flat. There is a simple method for avoiding these 'jagged' edges (see *Casting/Binding Off*).

However, on plain work turning is the most satisfactory method.

Turning Using the same garment as above, instructions for the back would read:
Work to last 10sts, turn.
Rep this row.
Work to last 20sts, turn.
Rep this row.
Work to last 30sts, turn.
Rep this row.
Cast off 36sts for the centre back neck.

Each needle now holds a complete shoulder. These stitches are worked across and then either cast off or left on a spare needle so that they can be knitted together with the shoulder stitches from the front (see the section on Knitted seams in *Seams*). Turned shaping which is then knitted together forms one of the neatest, flattest, and quickest shoulder seams, but see *Turning* before attempting it.
Note: Where a complicated stitch or colour pattern is being used casting off is the best method for shoulder shaping, since turning the work is likely to alter the pattern.

Non-shaped shoulders

Generally, non-shaped shoulders are not suitable for use with shaped

161

armholes. They are more properly used on garments which have a deep armhole that will not be affected by a lack of shoulder shaping. Baggy, drop-shouldered styles which have no armhole shapings and loose-fitting sleeves with little or no shaping are ideal. The drape effects created by deep dolman and batwing sleeves also require no shoulder shaping.

Saddle shoulders

These have a yoke or 'strap' across the shoulder which is knitted as an extension of the sleeve head/cap (see *Sleeves*). The armhole is shaped as for a normal set-in sleeve with standard shoulder shaping, but is shorter in depth to allow for the width of the shoulder panel.

On this type of shoulder, interesting decorative effects may be created by working a design, such as a cable, up the centre of the sleeve and then continuing it along the shoulder 'strap' to the neck.

Fully fashioned shoulders

Fully fashioned shoulders imitate the shapings most commonly seen on classic mass-produced machine knits. The back shoulder shaping is started earlier than on a standard shaped shoulder, while the fronts are worked longer than the back so that, when sewn up, the shoulder seam sits to the back rather than on top of the shoulder. This produces a very smooth shoulder line.

▪ SILK

Although not an animal hair, silk is a natural protein fibre rather than a cellulose one, for it is produced by certain caterpillars when constructing the cocoon which will envelop them during the chrysalis stage in their lifecycle. It is extruded from the spinneret of the silk worm as one continuous filament which is then wrapped around its body. The peanut-shell-sized cocoon takes the worm three days to produce, after which, if it lives on a silk farm, it is suffocated to prevent it emerging as a moth and damaging the filament.

The cocoons are then processed so that the filament can be unwound, intact, ready for spinning into the lightest and strongest natural fibre – silk. It is said that the process was discovered in ancient China when a cocoon accidentally dropped into a cup of tea and, indeed, the production of silk was a Chinese monopoly for many years. Now silk worms are reared throughout the world, but the price of silk remains high since the worms are delicate and prone to disease.

Like wool, silk is non-conductive to heat but it is strong enough to be spun very finely. This makes it the most versatile fibre, suitable for summer or winter wear. Compared with wool, silk does not have as much elasticity, is more sensitive to heat and will be weakened by prolonged exposure to light. Although silk has an affinity for dyes, the colour will also be affected by light.

When choosing silk knitting yarns, avoid those with a loose twist since they will 'pill' badly. A tightly twisted yarn is ideal, but these are rare since the tighter the twist, the heavier the yarn and the higher the cost. If you are working with a heavy silk yarn, double check that the tension is firm enough to support the weight of the finished garment without causing it to drop. As with all luxury yarns, there

The cocoons of the silk-producing moth.

are now some very interesting mixes on the market, both natural and synthetic, to improve price and wearability. Always take note of the percentages, however – some 'silk' yarns contain as little as 5 per cent silk.

▪ SLEEVES

The techniques involved in constructing a very basic straight-topped sleeve are dealt with in detail in *Designing*. Although it is not possible to give so much information on each of the main sleeve shapes described below, by referring to the sections on designing and shaping it should be possible for you to have a far greater understanding of sleeve construction, which will help when following a pattern.

When taking a measurement for a sleeve, measure the arm from the wrist to the underarm. This then corresponds to the sleeve seam measurement. (**Note:** On shaped sleeves measure the sleeve on the straight, not along the angle of the sleeve seam.)

Since the circumference of the wrist is much smaller than that of the upper arm any full-length sleeve which is to have a fitted cuff must have increases worked to widen it sufficiently (see *Designing*). When working increases at either edge of the sleeve, patterns which are planned using measurements rather than row counts will usually read 'inc. 1st each end of every X number of rows until you have Y number of sts. Now work straight until the work measures Z.' Allowance is made for a straight part of the sleeve in the pattern since knitters' row tension tends to vary, even when the stitch tension (gauge) is the same as quoted at the beginning of the pattern (see *Tension/Gauge*), so that it is impossible to calculate the exact sleeve measurement by the number of rows alone. If the sleeve shapings have been very gradual there is no problem, but if they have been worked close together to form a sharper angle, then working straight for more than a few rows will produce a very odd shape. To avoid this, measure the work several rows before the shaping has been completed and if it looks as if straight rows will be necessary to achieve the correct sleeve length, space out the remaining increases to prevent an abrupt stop to the shaping.

Sleeves which are not full length are worked in the same way but obviously require less shaping since they begin at a wider point on the arm. A wide sleeve which does not have a fitted cuff, such as a kimono shape, may be worked straight or with very little shaping. Remember that the wider the sleeve, the shorter it should be worked to avoid an enormous cuff.

It is extremely important to get the length of a sleeve correct. Always check the wearer's actual arm length against that quoted in the instructions and alter the pattern where necessary (see *Adjusting Patterns*).

Set/Set-in sleeves

This is the classic, curved-top, sleeve which is set into an armhole with similarly curved shaping (see *Armholes*), and may be worked to any length. It should only be used for fairly close-fitting garments since this shape looks wrong unless the seam which

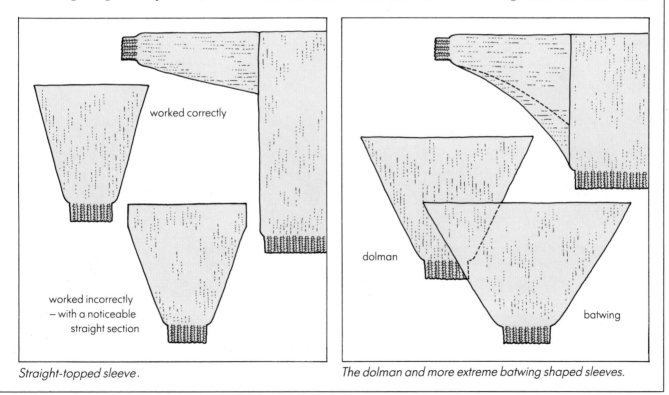

Straight-topped sleeve.

The dolman and more extreme batwing shaped sleeves.

worked correctly

worked incorrectly – with a noticeable straight section

dolman

batwing

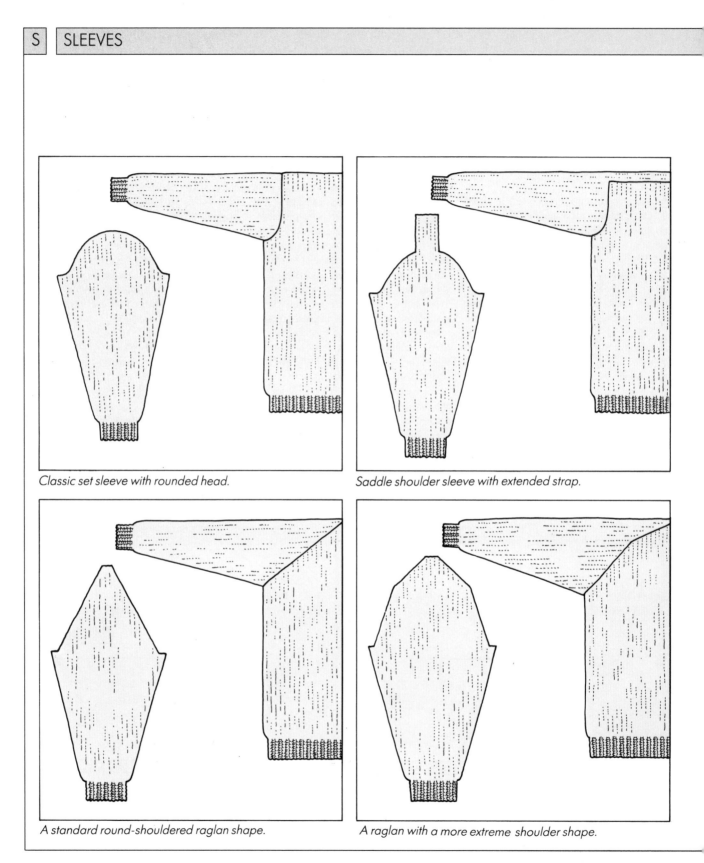

Classic set sleeve with rounded head.

Saddle shoulder sleeve with extended strap.

A standard round-shouldered raglan shape.

A raglan with a more extreme shoulder shape.

joins the top of the sleeve to the top of the armhole sits exactly on the shoulder line. An exception to this rule is when shoulder pads are used to support the shoulders. These may then extend slightly beyond the natural shoulder line.

When the sleeve is the required length the sleeve head (cap) is shaped. Cast (bind) off a few stitches at the beginning of the next two rows and then work decreases at both sides of the work to create a slope at both sides. These are then finished off with more acute shapings, usually sets of cast off stitches at the beginning of several rows, followed by casting off along the very top of the sleeve, producing a straight line which corresponds to the top of the shoulder when the sleeve is set into the armhole. Although the way in which this curve is created may vary a great deal, since every designer has a different idea as to what constitutes the perfect sequence of shapings, in principle the finished effect is usually the same.

When setting in this type of sleeve, complete the side and shoulder seams of the garment so that the armhole is fully formed. Work the actual sleeve seam and then set the whole piece into the armhole, taking great care to distribute any fullness in the sleeve equally around the armhole unless a puff sleeve effect is desired, in which case any fullness is eased to the top of the sleeve to form very slight gathers when sewn. To create a proper puff, the sleeve head should be worked wider than the standard shape to provide extra fabric.

Saddle sleeves

The shaping of the sleeve head which makes up a saddle shoulder starts as for a set sleeve, but when the top is reached the stitches which would normally be cast off are worked to a length which corresponds to the width of the shoulder. This strip forms the yoke which, when the garment is made up, sits on top of the shoulder.

This type of sleeve forms a square shoulder shape and is traditionally used more for menswear than womenswear.

Raglan sleeves

Raglan sleeves are probably the most versatile of sleeve styles. A deep raglan creates a loose-fitting sleeve which, in outline, may be as extreme as a dolman, whereas a shallow raglan produces a close-fitting, classic shape.

Whatever the depth of a raglan, however, the same sleeve shaping principle is used. This is a regular sequence of decreases which form an even slope corresponding to that on the back and front of a garment (see *Raglans*). When the number of stitches left on the needle corresponds to the actual width of the shoulder at the point where it reaches the neck, these stitches are cast off. When the garment is finished they form part of the neckline. Some purists angle this line slightly, casting off over more than one row, to take into account the shape of the neck.

The point on the sleeve where the raglan shaping commences varies according to how deep the raglan will be. If it is a classic, close-fitting one, then the start of shaping corresponds to the actual underarm point, as for a set sleeve. On a deeper raglan, you must make allowance for the fact that the underarm point on the garment will hang below the underarm of the wearer. The sleeve seam length should, therefore, be that much shorter to account for this.

On most traditional raglans the sleeve shaping will exactly echo the shaping on the body, giving a rounded shoulder shape. By adding extra width to the sleeve, extra shaping may be worked at the top of the sleeve, thus creating a larger shape to accommodate shoulder pads (see *Shoulder Pads*). This may easily be done, varying the angle of the sleeve slope by changing the decrease frequency – for example, a raglan which starts off as decrease one stitch each end of every third row would change to decrease one stitch each end of every row, producing two different angles in the same sleeve. The same effect can be produced by disposing of the extra sleeve stitches within a dart, positioned in the centre of the sleeve and started several centimetres or a couple of inches before the cast off point (see *Darts*).

Straight top sleeves

See *Designing* and *Drop Shoulders*.

Dolman sleeves

Dolman sleeves may be worked as separate pieces but are very often worked on garments knitted in one piece. This can be done vertically by working up the front and down the back, though it sometimes involves too many stitches as the body and both sleeve stitches are on the needle at the same time. Alternatively, the garment may be worked horizontally, from cuff to cuff. Both methods avoid a seam where the sleeves are attached.

Whichever way this sleeve is worked it entails a great deal of shaping, since the top widens out to a far greater degree than on most sleeves. If it is knitted separately the sleeve is cast off in a straight line when it is the required length. (Measured on the straight this should more or less correspond to the arm measurement from wrist to underarm, as on a set sleeve, since it is the width of the dolman sleeve which gives it its drape, not the length.) When worn, the sleeve meets the body somewhere between the waist and the underarm although dolman depths vary according to styling.

This is a very fluid shape with a great deal of fabric ending up in the underarm region, making it difficult to wear under a close-fitting coat or jacket. The style lends itself far more readily to evening wear than to everyday sweaters.

Batwing sleeves

Basically, a batwing sleeve is merely an extreme version of the dolman sleeve shape with an even wider sleeve top. When worn, the sleeve joins the body at the waist point so that the sleeve seam forms one long curve from the cuff point to the waist.

SLIPPED STITCHES

The technique by which a stitch is slipped from one needle to another, without working, has many uses, but whenever following the instruction 'sl 1' always slip the stitch in the manner of the stitch before it, unless instructed otherwise. On a knit row the stitch will be slipped knitwise, that is, by putting the point of the needle into it as for a knit stitch (see *The Knit Stitch*). Similarly, on a purl row a slipped stitch will be worked purlwise, that is, by putting the point of the needle into it as for a purl stitch (see *The Purl Stitch*).

Depending on how the following row is to be worked, the manner in which the stitch has been slipped will

make a difference to the way it lies in the finished fabric, either twisted or straight. It is, therefore, very important to take note of any 'knitwise' or 'purlwise' instructions, especially when working decreases where the angle of the finished shaping is often crucial (see *Decreasing*).

Slipped stitch patterns

With patterns which involve slipped stitches the fabric will be more dense than those where every stitch is worked, since the slipped stitches will have a 'pull in' effect on the surrounding

Two-colour pattern produced by slipping stitches, rather than working two colours across a row.

stitches. This will also affect the overall tension of the finished garment. So, although slipped stitches are far quicker to work than those which must be knitted, more stitches and rows must be worked to create the same area of knitting and no time is saved in the long run.

If the same stitch is slipped on every row it will have the effect of elongating the stitch, so that the work is pulled up tighter and tighter with each row (see *Ruching/Shirring*). When the slipped stitch is only being used to create a decorative vertical line of enlarged stitches it will be worked, rather than slipped, every few rows to avoid this puckering.

By keeping the yarn on the wrong side of the work every time a stitch is slipped, the strand of yarn which bridges the gap between knitted stitches will not be seen. Where a visible strand is required on the right side of the fabric, then the yarn should be put to that side of the work every time a stitch is slipped – the instruction 'yarn forward' or 'yarn back' may frequently accompany slipped stitches. Such strands are used for an enormous variety of patterns.

Practical uses for slipped stitches

Slipped stitches are often used in decreases (see *Decreasing*) and form the basis of most selvedge methods (see *Selvedges*).

They are also used to mark fold lines – for example, when working knitted pleats – since a line of slipped stitches produces a slight ridge. When working stocking (stockinette) stitch this is achieved by slipping the fold line stitch, purlwise, on every right side row and then working the purl row normally.

SMOCKING

Smock effects may be worked during the knitting stage or worked after the knitting is completed, as when smocking woven fabric. Both methods are usually worked on ribbing as the rib lines provide a guideline for the regular spacing of the smocking. Remember that the 'pull in' effect of either technique will reduce the width of the work by approximately one-third.

Knitted smocking
Knitted smocking is worked with the aid of a cable or lightweight double-pointed needle on to which a number of stitches are slipped so that the yarn may be wound around them before they are worked, thus bunching them together into a smock effect.

Worked on a k2 p2 rib, a smocking row would read:

(On a RS row) * P2, slip next 6sts on to a cable needle, wind the working yarn around these sts twice in an anti (counter) clockwise direction, then k2, p2, k2 off the cable needle, rep from * to last 2sts, p2.

Wind the working yarn round the next six stitches to bunch them.

The bunched stitches are then worked in pattern.

Work several more rows in rib, according to how far apart the smocking is required. Next RS row, work another smocking row:

P2, k2, * p2, slip next 6sts on to cable needle, wind yarn around and then k2, p2, k2 off cable needle, rep from * to end of row.

In this way a diagonal smocking pattern is formed.

This method creates a small hole either side of the bound stitches but is far quicker to work than embroidered smocking since it does not involve counting finished rows to position it on the work.

Embroidered smocking
When the knitting is complete the ribs may be drawn together using a needle and yarn. Two oversewn (overcast) stitches are enough to hold the ribs together. The position of the next line of smocking should be calculated by counting the number of rows.

This method allows the use of contrast yarn for decorative smocking, which is more popular on babywear. Additional embroidery stitches may also be added to it for greater emphasis.

Embroidered smocking: bunching lines of rib with needle and yarn.

SPINNING

In virtually every country of the world which has some sort of indigenous natural fibre, archaeological and other evidence points to a tradition of spinning. The process of spinning has often taken on a strong symbolic role: Gandhi, for example, emphasized the importance of 'homespun' cloth to the social economy of India.

The earliest recorded and most basic method of spinning is by using a spindle. The spinner teases fibre into a strand which is then twisted around the spindle. The spindle is either suspended on a string or used like a spinning top to facilitate this. Although primitive, this method is still used in many parts of the world.

The spinning wheel is a more familiar device in the West, although the first type was, in fact, invented in China where they were used to unravel silk cocoons. Although there are many different types of spinning wheel, their action is basically the same – to turn a spindle which twists the thread, which is fed by hand. The momentum provided by the wheel,

China is the home of the spinning wheel, invented for spinning silk.

however, allows the spinner to use both hands to control the fibres which are being pulled out. This gives the yarn a more consistent thickness.

When the factory system of spinning emerged in the 18th and 19th centuries, the spinning mills actually consisted of rows of spinning wheels, attended by female 'spinsters' (the derivation of the term). This is a far cry from modern spinning machinery where spindles are driven at around 14,000 revolutions per minute and the sophistication of techniques means that any number of different yarn textures can be produced by varying the manner and speed at which the fibres are spun.

SPLICING

See *Joins*.

SPLIT STITCHES

Split stitches should be avoided at all costs, both at the knitting stage and when seaming (see *Uneven Knitting* and *Seams*).

STOCKING/ STOCKINETTE STITCH

Stocking (or stockinette) stitch is probably the most commonly used knitting stitch. It is not the most basic stitch, however, since it involves two different types of rows, each right side row being knitted and each wrong side row being purled. These two rows are continually repeated to form stocking stitch. This creates a very different appearance on the right and wrong sides of the work: the right or knit side is often referred to as the 'smooth', while the wrong side has a ridged or 'rough' texture. If the wrong side of

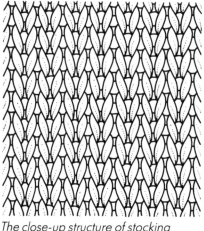
The close-up structure of stocking stitch.

the fabric is used as the right side of the work, it is called 'reverse stocking stitch'. This should not be confused with garter stitch since, although they look very similar from a distance, the structure is quite different. Reverse stocking stitch ridges sit next to one another, while garter stitch ridges are broken up with a gap.

Stocking stitch produces the flattest, smoothest finished fabric but has a pronounced tendency to curl, rolling under itself along selvedges and rolling up along the cast on and cast (bound) off edges. Stocking stitch work always needs finishing with bands, borders or hems to compensate for this.

Since it is the plainest of stitches, it also requires the highest degree of evenness when knitting, since any irregularities will be noticeable on the right side of the work.

Some knitters tend to work the purl row more slowly and at a slightly different tension (gauge) – this produces visible ridges within the work. There are ways of correcting this (see *Uneven Knitting*). Circular knitting is the perfect way to speed up the working of stocking stitch since, because the work is never being turned, no purl row is required.

As it is such a widely used stitch and because spinners' tension guidance is usually quoted over stocking stitch, it should be the first stitch for the beginner to master after plain knitting or garter stitch has been covered.

STRETCHING

Since knitting creates a fabric with a high degree of elasticity, compared to woven fabrics, the stretch factor must always be taken into account when planning a knitted garment.

Stretching inevitably takes us back to the golden rule of knitting – *getting the tension (gauge) correct*. If you are using a pattern for a specific yarn then, it is hoped, the designer will have taken the qualities of that yarn into account before deciding on the correct tension at which it should be knitted. If you are improvising, however, and are uncertain of how the yarn and/or stitch will stretch, work a decent-sized swatch so that you can put it to the test.

As styling has become baggier and yarns more exotic, the actual weight of the finished knitting has become an increasingly important factor in deciding how far the garment will drop when worn. Once again, this should have been calculated at the design stage, but if you are substituting yarns, common sense must be your guide. A knee-length dress, intended for a DK (worsted) wool, will probably end up floor length if knitted in heavy polyester ribbon. Although the yarns may be of the same thickness, they are most definitely not of the same weight per centimetre or inch.

Treat any knitted garments with care when you are wearing them and always store heavy knitteds flat rather than hanging them up. The worst stretching will occur if a garment is badly washed (see *Washcare*).

SUBSTITUTION

Substituting a yarn for a pattern which has recommended another need not be the minefield that many yarn manufacturers would have you believe. The mystique built up around only using a specific brand of yarn to

get the required results is largely a sales ploy.

Provided that the correct tension (gauge) can be produced using the substitute (see *Tension/Gauge*) and that you use your common sense when deciding on the suitability of the style of yarn for the style of the garment you wish to work, yarns can be freely swapped around (see *Patterns*).

Always bear in mind that the amounts of yarn required may vary considerably since all yarns differ in weight per metre. Unfortunately very few ball bands or labels quote this metreage so that comparison is rarely possible without knitting up part of the garment. A lightweight synthetic may go twice as far as cotton, for instance. If you are able to buy the yarn in two batches, buy a small amount first, work one piece of the garment such as a sleeve, and then by consulting the measurements on the pattern, you can roughly calculate how much substitute yarn you will need, compared to the quantity of specified yarn.

The rollneck sweaters pictured on page 158 illustrate exactly the same pattern knitted up in three completely different yarns – mohair, cotton and wool tweed – but which all produce the same tension. By following the golden rule of correct tension, all three garments are identical in sizing, regardless of the difference in yarns.

SWATCH

A swatch is a small sample piece of fabric, woven or knitted. It is essential to work a tension (gauge) sample or swatch before starting any knitting (see *Tension/Gauge*), and it is often

helpful to see exactly how a pattern will work out before attempting a larger piece of work.

HINT

If a small stain or burn appears on a knitted garment, provided it is in a suitable position, Swiss darning can turn the blemish into a decorative motif such as a monogram, a floral bouquet or any other design which will suit the style of the garment.

The same technique may be used to reinforce parts of a garment which are subjected to abnormal wear, such as elbows. The problem area may be worked in self-coloured (one colour) yarn or in a contrast if an obvious patch effect is required. By working in exactly the same way as the decorative version, the darning creates a double fabric and provides twice the strength.

SWISS DARNING

Although, strictly speaking, Swiss darning is an embroidery rather than a knitting technique, it is used so closely with knitting that it deserves to be included here.

As its alternative name of 'duplicate stitch' suggests, it is a method of embroidery that follows the exact path of the knitted stitch over which it is worked. It can, therefore, be used to create very neat mock fairisle effects on one-colour knitting. Naturally, this method is impractical for large areas of colour which are best knitted using the intarsia method, but where

SWISS DARNING

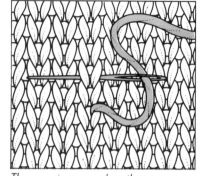

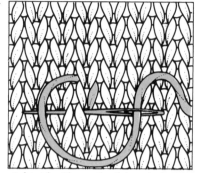

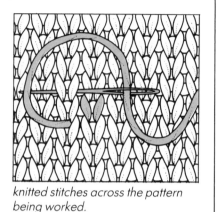

The yarn is secured on the wrong side, then brought through to the

right side. The path of the stitches duplicates exactly the path of the

knitted stitches across the pattern being worked.

small areas are involved it is an extremely useful adjunct to knitting.

Besides being added to plain work, Swiss darning may also be used to introduce additional colours to fairisle or intarsia work where it is not desirable to add them during the knitting stage. This means that a third colour may be added to a row of fairisle which is always worked using only two. When working an intarsia motif, instead of joining in another colour to knit a tiny area, it can be darned in

at a later stage.

It is sometimes tempting to Swiss darn complicated embroidery charts which are far too intricate and use too many colours to translate into knitting. But before starting, do bear in mind that these charts were made for the dimensions of certain embroidery stitches and they do not necessarily correspond to knitted stitches. The proportions will nearly always need adjusting (see *Charts*).

Swiss darning should be worked

with a blunt tapestry needle to avoid splitting the knitted stitches. Use a yarn that is the same weight as that used for the knitting as a finer one will not cover the original stitch properly and a heavier one will give the work a raised appearance. Follow the line of the stitches, keeping the tension (gauge) of the embroidered stitch exactly the same as that of the knitting. The knitted stitches will show through loose darning and the work will pucker if darned too tightly.

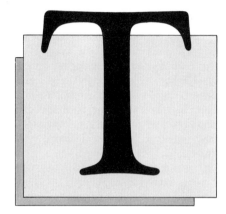

TENSION/GAUGE

Tension is the term used to describe the stitch size. Correct tension is not a gift: it is a technicality, totally under the knitter's control. As such, it must be tested for complete accuracy before commencing any work. *This is the most important rule in knitting.*

For a knitter to start knitting without working a tension sample or 'swatch' is rather like a dressmaker ignoring the printed outline when cutting out a paper pattern. 'Know-it-all' knitters who boast that they never check their tension are not demonstrating their expertise: completely the reverse. If the pattern which you are using has specific tension sample instructions, follow them to the letter. They are the basis of the precise mathematical calculations which have gone into the drafting of the pattern (see *Designing*).

If the tension is quoted as so many stitches or rows to a measurement – for example, 18sts and 24 rows to 10cm (4in.) – work a sample by casting on the quoted number of stitches plus at least two extra, since your edge stitches will not give an accurate measure-

ment. Always use the needle size quoted and the stitch – it is very little use getting your stocking (stockinette) stitch tension perfect if the garment is to be worked in moss (seed) stitch. Also make sure that you use the same method that you will be using on the garment. If the garment is to be worked in fairisle, for example, then work the swatch in the same manner, since your tension will be quite different from that achieved over one-colour work.

When it is finished, lay the 'swatch' on a flat surface (the arm of your chair will *not* do), and, taking great care not to squash or stretch it, measure the tension, using ruler and pins. A clear plastic ruler makes it easier for you to see the alignment of the stitches. Some people find that a tension gauge is of help but it merely takes the place of pins and ruler.

If your tension is loose – too few stitches per centimetre or inch – use smaller needles to work another swatch. If your tension is too tight – too many stitches per centimetre or inch – use one size larger needles to work another swatch. Even if you have to change needle sizes five times,

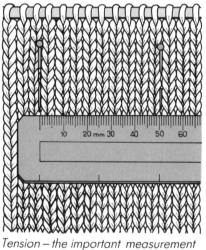

Tension – the important measurement of stitches, here 9sts = 5cm.

keep working swatches until you get it right. You save no time by skipping this stage of the work. A tension measurement which is only a fraction of a stitch out per centimetre will result in a wrongly sized garment since each fraction will be multiplied by the number of centimetres across the work. The choice is between spending a few minutes working a tension swatch or having to undo an entire garment.

Tips for different types of yarns

Unevenly textured yarns With slub finishes, for example, work a swatch twice as large as you would normally require and measure the work at several different points. As the measurements will vary, take an average to give you an accurate tension.

Fluffy yarns With mohair and angora, for example, where the individual stitches are difficult to define, hold the swatch up to the light to place the pins. Then lay the swatch flat and measure as usual.

Heavily textured yarns Where the stitch definition is almost non-existent, with bouclé for example, place small markers either side of the required number of stitches when working the swatch. The measurement can then be taken from marker to marker.

Slippery yarns With loosely knitted cottons and shiny synthetics, take extra care not to pull the swatch out of shape. Drop it lightly on a flat surface and measure it as it falls, without applying any pressure.

Always remember that your own individual tension will vary. Your hands will react to different yarns, needles and stitches in a unique way with each new piece of work. Even during a piece of work it is important to check that your tension is consistent since your mood can affect the way you knit. Always hold your work in the way that you feel most happy with so that you can relax. You can be sure that any 'tension' in your brain will most certainly be transmitted to your hands, and so to the tension of your work.

Details of row tension have been omitted since many people worry over this unnecessarily, changing their needle size even though they have achieved an accurate stitch tension. Although row tension is extremely important, it does vary considerably from yarn to yarn and knitter to knitter. If your stitch tension is spot on, your rows will only be slightly out but it is worth while measuring both so that you can keep an eye on the length (or width, if knitting sideways) as you go.

What to do with finished swatches

Many knitting books, especially older ones, will tell you to 'make colourful patchworks' by sewing all your swatches together. This may have been a good idea when virtually the only yarns used were 4-ply and double knitting (worsted), but with today's enormous range of yarn weights and textures the result could look gruesome unless great care is taken. A far more sensible idea is to staple each swatch to a piece of card upon which you can note exactly the yarn used, the size of needle and stitch details. These can then be stored away in a shoebox or something similar and used for future reference. Having that little piece of yarn on file can also come in very handy for emergency repairs at a later date since yarn can very rarely be matched long after the event. If you are nervous about washing your finished garment, you can also use the swatch to test for shrinkage, dye fastness, and so on.

The positive use of tension variation

Garments can be shaped by changing needle size to alter tension. This is very useful when decreases and increases are not desirable or might look unsightly, say on a ribbed collar when the outer edge needs to be slightly wider than the neck edge. It can also be used for figure-hugging garments and is much in evidence in old patterns from the thirties, forties and early fifties when the baggy sweater was anathema.

TRAVELLING STITCHES

A stitch, usually a knit stitch on a reverse stocking (stockinette) stitch ground, is referred to as a travelling stitch when it appears to move in a diagonal line across the work.

The technique can be seen as a miniature single stitch cable since it crosses over the stitch immediately next to it in the same manner. However, this is worked on every row to create a continuous line, rather than every few rows as in true cabling. The effect may be achieved in two different ways.

The first method is simply to use a small cable needle to create left or right twists (see *Cables*). The second method, which is rather faster, since it does not require the use of a cable needle, is to twist the stitches while they are on the working needle (see *Twisted/Crossed Stitches*).

Both methods may be used to create an enormous variety of fancy patterns, but travelling stitches are most suited to and most often used for the creation of diagonal lattice effects – a number of individual stitches may be used to create criss-cross and zigzag lines which interlace across a plain background fabric.

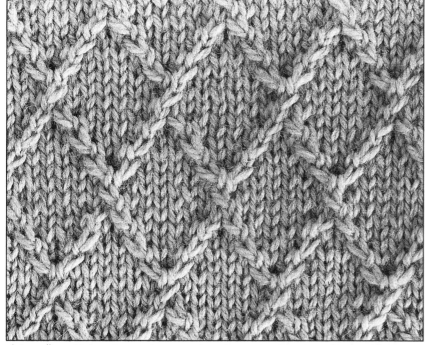

A travelling stitch pattern – the twisted stitches move them into diagonal lines.

TUBULAR KNITTING

See *Circular Knitting* and *Double Fabric*.

TUCKS

A tuck can be knitted into a piece of work in just the same way as a knitted hem, the only difference being that it is worked within the piece rather than at the very beginning or end. When the tuck row is reached, extra rows are worked which are then folded back on themselves. The stitches along the row at the start of the tuck are picked up on to a smaller needle and then

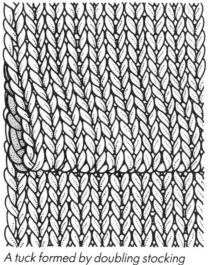

A tuck formed by doubling stocking stitch into a fold, then knitting the two rows of stitches together.

the two lots of stitches are knitted together, closing the tuck. The work is then continued as normal.

Although they create too much bulk to be worked with heavyweight yarns, tucks or knitted folds can produce very effective ornamental ridges on lighter weight yarns. They may be used to highlight features such as the line where horizontally knitted dolman sleeves join the body of a garment.

TURNING

The technique of shaping which involves turning the work before the entire row is completed is sometimes referred to as working short rows since this describes exactly what one is doing. Depending on how many turning points are being worked, the result is that one side of the knitting has a greater number of rows than the other. If the work is cast (bound) off afterwards, this results in a sloping cast off edge and is, therefore, most often used when shaping shoulders (see *Shoulders*). If the work is continued after

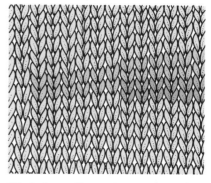

Work shaped by turning – coloured stitches show where short rows finish. A 'V' shape is produced.

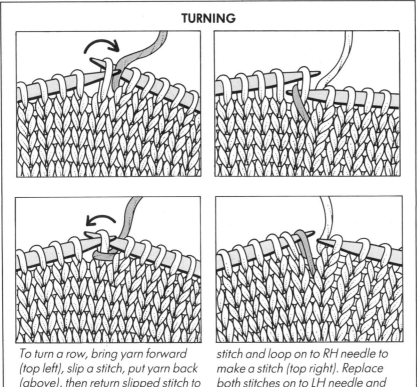

TURNING

To turn a row, bring yarn forward (top left), slip a stitch, put yarn back (above), then return slipped stitch to LH needle. On the next knit row, slip

stitch and loop on to RH needle to make a stitch (top right). Replace both stitches on to LH needle and knit together (above).

tween them, produces only a gradual slope. By dividing the stitches into smaller groups, with a greater number

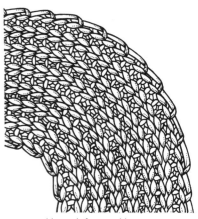

A curved band, formed by turning.

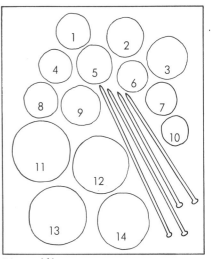

Natural fibres.
1. Pure silk; 2. pure cotton; 3. wool, silk and alpaca; 4. pure alpaca; 5. wool, silk and linen; 6. angora and wool; 7. linen and cotton; 8. silk and wool; 9. cotton; 10. silk; 11. tweed wool; 12. mohair, wool and nylon; 13. mohair, wool and nylon; 14. mohair, wool and nylon.

the turning has been completed then the shaping forms a dart (see *Darts*).

There is a tendency for noticeable holes to form at the turning points in the work unless the turns are made using a specific technique. It looks extremely long winded at first, but it is essential for a really neat finish.

The example used is a set of 18 right-hand shoulder stitches which are being turned in three groups of six to provide the shaping. They are worked in stocking (stockinette) stitch.
1. (Next RS row) K to last 6sts, bring yarn to front of work and slip the next st from LH to RH needle.
2. Return yarn to back of work and

return slipped st to LH needle.
3. Turn work, p to end.

Now repeat the last three steps but work to the last 12sts rather than 6sts.
Next row: K to first st which has had a loop made around it by putting the yarn forward and then back.
4. Sl this st from the LH to the RH needle, at the same time lifting the loop up on to the RH needle, making an extra st.
5. Replace the 2sts on to the LH needle and knit them together.

Continue the row to the next 'looped' st and repeat the process.

Dividing the work into three groups, with several stitches in be-

of turning points, the difference in row count at either side of the work would be far greater, creating a steeper slope.

If you are knitting a border which is being worked sideways and must fit around a curve or corner, then the turns are worked every other stitch all along the width of the band to produce an extreme curve (see *Bands or Borders*). Edging frills may be worked in the same way but with a few edge stitches left unturned to create a straight edge. The turning process is then repeated every few rows so that

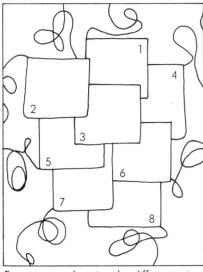

Fancy yarns showing the difference in effect between a single strand and the knitted fabric.
1. 88% viscose, 12% nylon; 2. 40% acrylic, 30% mohair, 27% nylon, 3% irise; 3. 45% cotton, 30% linen, 25% polymide; 4. 80% cotton, 11% nylon, 5% acrylic, 4% metallized; 5. 85% viscose, 15% polymide; 6. 50% viscose, 25% cotton, 15% linen, 7% polyester, 3% polymide; 7. 95% cotton, 5% acrylic; 8. 100% cotton.

one side of the band has far more rows than the edge which has been left straight.

If a curved edge is required, turning may often be used as an alternative to shaping the actual edge of a piece of work with increases, decreases, castings on and off, all of which will often leave an untidy selvedge, far from being a smooth curve. Naturally, the direction of the knitting must lend itself to this technique but the result is far superior to 'selvedge shaping'.

A perfect example of the technique is on a vertically knitted cardigan shawl neck where turnings, carefully placed, will give the correct shaping required (see *Collars*). By continuing to work turning rows at regular intervals, circular shapes such as those used for yokes and berets may also be produced.

When working a garment horizontally, the possibilities are endless since the predominant shaping principle is the number of rows rather than the number of stitches as on normal vertically worked knitting. Any number of flares, frills, darts and slopes can be knitted within the main work (see *Horizontal Knitting*).

TWISTED/ CROSSED STITCHES

Under normal circumstances, especially when knitting a very plain fabric such as stocking (stockinette) stitch, twisted stitches are to be avoided at all costs since they cause the stitch to lie at a different angle from those surrounding it. This is why, whenever you are picking up stitches, you should take great care in putting them all on to the needle in the same direction.

A miniature cable formed by twisting stitches, working the second, then the first on the left-hand needle.

Intentional twisted stitches have both an ornamental and practical use, however. They are made either by working into the back of the stitch or loop, a method which is usually abbreviated to 'tbl', or by twisting two stitches by working them in the wrong order – often abbreviated to 'tw2'.

Ornamental twisted stitches
A twisted stitch may be used to form a line of travelling stitches, if worked on every row (see *Travelling Stitches*), or a miniature cable effect, if worked on alternate rows. This two-stitch mock cable is worked on a basic k2 p2 rib, so that the two knit stitches are twisted every right side row.

To work a right twist:
1. Skip the first st (that is, leave it on the LH needle, without working it), and knit into the second st.
2. Rather than slipping the worked st off the needle, knit into the skipped

st, then slip both off the needle.

A left twist is made in the same way but the second stitch is worked through the back of the loop to change the angle.

Practical twisted stitches

Twisting a stitch by working into the back of the loop has two effects – to change the angle at which it will lie and to tighten the stitch.

The former is important in a number of decrease methods where the finished stitch needs to slope to the left rather than the right (see *Decreasing*). The latter is of great use when a particular technique has loosened a stitch which may then be tightened up by knitting into the back of it on the next row. It can be used anywhere that the neatening effect of a tighter stitch is required, as when knitting (picking) up a neckband where the back neck stitches are held rather than cast (bound) off. If you think that these stitches may have a tendency to stretch, work the first row 'tbl'.

UV

▮ UNEVEN KNITTING

When working a plain stitch or one with a small and regular repeat it is essential to work each individual stitch in a consistent manner in order to keep the overall effect even. On a stocking (stockinette) stitch fabric any change in tension (gauge), incorrect working of a stitch, or damage to the yarn, however slight, will be obvious. Although knitting that is being worked at a loose tension will be far more likely to appear uneven, as there will be more movement between stitches than in a fabric worked at a firm tension, uneven knitting should not be confused with the inability to achieve the correct tension (see *Tension/Gauge*).

Some knitters appear to have a natural ability to achieve even knitting, while others find it a constant effort. State of mind undoubtedly has something to do with it. As described in *The Knit Stitch*, the most important key to good knitting is feeling comfortable with the technique you have chosen. Even when working simple garter or stocking stitch, the manner in which the needles and yarn are held

and even the actual position in which you sit will all affect your knitting. First, feel happy and relaxed with the basic skills and then speed and expertise will follow naturally. Here are a few tips to help you along.

1. Never put knitting down when part way through a row as the stitches will stretch at the point at which you left off, making it visible when the knitting is re-started. Always finish the row that you are on and push the stitches down the needle so that they will not fall off while the work is put aside. If the needle is very full use a stopper on the point (a cork will do if nothing else is to hand).
2. Never put the needles through the work already completed or through the ball of yarn as they can easily split and damage the stitches and the unused yarn. To keep the work tidy and clean always use a work bag. If nothing else is available then use a pillowcase or a clean tea (dish) towel.
3. Although you should always wash your hands before starting work, don't overdo it as chapped hands will pill the yarn before it is even knitted, giving the finished work a fluffy,

well-worn appearance. Use a non-sticky hand cream to combat any roughness. Also, make sure that the needles are smooth and clean.
4. If more than one set of needles are being kept in the work bag, make sure that you pick up the right one each time that you take up your knitting – a needle of a wrong size will immediately alter your tension. For the same reason, turn down any offers of assistance, however welcome they may be, since every individual has a different personal tension and the changeover point will be apparent if there is a switch of knitters part way through a piece of work.
5. Some knitters find that when working stocking (stockinette) stitch the rows are not evenly spaced since they tend to work the purl row that much tighter than the knit row. This can be regulated by using a larger size needle for the purl row only or by working the garment in the round since, using this method, no purl row needs to be worked (see *Circular Knitting*).
6. When changing colours, many knitters lose control over the tension of their stitches and allow holes to

form and tight floats to buckle up the right side of the work. To perfect colour knitting techniques see *Fairisle* and *Intarsia*.

7. Always keep your eyes on your work, continually checking back over previous rows for possible mistakes. Dropped stitches, split stitches, stitches which have been missed or knitted from the previous row or the loop between the stitches are all caused by lapses in attention. They do not spring up in the work spontaneously. As the knitter, you are in charge of each stitch and each row, at every stage in the work.

Intentional uneven knitting

There is a method of knitting which utilizes an intentionally uneven tension from row to row. This effect is created by using two needles of odd sizes – one jumbo needle and one several sizes smaller. The large needle makes the knitting extremely speedy while the alternate rows worked on the smaller one give the work more firmness than if the entire garment were worked on enormous needles. The overall appearance is one of enlarged stitches.

UNRAVELLING

Taking back work can be a very tiresome experience, but do not let annoyance or loss of patience cause you to waste yarn or to spoil the remainder of a garment.

If only part of a garment needs unravelling, as when a mistake is spotted when the work is still on the needles, decide how far back you need to go and mark the row. Now take a spare needle and pick up the stitches

Steaming unravelled yarn removes the crinkles before reuse.

along this row before starting any unpicking. This will ensure that you do not pull back any further than is necessary and avoids dropping loose stitches as you try to put them back on the needle. This is particularly important with slippery yarns, such as those with a high viscose content.

As you unpick do not pull and tug as this will tighten difficult stitches, making them impossible to undo without cutting. Gently 'waggle' the yarn end, especially if it is a textured yarn, such as a bouclé, so that the stitches will ease themselves apart. With fluffy yarns have a very small pair of nail scissors handy as every once in a while it will be necessary to cut away the excess fibres which will form a knot around the yarn. But be careful not to cut through the yarn itself. With a textured yarn you may have to be very patient.

If the yarn has only just been knitted for the first time then it may be re-used straightaway, still attached to the work in one piece with luck. But if the work has been left for a

while and the knitted yarn has become crinkly, break it off and join in a new ball of yarn. Put the used yarn to one side in case it is needed later.

When unravelling a complete piece of work, do so from the cast (bound) off edge downwards, that is, in the opposite direction to the knitting.

If a great deal of yarn has had to be unravelled and it is in good condition and long lengths, making it worth recycling, then it may be salvaged and the crinkles removed in the following way. Using a frame such as a bent wire coathanger, wind the yarn so that it is under tension. Keep it evenly spaced to make drying easier. It should then be held over a source of steam or dipped into lukewarm water if drip-drying is no problem. Whichever method of reconditioning is chosen, allow the yarn to dry completely before winding it into balls (see *Winding*).

When you come to re-use the yarn, the fact that it has been stretched, re-stretched and its moisture content completely altered (an important factor with natural fibres such as wool which have a high water content) will make accurate weight estimates for a pattern difficult. To be on the safe side make sure that you have more than enough to complete the garment since if the yarn runs out it may have to be unravelled all over again.

'V' NECKS

A 'V' neck may be worked to virtually any depth and at any angle since the neckband is easily shaped to accommodate any neckline (see *Neckbands*). Extremely deep 'V' neckbands are often worked as a decorative feature

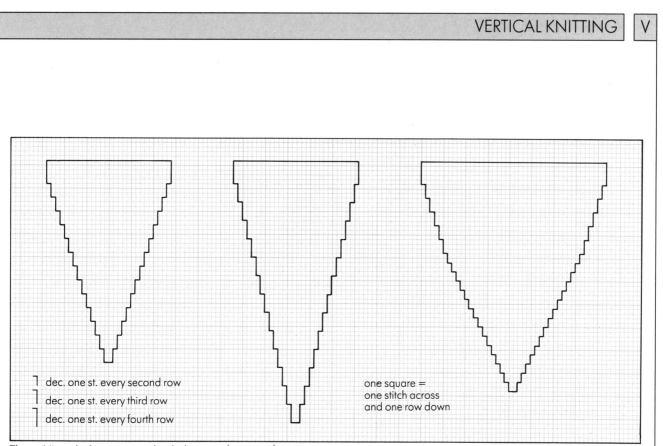

dec. one st. every second row
dec. one st. every third row
dec. one st. every fourth row

one square =
one stitch across
and one row down

Three 'V' neck shapes: standard, deep and very wide.

on a garment and may involve the use of colour stripes, as on traditional cricket sweaters which feature the team's colours here.

When the beginning of the neck shaping is reached on the front of a 'V' sweater, divide the stitches in half and shape each side of the neck separately. If there is an odd number of stitches to be divided, the central stitch is left on a pin. When the neckband is worked this is then picked up and forms the axial stitch, with shapings worked either side of it. Care should be taken not to stretch this stitch as it becomes the focal point of the neckline. If an even number of stitches are divided then an axial stitch may be knitted (picked) up from the central strand between the two sets of stitches. This is the quicker, neater method of the two.

The number of stitches which comprise the width of the neck at its widest point are then divided between the two sides and spread over the number of rows which makes up the depth of the 'V'. The manner in which these decreases are spaced depends upon the exact shape of the 'V' required. The graph shows a standard shape which would be worked over a depth of approximately 20cm (8in.) on an average woman's garment. It shows fairly gradual shaping at the bottom of the 'V' and finishes on several straight rows which eventually sit at the side of the wearer's neck.

The shape of the 'V' may vary enormously, however, depending on styling. An evening top with a very wide neck width would have a straight, broad angle formed from the point of the 'V' to the shoulder point,

while a deep 'V' with a standard neck width would form a tapering, gradual angle, giving a very narrow 'V' shape. Experiment with graph paper in order to get the shape spaced correctly to suit the individual wearer (see *Adjusting Patterns*). Remember to take into account the proposed depth of neckband.

◼ VERTICAL KNITTING

Vertical knitting is simply what most knitters think of as the standard direction of working for most knitting, that is, from the bottom of the garment up. This is in contrast to horizontal knitting which means knitting from side to side – from cuff to cuff on a sweater worked in one piece.

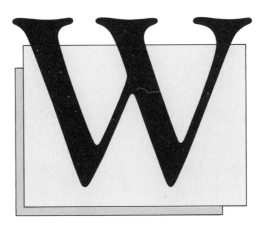

WAISTBANDS

When working a long-line garment such as a dress or coat that needs a definite waistline the easiest method is simply to incorporate several rows of rib to create a waisted effect. The nature of the stitch will pull in the garment at the required point.

On skirts and trousers, however, a waistband is actually required to keep the garment in place and it needs to be fairly snug fitting to avoid the item ending up around the wearer's ankles. It is possible to work a waistband by reducing the number of stitches and/or working the final rows at a much tighter tension (gauge) than the rest of the work. However, that also involves working an opening and then attaching fastenings so that the garment may be easily taken on and off.

The easiest solution is to reduce the amount of fabric very slightly to avoid bunching around the waistline and then use ribbon elastic, measuring the correct length around the wearer's waist. This may either be threaded into a tube, worked as for a hem (see *Hems*), or have a stitched casing worked around it (see *Elastic*).

WASHCARE

For a discussion of the relative merits of washing and dry cleaning, see *Dry Cleaning*. There are a few instances where washing is preferable to dry-cleaning, as when dealing with white or very pale colours which, if repeatedly dry cleaned, tend to acquire a slight dirtiness of colour. Washing also gives a far fresher smell to a garment.

Before washing always refer to the ball band or yarn label as this gives washcare instructions, usually including the internationally recognized symbols. Make sure that you thoroughly understand these before making any decisions regarding washcare. Never machine-wash knitteds unless the label includes the symbol that specifically indicates that this is possible. On pure wool this means looking for the term 'superwash' – indicating that the yarn has been specifically treated to withstand machine washing. Unless the symbol or the instruction is present, *always* hand wash.

Many synthetic fibres readily lend themselves to machine washing, but care should be taken in following the spinning and drying instructions as some yarns, such as acrylic, have a tendency to pull out of shape and crease badly if spun at high speed. Do not tumble-dry any fibres unless, once again, the instructions specifically state that this is acceptable and even if they do, be prepared for a high level of static electricity, especially on synthetic yarns.

The two main problems encountered when washing knitteds are shrinkage and stretching. Shrinkage is mainly associated with wool and wool mix yarns and it is usually accompanied by a degree of matting (see *Felting*). This may be caused by heat, friction, chemical reaction or a combination of all three. It is obvious why lukewarm water, a gentle washing agent and the minimum of handling are essential. Never allow natural fibres to soak since this allows the washing agent time to attack the fibre and may also result in colour loss. Instead, gently squeeze the garment to loosen the dirt, then immediately let the water out of the basin. Do not lift the garment out of the basin as the weight of the water which it holds will pull it out of shape.

Once again, gently squeeze the water out of the garment, pressing it against the side of the basin before running the first rinse water. Use at least two rinses or more if there are still traces of washing agent apparent. When not a trace of chemical is left, squeeze as much water out as is possible and then transfer the garment straight into a towel, still avoiding letting it support its wet weight. Lay the garment flat and roll the towel up, not too tightly, so that any extra moisture will be taken up by the towel. If it is a heavyweight garment, repeat this procedure with further dry

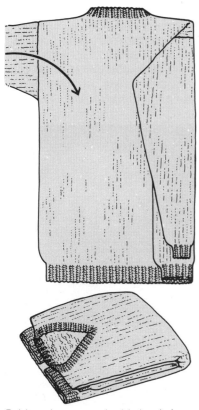

Folding knitwear, double back the sleeves and fold in two.

towels until you are satisfied that the garment is well past the dripping stage.

The garment must then be laid absolutely flat and pushed back into the exact shape which it should have when dry. Although this may be done by leaving it on a towel on the table or floor, it is far better to place it somewhere where the air may circulate, since a chunky sweater may take so long to dry that it starts to acquire a mildewed smell. An airing cupboard with slatted shelves is ideal, although a towel should also be used to avoid any stain being picked up from the wood. Alternatively, sweater drying frames may be purchased from specialist outlets. Do not put the garment into direct sunlight or near a very intense heat source such as a radiator. Leave it to dry naturally.

Just as knitwear should never be hung up to dry it should also never be stored on a hanger. Not only will heavy knits drop, sometimes to an alarming degree, but the elasticity of the fabric will stretch around the coat hanger and distort the shoulders. Always store knitwear carefully folded to avoid creasing. If storing wool, always make sure that the garment is put away clean as any soiling will attract moths. These may now be discouraged by pleasant-smelling sprays rather than the gruesome mothballs of days gone by.

If washing has flattened a fluffy yarn, such as mohair, the fibres may be teased back with the use of an average bristle hairbrush. Do this with short, light strokes to avoid pulling the stitches. Only press a knitted garment if it is essential and then only after consulting the ball band (label) for instructions (see *Making Up/ Assembling*).

WEAVING

Weaving refers to one of the techniques used in fairisle colour knitting whereby the yarn not in use is carried across the back of the work, and looped in behind every stitch. The method of achieving this is covered in detail under *Fairisle*.

By working the same technique, but using what would normally be the wrong side of the work as its right side, interesting woven effects are created in colour, or simply in texture if self-coloured (one-colour) yarns are used. Naturally, there is very little point in using complicated fairisle patterns since much of the intricacy will be lost on the wrong side of the work, but effective woven looks can be created by using fairly basic large, geometric shapes as guidelines.

WELTS/ FINISHING BORDERS

The dictionary definition of a welt is a band or border and, as such, all the points discussed in *Bands or Borders* are applicable. It is, very often, a far more important part of a garment than one would imagine since it can affect the shape of the entire body. Before deciding on the most suitable welt stitch and how close fitting it should be, take into account the precise length of the garment so that you know exactly where the welt will sit when the garment is being worn. A deep, tight rib may be ideal for a sweater that stops at the waistline but quite unsuitable for a long cardigan, where the

183

strain will be taken across the bottom, pulling the fronts apart. In this case a short, loose rib or a non-'pull-in' border stitch such as garter stitch may be preferable to ensure that the cardigan hangs correctly.

The cast on edge of a welt is also the point on almost any garment which takes the greatest amount of wear and tear, not to mention strain. Ensure that a suitable cast on method has been chosen for the yarn which you are using and take great care over working strong, secure welt seams. If the welt finally does give up then a new one may be knitted to take its place (see *Alterations to Finished Garments*).

WINDING

Whenever you are winding yarn with a natural elasticity, such as wool, do so loosely to avoid unnecessary stretching. Yarn that has been pulled out of shape may lose some of its elasticity altogether or may return to its original condition, after the knitting is complete, causing the tension of the garment to tighten up.

If you are winding a ball by hand do so around your fingers. Once you have withdrawn your fingers the wraps of yarn will have the correct degree of looseness. If you use a ball-winding machine, make sure the yarn is being fed loosely and evenly. Skein holders (the mechanical type, not the human variety), are very useful since they spin around, unravelling the skein as they go. Both winders and skein holders can be bought at specialist craft shops.

For winding yarn that has already been knitted up, see *Unravelling*.

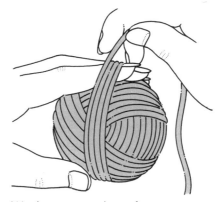
Wind yarn around your fingers.

WOOL

Ever since the first, primitive attempts at knitting were made, thousands of years ago, wool has totally dominated the craft, as it still does. Even though a vast array of different fibres are now spun for the hand-knitting market, many knitters still insist on referring to any type of yarn as 'wool', regardless of whether it is 100 per cent polyester or a linen and cotton mix.

Wool's extraordinary qualities of elasticity, durability and ready availability have made it the number one choice for hand knitting. While still in fleece form, it will protect a sheep from the harshest of climates. The natural 'crimp' of the wool fibres gives excellent insulation by trapping air, allowing the animal to keep warm in winter, cool in summer.

Sheep also produce a natural oil, lanolin, which makes the fleece totally weatherproof. This is largely removed during the initial cleaning process or scouring, but wool is still capable of absorbing up to 33 per cent of its own weight in water before starting to feel wet. Even more amaz-

Wool-producing sheep: the Shetland (left) and the Devon and Cornwall long wool (right).

ingly, the absorption process itself produces heat so that a woollen sweater will not feel cold, even if you are caught in a shower. This, along with its ability to absorb any perspiration exuded by the wearer and thus regulate the temperature of the skin, makes wool by far the most comfortable yarn to wear when compared to synthetics, most of which have minimal absorbency (approximately 5 per cent their own weight in water), and give off no heat.

To illustrate the moisture content of wool one only has to reverse the process by leaving a woollen garment in a polythene (plastic) bag close to a source of heat. Very soon, the inside of the bag will become covered in droplets of condensation.

A single wool fibre, when seen under magnification, is covered in scales and it is these which make matting or felting irreversible – when opened out or rubbed the wrong way, they act as barbs becoming interlocked with the surrounding fibres (see *Washcare*). It is the size of these scales, the thickness of individual fibres and their length which affect the softness of a wool. This varies from breed to breed of sheep and often according to the part of the fleece used. Sheep are now specifically bred either for meat production or wool production with the Merino and Merino cross-breds growing the most abundant, high-quality wool. These breeds dominate wool production; the more specialist breeds, such as Shetland, only account for a small percentage of world production. By far the world leader in wool production is Australia – a stunning 789 million kg were produced in 1984–5. Next on the table is the Soviet Union, producing approximately half that amount, followed by New Zealand, China and Argentina.

Fibres come and go according to the dictates of fashion and economy, but there has never been a yarn which comes anywhere close to challenging wool's supremacy in the hand knit market.

YARN COUNT

The count is the precise measurement of a yarn's size and can be defined as 'a number indicating the mass per unit length or the length per unit mass of a yarn'. There are numerous different count systems in use but the one supposed to be taking over universally is the tex system. The tex of a yarn is the weight, in grams, of 1000 metres, so the smaller the tex, the finer the yarn. Spinners and industrial knitters and weavers are more likely than hand knitters to talk of counts. It is, however, useful to know the term, if not the specific system, so that if you are asked what count you require when buying direct, you will not be completely at a loss.

YARNS

A separate consideration of yarns is largely unnecessary here. Since yarn is the main tool involved in the art of knitting, and without reference to it no knitting technique can be adequately covered, almost every section

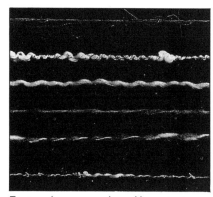

Textured yarns produced by spinning strands at different speeds.

of this book includes hints and tips regarding the uses and treatment of various yarn types. In addition, the main natural fibres and yarn thicknesses have all been individually listed.

A detailed consideration of the synthetic yarns and the vast selection of yarn mixes and fancy effects which are now available on the market has been avoided. Fashion dictates that these change and develop so fast that any detailed list would be out of date almost before the printer's ink dried. The technical advances in synthetic

fibre production have been such that many now appear almost identical to natural fibres. When worn, however, the qualities of insulation and absorption that most of the natural fibres possess can never be matched and so the choice today is often down to comfort rather than aesthetics (see *Wool*).

It does, however, seem pointless to spend hours of loving care producing a hand knit and not to use the very best-quality yarn available to do the craftsmanship credit. If economy is the only consideration, then shop around. Yarn bargains are always available with many shops reducing the price of discontinued qualities or colours and mail order companies offering extremely competitive 'cash and carry' prices.

The faster pace of modern life has meant that very few knitters now have the patience to work in the fine yarns which even up to the mid-fifties were virtually the only yarns available. Yarns have become thicker and thicker so that a chunky garment can be knitted in a fraction of the time it would take to knit a 4-ply equivalent. The fact that most younger knitters are self taught has meant that styling has had to become far more basic. In turn, yarns have had to become quite diverse to compensate. The mixtures of texture and colour have become so fantastic that even a sweater that is a plain rectangle of stocking (stockinette) stitch can appear to be a fascinating work of art.

Yarns made from such varying materials as raffia, suede, rags and fur have all come on to the market in recent years and the spinners are having to become far more innovative than they ever were in the past in an attempt to keep up with demand. As with anything related to knitwear, the Italians lead the field in yarn design – the twice-yearly Pitti Filati trade fair in Florence attracts attention from all over the world.

When choosing a yarn do not get carried away by how lovely it may appear in a ball. Its suitability to the style and stitch which you will be working, and its compatibility with your skill as a knitter and the lifestyle of the wearer, are all of prime importance.

A heavily textured yarn will be useless for a fancy stitch pattern – the stitches will become totally obscured by the busyness of the yarn. Equally unsuitable is an evening top in mohair, one of the warmest yarns in existence. Remember that designers are not infallible – it is extremely unlikely that they have ever had to wear the garment which they have designed in order to test its feasibility. A chunky tweed sports sweater may look effective with a plunging 'V' neck but when you are out walking the dog in the middle of winter, a roll neck will suddenly seem far more attractive. Never be afraid to substitute yarns, but always check the tension.

If you have never used a particular type of yarn before and you are unsure whether or not you will be able to cope with it, buy a single ball and experiment before going the whole hog and investing in a garment's worth. Many knitters have difficulty with the lack of elasticity found in cotton. There are those who find many fluffy yarns quite impossible for health reasons. Some knitters cannot face working with fine yarns, while others cannot handle the great thick needles required for heavyweights. Get on friendly terms with your yarn as a priority.

Should a yarn supplier not have the yarns that you want, only have a limited selection of colours or a range of patterns that are ten years out of date (or all three!), then tell the manager or owner exactly what you are looking for, before you leave to find a better stocked store or send for a mail order catalogue. It is only through customer feedback to retailers and, in turn, to wholesalers and spinners that the choice of any merchandise ever improves.

Synthetics

The production of synthetic fibres in recent years has become increasingly sophisticated and advanced. Research and development continues at such a pace that it is barely possible to keep up with the new fibres on the market, many of which are known by the names of specific manufacturers rather than generic terms.

The main group of synthetic yarns in use are the hydrocarbon compounds of which acrylic and polymide are the most commonly used varieties. These, along with viscose or viscose rayon – a cellulose derivative – are the fibres which crop up over and over again

when reading the fibre content on the ball bands of modern yarns, which sometimes contain up to ten different fibres in order to produce a new effect. Clever mixes of synthetic and natural fibres make it possible to produce yarns which bear no relation to the primitive synthetics of a few years ago.

Although they still lack many of the features of natural fibres, these new synthetics are strong and durable and lend themselves to a huge variety of fancy finishes, making them very hard wearing. Many also tend to be very lightweight compared to their natural counterparts. So-called 'high bulk' acrylic is the most extreme example, spun to provide the maximum thickness of yarn with the minimum of weight. It is possible to complete a garment using half the weight of the equivalent thickness of wool. The 'handle' or feel of the yarn, however, is another matter.

As with the advances in synthetic fibre development, so fancy spinning techniques are changing at such a rate that it is difficult to keep up and impossible to enumerate all the new methods of fringing, coiling, fraying and bonding which are being used to create novelty yarns. In the past it was only possible to vary the texture of a yarn in a limited number of ways, most of which depended on the speed and tension with which the different fibres were plyed with one another. Bouclé, gimp and loop finishes are all produced by feeding one ply at a faster rate than another so that one buckles up to a greater or lesser degree. Mohair is, in fact, produced as a loop yarn, and the loops are then broken by the brushing process to create the fluffy finish. Slub yarns vary in thickness along one or more plys to produce lumps, and tweed type yarns have coloured lumps

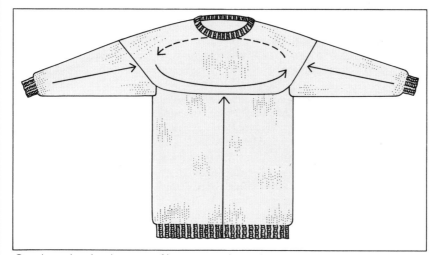

Circular yoke, the direction of knitting is indicated by the arrows.

or 'knops' added to the longer fibres during spinning. The skill of the spinner has now gone far beyond these techniques, however, and some very recent yarns look like something from the realms of science fiction.

YOKES

Straight yokes speak for themselves since no specific technique or shaping is required to produce them. They very rarely serve a purpose other than that of decoration, which may mean that they are worked in a different stitch or yarn and are not actually worked as separate pieces as they would be on a tailored garment. If the

body of the garment is to be gathered on to a yoke then it is advisable to knit downwards, from the bottom edge of the yoke, working a row of increases to form the gathers (see *Gathers*).

Circular yokes are more complicated, however, since they involve a considerable amount of shaping to produce a curve that will accommodate the shoulders. They may be knitted sideways, the shaping being worked as turning rows (see *Turning*), but this necessitates joining the final row to the cast on row and then attaching this separate circle to the body and sleeves of the garment.

The more usual way of working a circular yoke is to work the body and sleeves of the garment as if a set-in sleeve style were to be created, but to

stop a few rows after starting the armhole shapings on the front and back and the sleeve head (cap) shapings on either sleeve. The stitches from the back, then one sleeve, the front and, finally, the other sleeve are all placed on to a circular needle or set of double-pointed needles. Some knitters prefer to put these stitches on to holders and then sew up the side and sleeve seams before starting the yoke; the finished effect is exactly the same.

By calculating the number of stitches required around the finished neckline and then subtracting this figure from the number of stitches now on the needle, you will arrive at a figure representing the number of stitches which have to be decreased during the working of the yoke. Divide the number of rows which will be worked (the diameter of the yoke), by the number of decreases to give you the number of stitches which will have to be decreased over each row. The difficult part is in distributing all the shapings evenly around the circle, since if any of them are bunched it will result in a most peculiar and unwearable garment. As with all matters of shaping, graph paper is invaluable in charting the decreases before experimenting with the knitting itself.

For those of you who cannot face the thought of keeping track of so many shapings there are 'cheaters' kits available which include ready-knitted fairisle yokes which you can add to garments you knit yourself.

BIBLIOGRAPHY

This bibliography is not intended to be exhaustive, but to give those interested in the history and development of the craft ideas for further reading. For obvious reasons, books of modern patterns have been excluded; those which offer a more historical approach are included.

Felkin, W. (1867, reprinted 1967) *History of Machine-Wrought Hosiery and Lace* David & Charles, Newton Abbot, Devon; B. Franklin/Kelley Augustus M. Publications, New York.

Hartley, Marie and Joan Ingilby (1951, reprinted 1969) *The Old Hand Knitters of the Dales* The Dalesman, England.

Henson, Gravenor (1831, reprinted 1970) *History of the Framework Knitters* David & Charles, Newton Abbot, Devon; Kelley Augustus M. Publications, New York.

Lind, Vibeke (1984) *Knitting in the Nordic Tradition* Lark Books, US.

Menkes, Suzy (1983) *The Knitwear Revolution* Bell & Hyman, London.

Pearson, Michael (1984) *Traditional Knitting – Aran, Fair Isle and Fisher Ganseys* Collins, London.

Phillips, Mary Walker (1971) *Creative Knitting* Van Nostrand Reinhold, New York.

Probert, Christina (1982) *Knitting in Vogue: Patterns from the '30s to the '80s* David & Charles, Newton Abbot, Devon; Viking-Penguin Inc., New York.

Thomas, Mary (1938, reprinted 1985) *Mary Thomas's Knitting Book* Hodder & Stoughton, Sevenoaks, Kent.

Thomas, Mary (1943, reprinted 1971 US, 1985 UK) *Mary Thomas's Book of Knitting Patterns* Hodder & Stoughton, Sevenoaks, Kent; Dover Publications Inc., Mineola, New York.

Thompson, Gladys (1971) *Patterns for Guernseys, Jerseys and Arans* Dover Publications Inc., Mineola, New York.

Waller, Jane (1972) *A Stitch-in-Time – Knitting and Crochet Patterns of the 1920s, 1930s and 1940s* Duckworth, London.

ACKNOWLEDGEMENTS

Swallow Publishing Limited wish to acknowledge the assistance given to them in the preparation of *The Encyclopedia of Knitting Techniques* by the following people and organizations. We apologize to anyone we may have omitted to mention.

Garments/Knit kits
W. Bill Ltd, 93 New Bond St, London W1 18, 22, 68; Joan Chatterley Knitwear; Melinda Coss, 1 Copenhagen St, London N1 67, 140; The Hand Knit Company, PO Box 148, Wembley, Middx cover, 22, 50, 67, 99, 158; Patons and Baldwin Ltd, McMullen Road, Darlington, Co. Durham 98; Pilot, 34 Floral St, London WC2 140; Rococo at Harvey Nicholls & Co, Knightsbridge, London SW1 22, 39, 40; Scottish Merchant, 16 New Row, London WC2 103; Westaway and Westaway, 92–3 Great Russell St, London WC1 68, 122; Yarnworks, 4th Floor, Waring and Gillow Building, Western Ave, London W3 40.

Photographs
Ardea 35, 125, 184; The American Museum in Britain 133; BBC Hulton Picture Library 21; Biofotos/Heather Angel 55; Bruce Coleman 15, 17, 162; Hamburger Kunsthalle 12; Michael Holford 168; The London Illustrated News Picture Library 21, 103; Patons and Baldwin Ltd 21; Patricia Roberts 21; The Victoria and Albert Museum 104, 114; Werner Forman Archive 11.

Patterns
Bestway Knitwear 157; Robert Glew & Co Ltd 157; Patons and Baldwin Ltd 157; Scheepjeswol, Holland 105; Stitchcraft 157; Vogue Knitting 157; Wendy Wools 157.

Yarns/Gadgets
Liberty & Co. Ltd, Regent St, London W1 86, 175, 176; Reis Wools at Holborn, 242 High Holborn, London WC1 86, 175, 176.